DISCARDED

STORIES OF THE GREAT RAILROADS

BY
CHARLES EDWARD RUSSELL

CHICAGO
CHARLES H. KERR & COMPANY
1914

Copyright, 1908, 1909, 1910, by HAMPTON'S MAGAZINE
Copyright, 1912, by CHARLES H. KERR & COMPANY

PREFATORY ANECDOTE.

Most of the matter in this book originally appeared in Hampton's Magazine in the form of separate articles.

After the manuscript of Chapter III had been taken to the magazine office, before there had been any publication, and when the article, in fact, had advanced no farther than the proof stage, I received a letter from a railroad agent in a western city, displaying an intimate acquaintance with the article, attempting to refute some of its statements, and urging me not to print them.

Again, while the chapter on Death Avenue was lying at the office in proofs, and two weeks before the magazine that contained it had been made up, a gentleman declaring himself to be a representative of the New York Central railroad and known in the office to be such, called with the information that he knew the nature and scope of the article the magazine intended to publish about the New York Central, and he plainly intimated that unless it was suppressed the railroad company would withdraw all its advertising from Hampton's. The article was published and railroad advertising was accordingly withdrawn.

About two weeks before the publication of Chapter XIII, and while it, too, had advanced no farther than the proof stage, there came to the office of the magazine a gentleman that introduced himself as coming from Mr. Charles S. Mellen, president of the New York, New Haven and Hartford Railroad company, which is made the subject of that chapter. He said that Mr. Mellen understood that an article attacking the railroad company was about to be published in Hampton's; that it was as he expressed it, "full of lies," and he came to warn the editor not to publish any such matter. In describing the article, he showed such familiarity with it as a man could hardly have unless he had read it, although Mr. Hampton had believed that no one outside of the office (except myself) knew of the existence of the article.

Proofs of the matter were now produced and the caller requested to indicate which of the statements were "lies." Each important sentence was read to him separately, and he was asked whether it were true or false. In every instance, except four, he was obliged to admit that it was true. The four instances to the contrary were either trivial or they were matters that Mr. Hampton himself knew to be accurately stated.

He had told his caller at the beginning of the interview that he would change or omit every statement in the article that could be shown to be false. After spending the better part of the day in the careful consideration of the matter sentence by sentence, there appeared to be nothing material to change.

Nevertheless the visitor demanded that the article be not printed. He said that if it should be, the financial powers back of the New Haven railroad would ruin the magazine and Mr. Hampton.

The article was printed in the issue of November, 1910. From that time Mr. Hampton found it increasingly difficult to get any money at the banks. Even when he offered paper of the best kind, endorsed by four men of wealth that had no trouble about borrowing money on their own account, the banks refused him all accommodation. Twenty-one banks and trust companies were approached with the same result. More than one declared a willingness to accept the paper for any other purpose than Hampton's Magazine. Several times the paper was accepted and subsequently, at some mysterious signal, rejected. The result was that Mr. Hampton was ruined according to prediction and his magazine was swept out of his hands.

It had a circulation of more than 400,000 and a very large advertising business, and not a bank in New York would advance to it one dollar.

Meantime, spies had made their way into the business office of the magazine, copied the list of stockholders, and these were besieged with circulars intimating that the concern was about to fail, and they had better protect themselves, with the inevitable result of destroying the magazine's credit and bringing upon it a swarm of frightened stockholders.

These are the facts.

The author earnestly desires opinions upon them from unprejudiced sources—and others. They seem to him to represent a condition incompatible with any assertion of a free press in America, and a state of espionage by the corporations that deserves the thoughtful attention of every citizen.

CONTENTS

	PAGE
PREFATORY ANECDOTE	5
THE ROMANTIC HISTORY OF THE DUTCH BONDHOLDERS AND THE ST. PAUL AND PACIFIC	11
THE ROMANCE OF THE INLAND EMPIRE	33
THE GREATEST MELON PATCH IN THE WORLD	57
THE ROMANCE OF DEATH AVENUE	80
ROMANTIC DAYS IN EARLY CALIFORNIA	102
UNCLE MARK PACKS UP THE BOOKS	128
MR. HUNTINGTON WRITES TO FRIEND COLTON	158
MRS. COLTON LEARNS ABOUT PHILANTHROPY	197
SPEAKING OF WIDOWS AND ORPHANS	212
WHAT THE LAW DOES FOR US	226
THE STORY OF THE HARBOR FIGHT	255
THE STORY OF THE LEMON RATE	281
THE STORY OF THE NEW HAVEN	309

Stories of the Great Railroads.

CHAPTER I.

THE ROMANTIC HISTORY OF THE DUTCH BONDHOLDERS AND THE ST. PAUL AND PACIFIC.

Sir George Stephen, Knight Grand Cross of the Royal Victorian Order, Baron Mount Stephen in the Province of British Columbia, Dominion of Canada and of Duffstown, Banff, in the Peerage of the United Kingdom; so created June 23, 1891; and Baronet, so created March 3, 1886; late President of the Canadian Pacific Railway, Deputy Lieutenant, County Banff, Motto, Contra Audentior. Seats, Grand Metis, Quebec, and Brocket Hall, Hatfield, Herts. Town House, 17 Carlton House Terrace.—*Burke's Peerage*, 1909.

The Baron Strathcona and Mount Royal, Sir Donald Alexander Smith, G.C.M.G., F.R.S. (Cross of the Order of St. Michael and St. George, Fellow of the Royal Society) of Glencoe, County of Argyle, Quebec, Canada; late Resident Governor and Chief Commissioner at Montreal of the Hudson Bay Company, President of the Bank of Montreal, Vice-President Dominion Rifle Association, Honorary Colonel 8th Vol. Batt. Liverpool Regiment, some time member for Montreal in the Dominion Parliament, Chancellor of Aberdeen University since 1893, and of the McGill University, Hon. LL.D. of the Universities of Cambridge, Yale, Glasgow, Aberdeen, Toronto, etc., and Hon. D.C.L., Oxford; F.R.S. High Commissioner for Canada in London since 1896, member of Royal Commission on War in South Africa, 1902, etc. Seats Glencoe, Argyleshire; Silver Heights, Winnipeg; Norway House, Pictou, Nova Scotia; Residences, Knebworth House, Stevenage, Herts, and Debden Hall, Newport, Essex. Town Residences, 1157 Dorchester Street, Montreal; 28 Grosvenor Square, W.—*Burke's Peerage*, 1909.

As a rule, the luminous pages of the estimable Mr. Burke have for us in this country but slight concern (except very likely for those of us that have marriageable daughters ready for the title market), but about the two peerages above noted, there should dwell for Americans all the keen interest that pertains always to the work of our own hands; because these two peerages we have made. In that sense they are far more truly American than British; and the tourist from Minnesota or Montana, straying through the awful precincts of Carlton House Terrace or Grosvenor Square, can look with peculiar, and in a sense proprietory interest upon two of the stately houses there, since we conferred them upon their present inhabitants. If he be philosophical, also, the spectacle may properly spur him to much profitable thought, one subject powerfully suggested being a question whether, after all, we Americans are really as smart as we think we are.

Lord Mount Stephen and Lord Strathcona began as poor boys and humble commoners. Look upward and observe the dizzy heights to which they have climbed; the lofty distinctions, the great wealth, the many palaces, the station where in a long sonorous rumble a row of titles must follow each utterance of their names, lords and peers and baronets and what not—each referred to in the English press as His Lordship, each loaded with honors, decorated by universities, including our own. What an apparent splendor of achievement! What grandeur! As we ordinarily view these matters, what a lesson to the young! And all done with American dollars!

About this sort of thing there clings in our minds the traditional halo and allurement of romance. Beyond any exploit of any soldier on any battlefield, beyond all physical daring or prowess, our hearts acclaim the glorious record of the boy that begins desperately poor and wins fortune, fame, eminence, power; and among such histories the instances I mention here leave for romantic splendor nothing further to be conceived. Donald Smith, for example, was once a poor and obscure drudge in the service of the Hudson Bay

Company; he spent thirteen years in the humblest labor, almost marooned among the savages of Labrador; he endured countless vicissitudes and dangers; he made his way to affluence; he became a peer of the realm. At his own expense he raised, equipped, and maintained a body of efficient troops that greatly helped to save his country when in the crisis of her imminent peril at the hands of 25,000 Boer farmers. To him, therefore, the whole nation gives praise and honor. Novelist never conceived a career more inspiring to persons of our predilections, and not the least of its attractions is the fact that we gave so much to assist it; even if our contributions were involuntary.

But have we on our side of the international boundary no careers comparable with these, even if of necessity they be uncrowned with peerage? Most assuredly have we. There is Mr. James J. Hill, distinguished as easily the greatest and most admired of our railroad kings, who though still without a lordship (by name) is well known to deserve this and even greater honor. His is the life of achievement most often and most reasonably held up as the perfect model for our aspiring youth. In solidity of performance, in the making by irreproachable methods of a great fortune, in application, industry, zeal, ability, fidelity, integrity, in short in all the most laudable traits of manhood, here we are informed is the ideal type. He began very poor and with every disadvantage, including uncompleted schooling; he appears now in possession of a colossal fortune, at the head of a vast system of railroads, endowed with truly imperial power, praised by the press and by educators, cited by the pulpit as the conspicuous exponent of wealth honestly acquired, admired of all men (or nearly all), embalmed in literature as the typical example of the romance of success. What could be beyond all this?

I know not how these things can be better said than in the words of one of his most eloquent panegyrists, Mr.

Henry Lee Higginson, of State Street, Boston, in the Atlantic Monthly for January, 1908. "He was," says Mr. Higginson, " a poor boy who passed through one stage of honest industry after another, never fagged in his task, * * * using his knowledge and skill to win success; who has toiled without salary, allowing neither to himself nor any of his officials side profits or interest in adjoining lands, factories, or mines contributing business to his railroad; who has distributed throughout his country at his own cost the best live stock and has helped in divers ways everybody within his domain."

Good! Let us then betake ourselves to profitable study of the man to whom are thus frankly ascribed regal powers and attributes in "his domain," and whose career can hardly fail to be a suitable companion piece to the careers of his friends, Lord Mount Stephen and Lord Strathcona. With the more good will since it happens that we can observe all these admirable exploits compendiously and at one glance. Because Lord Mount Stephen and Lord Strathcona made their fortunes at the same time that Mr. Hill made his, in the same operations and from the same people, who are ourselves—a happy and rare conjunction of circumstances for which we can hardly be too thankful.

Mr. Hill was born in a log house on a little farm near Rockwood, Ontario, September 16, 1838. Fourteen years later his father died, and young Hill left school to go to work in the village store, the family being in extreme poverty. At eighteen, he joined the western flowing tide of emigration, and was carried by it as far as St. Paul, where he secured the place of shipping clerk with the agents of a Mississippi River steamboat line. He was both industrious and thrifty; it was noted then that for some reasons of personal economy he used to get his dinners aboard the incoming steamers, where they were free. In 1867 he became the local freight agent of the St. Paul & Pacific Railroad, and held that place until 1873. For a short time he was engaged in steamboating on the Red River of the North, and next he had much experience in the forwarding and commission business; with a side line in fuel. At the time this romantic story really begins, he was nearing forty, a stocky, spade-bearded man, active, a keen trader, fairly well known in St. Paul, and not, as a rule, taken very seriously. He was just Jim Hill, shrewd bargainer, a good judge of butter and a commission man.

Our enthusiasm concerning the romantic phases of American railroad history should not lead us to overlook the extraordinary liberality wherewith our government once bestowed the public domain upon any gentlemen that happened to be in the railroad line of enterprise. Therefore, we shall do well to introduce the first chapter in this greatest of all railroad romances, by reciting that in 1857 what is now the State of Minnesota was a territory, and that on March 3rd of that year, the Congress of the United States granted to the territory of Minnesota a vast area of public lands to be used to encourage the building of railroads. Nineteen days later, which at that time was about as quickly as the good news could be hurried to St. Paul, the territorial legislature chartered the Minnesota & Pacific Railroad company, which patriotic gentlemen had formed in expectation of congressional generosity, and to them, therefore, was conveyed much of the land bestowed by Congress—subsequently enhanced by further largess of the same kind.

What this was, I hesitate somewhat to say. because I doubt if in these days I shall be believed. I can only assure you that I have examined the records in the Federal Court at St. Paul, and what with diffidence I transcribe here, is taken from official documents. From these it appears that in its final state, the gift of public property upon the patriotic gentlemen in the railroad way was, free of all charge, all the odd-numbered sections of land for a distance of ten miles on each side of the line of the railroad. A section, let me remark in your ear, consists of six hundred and forty acres, and the land was the richest, the most fertile, the most desirable in the northwest.

Few facts seem more romantic than this.

In other ways the Minnesota & Pacific might have succeeded admirably; as a railroad its achievements were not notable, being confined to a track from St. Paul to St. Anthony Falls (now Minneapolis), ten miles long—which for an enterprise with a name so ambitious and a land grant so prodigal, hardly seems all that might have been expected.

In 1862, there was a reorganization and all the rights and properties of the Minnesota & Pacific passed to a new company called the St. Paul & Pacific, which proceeded to do many things, including the building of some real and much imitation track, and the issuing of many bonds, all of which were sold to the lowly and ignorant European, and chiefly to him of Holland.

But observe that by an act of the Minnesota Legislature in 1864, the St. Paul & Pacific was, in the most singular way, divided, so that thereafter it seemed to be possessed by two companies, one called the St. Paul & Pacific Railroad company, and the other bearing the remarkable title of The First Division of the St. Paul & Pacific Railroad company. Inasmuch as the officers of the companies remained the same and the trackage to be divided (real and imitation) was a trifle, this performance seems very mysterious until you learn that one of these companies operated as a construction company for the other. Then if you know anything about the true romance of the American railroad, you begin to understand the mystery, an enlightenment much facilitated by carefully considering the alleged cost of construction (to be given later in these pages) and incidentally remembering that the money for the construction came from the lowly and ignorant European.

There were five successive issues of bonds, and on the proceeds of these, when sold as above noted, the building of the road was, in the classic phrase, pushed (more or less) from St. Paul toward the North and Northwest. Until 1872, that is. Then the lowly Hollander ceased to produce funds and consequently the building stopped. Also the payment of interest. Inasmuch as the last bond issue of $15,000,000 had been made so late as April, 1871, and the proceeds could hardly have been in that time expended upon construction at least, these romantic facts occasioned some astonishment and unpleasant comment.

Of these $15,000,000 of latest style bonds, $10,700,000 had been sold in Holland through the banking house of Lipmann, Rosenthal & Co., Amsterdam, and $4,300,000 were held by the same firm as security for advances made. Nobody knows what had become of these advances.

The firm of John S. Kennedy & Co., New York, was trustee for some of the bonds. In consequence of the default on them, it brought suit and on August 1, 1873, Judge John F. Dillon of the United States Circuit Court appointed Jesse P. Farley, of Dubuque, Iowa, to be receiver for the St. Paul & Pacific company.

Mr. Farley was of long and varied railroad experience. At the time of his appointment, he was superintendent of the Iowa Division of the Illinois Central. He went to St. Paul and proceeded to receive—also to operate the property as a railroad, the which I judge to have been an innovation in its history. Hitherto its function had been chiefly to get money from the Hollanders. Mr. Farley seems to have come upon some of the most romantic junk that even the picturesque annals of the American railroad have revealed. When he arrived in St. Paul, he notified his predecessor in the control of things to turn over to him the property of the road. "If you can find any property belonging to the St. Paul & Pacific," his predecessor replied, "you had better seize it." But even at that it would hardly have seemed worth seizing, except possibly for museum purposes. In some places the tracks looked like a Virginia rail fence and nothing but a squirrel could run over them; elsewhere the receiver had no locomotives nor cars and must rent all his equipment from the Northern Pacific.

Yet, being of undoubted capacity and dogged resolution, he worked his way through all these troubles. He patched up the road bed and put all of it in good working order; he secured equipment and material; he supplied a service, developed the traffic, increased the revenue and diminished the outgo; he enhanced the through business to Manitoba by the way of the Red River, in which he made his road an important link. Settlers began to arrive in large numbers, the country was filling up, the railroad traffic kept pace with and shared in the resulting prosperity; the poor old St. Paul & Pacific began to get upon its legs.

When Farley came into the road the First Division company (of which he was General Manager, but not Receiver) had the line from St. Paul to Breckenridge, and the branch to Sauk Rapids; the other company had the extension from Watab to Brainerd and the line from St. Cloud to St. Vincent, in all something more than four hundred miles of track. Farley not only put these in order, but he completed connections with the Canadian railroad at the frontier. He still further proved his capacity when after three or four years of his receivership, the Minnesota legislature (in a moment of unprecedented righteousness) passed an act providing that unless the road should be completed to a certain point within a certain time, it must forfeit part of the rich land grant whereof the people's representatives had been so liberal. Judge Dillon authorized the receiver to construct this extension and to issue receiver's debentures for the expense. So the receiver built one hundred and twelve miles of new road and saved the land grant.

Four facts connected with this operation are important to you:

First, Judge Dillon limited the cost of construction to $10,000 a mile, and this sum must include station buildings, grounds, side tracks and equipment.

Second, The Receiver built and equipped the one hundred and twelve miles for less than the limit fixed, expending only about $9,500 a mile, some stretches being done for $8,225 a mile. Kindly remember this. You will have reason to refer to it later in these chapters, and it is a good fact to have handy when you encounter the assertion of gentlemen in the railroad way that it costs $60,000 to $75,000 a mile to build a railroad.

Third, The Receiver filed with the court detailed accounts of every item of expense connected with this work, and every citizen can go now and see in the office of the clerk of the United States Circuit Court at St. Paul, Minnesota, exactly what it costs to build and equip a railroad when the work is honestly done.

Fourth, The construction company with the alias, as before noted, expending the money of the lowly and ignorant foreigner, had charged up $30,000 a mile for construction in the same region and had done the work so badly that when the Receiver took charge, the track was unsafe.

Do you begin now to see something of the real romance of these things?

Mr. Hill, as we have before observed, had been for six years the local freight agent of the St. Paul & Pacific. His experience in the commission business had made him familiar with the farm products and agricultural possibilities of the Northwest. He himself had been born on a farm, and a tough one. Having been agent for the railroad, he knew also about the rich land grants on each side of the railroad line. It has been supposed that because of these items of knowledge and by reason of marvelous gifts of ability, he foresaw the vast agricultural wealth of the Northwest and determined now to take advantage of it. All of these matters came subsequently under judicial inquiry, when there appeared no reason to believe that Mr. Hill foresaw anything beyond what he himself described as a good speculation. But, however that may be, his were the next moves that completely changed the history of the railroad and laid the foundation for these admired peerages and Mr. Hill's own regal state.

Mr. Hill is a Canadian. Among the interesting traits of the truly admirable people of Canada, is their touching sense of loyalty. No Canadian ever forgets the tie that binds him to every other Canadian, and not even Scotland has produced a stronger feeling of the clan. I do not know why this is so; I think nobody knows; but the fact itself must be familiar to all observers. As soon as it occurred to Mr. Hill that he had what he called a good speculation, his first impulse was to bring into the good thing another Canadian. There was one then living in St. Paul that was a conspicuous figure of his times, Norman Wolford Kittson, native of Sorel in the Province of Quebec. Hr. Hill broached his speculation to his compatriot Kittson.

His second impulse seems to have been to confer much with the Receiver. Mr. Farley subsequently testified that one day in the summer of 1876, Mr. Hill came into his office and, after many prolegomena, outlined a scheme by which bonds of the railroad could be obtained at cheap prices, foreclosure forced, the company reorganized, and much profits secured. Mr. Farley conceded that the scheme was fair to look upon if anyone could get the money wherewithal the bonds were to be bought. Mr. Hill said he believed he knew where the money could be had.

As to what followed, the record shows divergent testimony.

The one fact that is clear, is that Mr. Hill and Mr. Kittson, Canadians, drew into the combination Mr. Kittson's friends, George Stephen of Montreal, and Donald Alexander Smith of Winnipeg, also Canadians, and that these gentlemen executed a document afterwards known as the "Montreal agreement," by which Mr. Hill's suggestion was indorsed and amplified and the spoils of the Yankees decently apportioned. Some money seemed to be required. None of the signatories had money, but Mr. Stephen, who was manager of the Bank of Montreal, and Mr. Smith, who had been an active and romantic adventurer in the Northwest, had financial connections from which they believed they could secure what was needful.

In the benevolent partnership thus formed Mr. Farley believed he had a full and equal share. The profits had been divided in advance into five equal parts, and one of these shares, he said, was assigned to him. He had been taken into the deal, he said, in return for his services, and he had continually guided the combination with advice founded upon his superior knowledge as Receiver and Manager of the property. Thus, for example, Mr. Hill wished to send quietly to Holland and buy the bonds from the lowly foreigners. Mr. Farley, as Receiver, knew the location of practically every bond, and negatived Mr. Hill's idea as unwise and unnecessary. He said the bonds could be obtained without sending to Holland.

In a short time there appeared in St. Paul a man sent by the unfortunate bondholders to see what had become of their money. Mr. Farley introduced this man to Mr. Hill and Mr. Kittson. They carried on some negotiations with him, as a result of which they entered into an agreement to purchase bonds on these terms:

For the $1,200,000 Branch Line issue of June 2, 1862, seventy-five per cent of par value.

For the $3,000,000 Main Line issue of March 1, 1864, thirty per cent. of par value.

For the $2,800,000 Branch Line issue of October 1, 1865, twenty-eight per cent. of par value.

For the $6,000,000 Main Line issue of July 1, 1868, thirty-five per cent. of par value.

For the $15,000,000 Extension issue of April 1, 1871, thirteen and three-fourths per cent. of par value.

All unpaid coupons to be included in the sales.

These bonds were first mortgages on more than five hundred miles of operated railroad, and two million five hundred and eighty thousand six hundred and six acres of the best land in the world. The romance involved in these facts would almost bring tears to your eyes.

Having secured such of these bonds as were necessary to the genial plans of the five partners, and chiefly on the understanding that the purchases should not be paid for until the road should be reorganized, the Canadian brotherhood proceeded, on May 23, 1879, to form the St. Paul, Minneapolis & Manitoba Railroad company, of which George Stephen was president, Norman W. Kittson and Donald A. Smith, Directors, and James J. Hill, General Manager. Whereupon there was appointed a Master in Chancery, who, on the 14th day of June, 1879, sold all the property of the two St. Paul & Pacifics to the St. Paul, Minneapolis & Manitoba Railway company for $3,600,000—which happened to be less than the total of the bonds secured at the agreeable rates quoted above. Some outlying piece of junk purchased at the same time, brought the exact cost to $4,380,000. In making payments, the purchasers were allowed to turn in receiver's debentures and also the bonds, for all the purchase price, except a small percentage in cash.[1]

---

[1] It is unfortunate that the court records at St. Paul are in a condition so incomplete and unsatisfactory that no one now can trace with entire accuracy the successive steps in these proceedings. There is no question, however, that foreclosure was accomplished and the road sold to the new company as outlined here.

This cash is an exhibit of historic interest being all the money the partners ever invested in the enterprise and that not of their furnishing.

Then were the happy days before those vile creatures, the muck-rakers, had begun to cast their baleful shadows upon our fair land, but even at that halcyon time the romantic nature of these transactions seems to have occasioned unpleasant remarks, and some of the holders of bonds outside of the circle affected by the Canadian brotherhood, brought suit to have the sale set aside and the litigation reopened. Here were five hundred and sixty-five miles of operated railroad and two million five hundred and eighty thousand six hundred and six acres of the best land out of doors, all sold for $4,380,000—mostly in promises to pay—one of the most romantic events in railroad history, and too romantic for those that did not share in it.

Two developments of later years tended to enhance even this delicious romance. The first was the sale by the St. Paul, Minneapolis & Manitoba Railway company of the greater part of the land for $13,068,887, and the other was the sworn testimony of the Receiver that the railroad property sold for $4,380,000 was worth at the time more than $15,000,000.[2] He ought to have known; he helped to sell it.

However, the railroad and the rich lands passed into the hands of the partners, and at once the new owners issued upon the property $8,000,000 of new bonds with which they paid for the old bonds they had secured, returned to their friends in Canada what sums had been advanced for necessary expenses, and in this highly agreeable manner began their operations on American soil; having secured from the simple-minded Americans, five hundred and sixty-five miles of railroad, two million five hundred and eighty thousand

---

[2]Farley v. Hill et al., Supreme Court of the United States, about which see succeeding pages.

six hundred and six acres of fertile land, and $3,620,000 of surplus bonds (worth 104), representing additional profits. All without investing a cent—a romantic triumph, as you will readily perceive, of a truly touching nature.

There was also issued by the brotherhood $15,000,000 of St. Paul, Minneapolis & Manitoba stock, for which not one cent was ever paid into the company's treasury, being in fact, the purest water that ever gushed and gurgled from the financial rocks. Of this stock, Mr. Hill, Mr. Kittson, and Mr. Smith took twenty-eight thousand eight hundred and twenty-three shares each, being about one-fifth. Mr. Stephen took two-fifths, one of which he held in trust for some person or persons not stated—a curious fact to which we shall have occasion to refer later.

You will observe now that this is one of those romances that deepen in interest as they progress, for the $15,000,000 of stock thus neatly created out of nothing by the mere waving of the wand of financial wizardry presently became an enormously valuable possession, and is therefore to be added to the spoils secured from the outwitted Yankees.

On this pellucid water stock, the first dividend from the Yankees was declared August 1, 1882. It was at the rate of seven per cent a year, and the stock was then worth 140: which was doing fairly well, everything considered. Through the issue of more bonds, the mileage of the road had been increased to 1,058, the fat lands were being sold for fat prices, and, of course, every time a farm was carved out of them some tons were added to the freight traffic. The Canadians were perfectly right; they had a Good Thing; one of the best Good Things in this world.

Still, this life here below affords few instances of perfectly unalloyed joy. The loyal Canadian brethren were reaping seven per cent dividends on stock that cost absolutely nothing beyond the expense of printing it, and other emoluments were theirs or loomed large ahead; but in the precious ointment of content was still the noxious fly. There was the Receiver. Great Scott—yes! We almost forgot the Receiver. What became of him?

Well, Mr. Farley, the Receiver, did not a thing but clamor day and night for what he said was his just share in these goodly profits. He said that from the beginning he had been a full partner in the enterprise; one American in the same boat with four Canadians; that he had helped to plan, devise, and consummate the operations; that his advice, co-operation and knowledge as Receiver, had been indispensable; that his full and equal partnership had been recognized by the others, although, because of his position, it had been kept a secret; that he had been promised a one-fifth share of all the profits, the same as the others received; but that when the road had been sold and the new owners had taken possession, the Canadians had coldly refused to recognize his claims; had repudiated the contract that he alleged existed among them; and had thrown him out of the boat.

How in the world a Receiver, who is a court officer and certainly has sacred relations to the court and to his trust, could properly enter upon any such arrangement as Mr. Farley asserted, or how he could perform any proper service to such a combination, I do not pretend to say; but these were his allegations, and after a time he brought suit against Mr. Hill, Mr. Kittson, and the St. Paul, Minneapolis & Manitoba company to secure an accounting of profits and to enforce his contract.

This strange suit, which you will find fully reported as No. 287 in the October term of the Supreme Court of the United States, 1893, dragged on for thirteen years, being twice fought from St. Paul to Washington and back. You might think it of a nature to cause a national scandal, in view of the position of the Receiver and the significance of his allegations. If he told the truth, he had made with the Canadian brotherhood a bargain of a kind wholly incompatible with our cherished conceptions of our courts, and one that should have had the prompt attention of a district attorney.

Also, if his allegations were true, the romantic gentlemen from Canada were put in a light still worse and highly inconsistent with the true spirit of any other romance than that of the card-sharp. For even the most desperate devotee of railroad romanticism will hardly go so far as to admire a greasy, sinister and utterly illegal bargain with an officer of a court and a bargain that was not kept. This, of course, is the conclusion suggested by Mr. Farley's allegations. Perhaps those allegations were unfounded. Thirteen years of litigation failed to produce any definite judicial decision on this point, but it brought forth other things of almost equal value to those that believe in great fortunes "honestly acquired."

When the case was tried in the lower court, Mr. Farley took the stand and told an extraordinary and detailed narrative of the many conferences at which (he said) the plan to secure the road had been discussed, including his own share therein. He said that he was, in fact, absolutely necessary to the enterprise, because as Receiver he "had knowledge not possessed by the others as to the whereabouts and situation of the bonds, their rated value by the holders, the mode whereby they could be reached and procured, the situation, amount, character, and value of the lines of railroad and other property, and in respect to the pending foreclosure suits." He quoted Kittson as insisting upon Farley's participation and refusing otherwise to join the brotherhood.

"I know nothing about a railroad and don't care to know," Kittson was alleged to have said. "Jim Hill knows nothing about the management of a railroad, and it would be folly for men to go into an enterprise of this kind even if they were successful, without some person with them with railroad ability and experience to manage the property."

On this, according to Farley's testimony, he agreed to join the enterprise if Kittson could get the money required. Kittson, Farley testified, undertook to get the money from his Canadian connections, and an agreement was made that Farley should have share and share alike with the others. On June 3, 1876, Farley wrote to John S. Barnes of New York, a member of the firm of John S. Kennedy & Co., with which he regularly corresponded, that "he (Kittson) can get the money," and on August 23rd, same year, he wrote:

"His friend, who is expected to furnish the money, has unlimited control of Canadian politics. It might become a Canada project, but that would be a matter of no moment to you or me if we could make some money."

Here are bits of alleged conversation at the conferences taken from the testimony in the case:

Kittson—I won't have anything to do with it, unless you [Farley] are interested. We don't know anything about railroads.

Farley—I have no money, Mr. Kittson.

Kittson—We don't want you to furnish any money.

Hill—Certainly not.

Kittson—We will furnish the money.

On another occasion.

Farley—If you cannot get the Litchfield stock [in the old company], why, you will have to step into the Dutch shoes, take the place of the Dutch bondholders, and go ahead and foreclose—organize a new company, put on all the securities the property will bear, use enough of the securities to pay back what the bonds cost, and the balance is profit on the thing.

Which, as we have seen, is exactly what was done.

On another occasion, according to the testimony, Farley's position as Receiver was discussed.

Kittson—We will have to keep this thing to ourselves.

Hill—Certainly; it won't do to let anybody know anything about it.

Farley [to Fisher, his assistant, who participated in many of the conferences]—Now, Mr. Fisher, we will have to keep this thing perfectly quiet.

It seems that at first Mr. Stephen went to England and tried to raise money there, but failed. It must have been later, then, that the scheme of conditional purchase of the bonds was hit upon and proved eminently successful.

One of Farley's letters taken from the record of the case, may serve to lighten these matters with a passing ray of grim humor. It was written after the sale of the property and read thus:

"Since the election of Bigelow and Galusha as Directors in the New Company, men of no Money, railroad experience or Influence, And myself left out in the cold, I am forced to the conclusion that My time and claims on the St. Paul & Pacific is Short. I did expect better things of Hill and Kittson. I had a talk with Jim Hill last knight. He disclaims any intention on his part to ignore my claim. But he is such a Lyer can't believe him. It is a matter of astonishment to every Person in St. Paul, to see the way Jim handles Mr. Stephens. * * * You must not blame me if I should try to get even with Jim Hill before I leave here."

Mr. Farley's story was supported on the witness stand by Mr. Fisher, who at the time he testified, was President of the St. Paul & Duluth Railroad. Mr. Kittson had died before the case came to trial, but Mr. Hill, in his testimony, denied emphatically that there had been an agreement with Farley, and that Farley had been in any way a partner in the enterprise. In this he was supported by depositions from Stephen, Smith and others. Certain letters that it was said Farley had written to John S. Kennedy in New York, letters that, according to his lawyers, would help materially to establish his case, he was not able to put in evidence because, as was asserted at the trial, Mr. Kennedy went to Switzerland when the suit was begun and remained there out of the court's jurisdiction, refusing to furnish the letters or copies thereof. Mr. Kennedy died not long ago, leaving a great fortune, much of which was bequeathed to charity, causing many enthusiastic panegyrics. In the list of his possessions, published at that time, appeared quantities of securities in what are known as the Hill properties. His name occurs frequently through this narrative; through his firm, for example, the first foreclosure suit was begun which resulted in the receivership.

When Mr. Farley's suit was tried in the United States Circuit Court, it was dismissed on the ground that the alleged agreement had not been established, and even if it had been, it would have been improper and illegal, because it was made with a Receiver, who was an officer of the court and the guardian of the property. Farley appealed and secured an order for a new hearing. Finally, the case came for decision on its merits to the Supreme Court, which, on December 11, 1893, ruled against Farley. Justice Shiras wrote the opinion, which was based solely on Farley's failure to establish the agreement, the Justice pointing out that nothing in the nature of a written contract or memorandum of the agreement had been submitted, and that Farley being a man of affairs, "it was unlikely he would rely in an affair of such magnitude upon a merely verbal agreement." How, being a Receiver, he could have put his name to a written agreement of that character, did not appear.

After this final disposition of the matter, the Canadians were left in undisturbed possession of the property. Meantime the great tide of settlers into the Northwest had filled the country; cities and towns grew almost overnight on the prairies; the fertile land began to produce monster wheat crops; Minneapolis and St. Paul developed into a great metropolis; the railroad traffic piled up; the line was extended year by year; Winnipeg and the Canadian Northwest began to attract a great population; this railroad was the grand highway of Manitoba travel; a flood of profits rolled in upon the fortunate owners.

Mr. Stephen and Mr. Smith used theirs in furthering their social ambitions in England; Mr. Stephen becoming Lord Mount Stephen, Mr. Smith becoming first Sir Donald Smith, and then Lord Strathcona. Mr. Hill used his share to extend his railroad holdings. First he built his railroad (now reorganized again into the Great Northern) through to the Pacific coast. Then he secured, with his share of the profits, control of the Northern Pacific, and of the great Burlington system. To these he added road after road until in December, 1908, he completed his gigantic system with the Colorado & Southern, and held in his control trunk lines from the Great Lakes to the Pacific Ocean, and from the Canadian border to the Gulf of Mexico, approximately twenty-five thousand miles of track, traversing and dominating an area fitly termed the Inland Empire, of which, as he owns the highways, he is the practical ruler. When to these advantages you add newspapers, politicians, conventions, parties, houses, lands, farms, sycophants, praise-chanters, knee-crookers, legislatures, senators, and other matters, here appears one of the most colossal figures of the times.

Why recite these things now? The Past is past: let it be.

True. But I recite them because they have direct and absolute bearing upon the greatest public question that this generation will have to deal with. We cannot think that much longer we shall be able to dodge that issue: it is too insistent and too important.

Some other considerations are also to be noted.

Mr. Hill is admitted by most of his adulators to have some slight imperfections, but these are generously overlooked because he is alleged to have used some of his vast profits (made out of nothing) to develop the Northwest. I purpose to show in a succeeding chapter, exactly how he has developed the Northwest, and to that showing what has been recalled here from his other achievements was an indispensable preliminary.

Furthermore, Mr. Hill, being declared so loudly to be able, generous, honest and successful, and having risen in this marvelous fashion from penury to great wealth, may well be taken as the perfect type of the product of that free opportunity that America is said to offer to all men and of which we are so proud. Therefore, it should be well to see exactly what the gathering of this great fortune and great power has meant for Mr. Hill and meant for other persons —to the end that we may the better judge whether this free opportunity is all of the public benefit we have held it to be.

In the next place Mr. Hill is much admired because he has served, without salary, as General Manager and as President of his railroad. If he had been paid a salary of $50,000 a year, he would by this time have drawn from the enterprise $1,600,000.

He has had no salary, but he has, with Lord Mount Stephen and Lord Strathcona and others, drawn from the enterprise his share of a very much larger sum.

To-wit, four hundred and seven million dollars.

This sum, with which the partners have been endowed as one of the results of the original agreement, is exclusive, please note, exclusive of all dividends, interest, or other emoluments—four hundred and seven million dollars in thirty years. Does that amount seem incredible or stupendous to you? I assure you it is only a part of the colossal profits coined from an investment of nothing by this most wonderful of all machines, and when you come to see the full balance sheet of these operations, you will agree with me that never before have there been such marvelous results from a beginning so inconsiderable.

I propose next to show just how the partners were put in possession of this money, and who furnished it.

Will the showing be interesting to you? It will be if your monthly rent interests you, or your butcher bill, or your coal bill, or your grocery bill; because to each of these items the story I have to tell has a direct relation.

Finally, the transcontinental railroads of this country adopted on January 1, 1909, an increase of freight rates ranging from three to eighteen per cent. and calculated to produce for them an increased annual revenue of many millions of dollars. When we are through with the study of these matters you will see exactly how fair, reasonable, and necessary is this increase, and how just it is that to furnish this additional income, you should pay more for your meat, your fuel, and your shelter.

CHAPTER II.

THE ROMANCE OF THE INLAND EMPIRE.

And now for the exact way in which this tremendous, incalculable power we bestowed upon Mr. Hill and his friends, "builds up the Northwest"—also other regions.

Take a map of the United States and study attentively the distribution of the large cities. You will observe that after you leave the Atlantic seaboard, the natural population centers are about equidistant.

Pittsburg is about as far from the coast as Buffalo is, Cleveland is situated relatively much like Detroit; you go four hundred and twenty miles northwest of Chicago and find the metropolis of St. Paul and Minneapolis, or you go five hundred miles southwest and you find Kansas City, or five hundred miles due west and find Omaha. Denver is as far from Omaha as Omaha is from Chicago; Salt Lake City is another five hundred miles' remove. Portland, Oregon, is about seven hundred miles north, and Los Angeles about five hundred miles south of San Francisco. Cities like Atlanta and Fort Worth, even though inland, are clearly destined to be great central points for production and distribution. Streams of trade head for such places; inevitable markets for vast areas of rich country, they are noted of men as the industrial capitals to be.

In the far Northwest the obvious inland center, having not alone the favored situation, but a marvelous combination of natural advantages, is the City of Spokane, Washington.

It is about three hundred and forty miles inland from any

Pacific Coast City;[1] it is fifteen hundred miles west of St Paul and Minneapolis; there is no indication of any other metropolis within three or four hundred miles.

Beyond all this, it is the natural center and market place for an enormous area of marvelously fertile and very beautiful country, the true garden spot of the Northwest, the granary and orchard of that part of the national territory, one hundred and fifty thousand square miles, so rich in so many different ways that probably twenty million people could be supported there.

Of all this magnificent region, Spokane is the cross-roads and supply depot. Eastern Washington, eastern Oregon, northern Idaho, western Montana and part of British Columbia are embraced in the Spokane country. Here the wheat fields grow more than forty-five million bushels of wheat every year, the orchards yield nine or ten million dollars' worth of fruits, the dairies yield about five million dollars' worth of their products, there are lumber, lead, silver, gold and copper; coal is not far away.

Three hundred billion feet of timber stand in this region and a great lumber industry is indicated.

Above all, Spokane, situated at the falls of the Spokane River, has the incalculable advantage of water power. It is perfectly equipped, therefore, to be a great manufacturing as well as a great commercial center. In the sanguine local literature, it is termed the Power City.

Taking a comprehensive view of the Spokane country, its fertility, extent, resources, location, you would naturally expect Spokane to be a great city. You would look for 200,000 or 250,000 people in a city so blessed with every natural advantage.

---

[1] Four hundred miles from Seattle by the Northern Pacific Railroad, five hundred and forty-one miles from Portland, three hundred and thirty-nine miles from Seattle by the Great Northern Railroad.

Spokane has not 250,000 people, nor 200,000. The census of 1910 gave its population as 104,402.

Not alone is the population of the city below the normal, but the industrial development is impressively small.

The magnificent water power largely goes to waste. Of all kinds of production that can be called manufacturing, the annual total is only about $9,000,000. With such a country about it, with such natural wealth poured into its lap, a total twenty times as great would not be by this time an unreasonable expectation. Yet Spokane sticks at 104,402 people and $9,000,000 of manufactures.

So sticks all the Inland Empire.

What is the trouble? Why does it not grow? No natural disadvantage interferes. Location most charming; climate mild, healthful, invigorating; a beautiful city in a beautiful environment; nothing is lacking here. Nor is one known quality of progress deficient in this people; for pertinacity and public spirit, for industry and zeal and all the other civic virtues, I know not how or where they can be excelled. And yet the capital of the Inland Empire sticks fast. What is the matter?

This is the matter:

It is strangled with railroad rates.

That is all—Spokane and the whole Spokane country.

How? Thus:

Spokane is reached by four great trans-continental railroad systems and several branch lines.

Towns are accustomed to view such facilities as an asset of great value. In the case of Spokane and the Spokane country, it has been no asset, but a terrible injury.

The transcontinental systems are the Great Northern, the Northern Pacific, the Canadian Pacific, and the Union Pacific (Oregon Railroad & Navigation company).

These lines, supposed by a convenient fiction to be rivals and to furnish the shipping public with what we are pleased to call the advantages of competition, are practically one so far as the Spokane country is concerned.

That is to say, they have formed an iron-bound compact the essence of which is to throttle Spokane and the whole Spokane country—obligingly referred to by Mr. Higginson as "Mr. Hill's domain." This compact is doubtless facilitated by the fact that two of the lines mentioned are the property of Mr. Hill, being part of the wealth we conferred upon the Canadian brotherhood, as related in the foregoing chapter of this chronicle.

If you are a merchant, or manufacturer, or farmer in this domain, it makes not the slightest difference which of the lines you choose for your shipments. By one or by all you are subjected to exactly the same extortionate rates.

This is the extortion: Spokane is 340 miles east of Seattle; the haul from Chicago to Seattle is about 2,248 miles; the haul from Chicago to Spokane is only 1,980 miles. The lines by which freight is hauled from Chicago to Seattle pass through Spokane and go 340 miles farther to reach Seattle.[2] Is that clear? Good. To a traveler passing from Chicago to Seattle, Spokane is relatively like Syracuse to one passing from New York to Buffalo.

Let us say that you are a dry-goods merchant in Spokane and you have shipped to you from Chicago, a carload of calico and other fabrics in your line. On that carload the freight rate that you will pay is not the normal freight rate from Chicago to Spokane, 1,980 miles, but the normal freight rate from Chicago to Seattle, 2,248 miles, plus (approximately) the normal freight rate back again from Seattle to Spokane, 340 miles. Thus if the rate from Chicago to Seattle is one dollar a hundredweight, and the local rate on the same commodity from Seattle to Spokane is thirty-five cents, the rate from Chicago to Spokane, 340 miles nearer to Chicago, and on the same line, is usually about

---

[2] I have used in all these calculations the shortest distances.

$1.35 a hundredweight. I know full well that if you have never looked into the subject of railroad rates in America you will think that I am in this either mad or imagining a vain thing. Yet I am but reciting the certainties of the tariff sheets. All the railroads actually do charge to the Spokane country what they charge to the Pacific coast, plus the rate back from the Pacific coast to the Spokane country. They do it now, they have been doing it for many years, they will probably keep on doing it; and so long as they do it the Inland Empire will stick where it is. This is the way the railroads develop the Northwest.

Merely as an illustration I have supposed a shipment from Chicago. The rule holds good on shipments from all other eastern points; shipments from New York, Boston, Philadelphia, Pittsburg, or other cities to the Spokane province of "Mr. Hill's domain" must pay the rate to the Pacific coast and then the rate back from the Pacific coast to their destination. A wholesale dealer in a Pacific coast city can get his goods from New York and have them shipped to his own city and reshipped to towns in the Spokane district, and the total freight rate is substantially the same as if they had been shipped originally to Spokane, although meantime they have traveled 680 miles farther than they would have traveled if they had been sent direct to Spokane, through which city they were actually hauled when they went to the Pacific coast and to which they now return.

In other words, if the rate from New York to Spokane is fair, then the rest of the haul from Spokane to the coast and back, 680 miles, is performed for nothing. To this practice all the railroads are equally committed.

But, you say, what is the reason for this most singular performance? Railroads are not ordinarily conducted on whim or caprice. There must be some reason for this discrimination. Surely. There are, in fact, not one but three reasons. The first is that the railroads have the power and can lay the Spokane or any region under such tribute as they may be pleased to exact. They can; therefore they do. You will not find this reason mentioned in the arguments for the railroads, but be not disappointed; it exists, nevertheless.

The second reason, on which the railroads lay great stress, is that their capitalization and value are such that if they were to reduce the rates to the Spokane country by no possibility could they earn a fair interest on their capital. You will see a little later how just and fair is this reason.

The third reason is that there is water competition to the Pacific Coast points and none to Spokane.

Water competition? How is that? Why, a shipper can sometimes send something from New York around Cape Horn to San Francisco. The plea of the railroads is that they made a low rate to the Pacific coast cities to meet this competition.

I invite careful attention to this plea, because it shows us exactly how freight rates are made in this country.

Water shipments via Cape Horn at the time the railroads began this practice, were made in sailing vessels. Very few vessels[3] were engaged in the trade, and these sailed irregularly. From New York to San Francisco averaged about one hundred and fifteen days. The merchandise that could be transported, subject to such delay, was limited in character and of small amount. Not one shipper in ten thousand knew of the existence of the water route; not one in twenty thousand could use it. Yet because of this competition, which existed only in name, the railroads put on an extra rate to the interior points, asserting that the lower rate to the coast cities was the result of water competition.

This seems sufficiently ridiculous, and yet it is only a

---

[3]The navigation laws compel such shipments to be made in American vessels, and there are very few American vessels.

small part of the story. Admitting that a man could ship something from New York to the Pacific coast by one of these occasional sailing vessels, he certainly could not so ship it from Pittsburg, Chicago, Alabama, Muncie, Columbus, Atlanta, or St. Paul. And yet the discrimination in rates was applied to shipments from all these places exactly as to rates from New York.

Again, admitting that the bugaboo of an occasional old hooker beating her way through the Cape Horn squalls was sufficiently terrifying to excuse a rate to Seattle as low as the rate to Spokane, what excuse could any ingenuity find for the addition of the local rate back from Seattle to Spokane on shipments made directly to Spokane from Eastern points?

I do not know. Except for the explanation contained in the first reason, that mystery remains insoluble.

But at least there the rates were, and there they remained, and because of these rates Spokane did not fulfill its obvious destiny, it did not become a great metropolis, the Spokane country did not become populous, the almost unexampled resources were not developed, the region capable of supporting many millions, had a population of three hundred thousand.

Of course! What good lies in fertile soil if you cannot market its products? Of what use is water power if it makes nothing that can be sold? Of what use is any advantage of situation if the railroads embargo shipments?

Against this deadly condition the people of Spokane groaned and protested. To the injustice from which they suffered was added a needless aggravation: they had been fooled and disappointed. Having been brought up in the school of economics that resolutely holds competition to be the infallible cure-all, they had believed their rate troubles to arise from having too few railroads and too little competition. They welcomed the coming of a new line only to find it joined hands with the oppressor. The more railroads, the stronger the combination to maintain the oppressive rates. Whenever their hope has been raised by the promise of competition, it has been immediately disappointed when the new line began to be operated.

Yet the very suggestive fact remains that in all these years of struggle the policy of the railroads has steadily violated the intention and, so far as a mere plain citizen can see, the letter of the Interstate Commerce Act.

By the fourth clause of that act a railroad is strictly forbidden to charge more for a short haul than it charges for a long haul. This is precisely what the railroads do here. They charge more for a haul to Spokane than they charge for a haul to Seattle, three hundred and forty miles farther.

How, then, if it is so clearly illegal, do the railroads manage to continue this practice?

Quite simply. In every one of these regulative laws there is a joker. The joker in this law is a provision that the fourth clause is suspended when "controlling competition" exists. The railroads merely said that this was such a case, and that the possibility of shipping some things occasionally around the Horn in a sailing vessel was "controlling competition." What it controlled, or how and where, when or with what it competed, no one ever explained. The ghost of an American clipper was seen at long intervals off the Cape, and that was a reason why freight from Chicago to Spokane should bear an extra rate of thirty per cent.

To what extent it is "controlling" may be readily gauged. In recent years the phantom clipper has disappeared and there is now operated from New York to Hawaii, calling at San Francisco, a line of steamers.

The utmost capacity of these steamers, including what they carry to Hawaii and what they carry to San Francisco, is stated in the brief of the Great Northern Railway Company to be 250,000 tons a year, and when their freight is landed at San Francisco it is still nine hundred miles from Seattle. When you contemplate these facts you will be lost in wonder at the supreme and unsurpassable audacity of the American railroad management. You should not let your admiration obscure from you the fact that the fruits of this audacity are reflected daily in your grocery bills, meat bills, tailor bills and rent.

But to return to the long-suffering people of Spokane, who are, after all, but a type of the American community in the hands of the American railroad. From the somewhat despondent and cynical mood that I have mentioned as the result of the failure of competition to relieve their distress, they were now happily aroused by the appearance of a new and rosy harbinger of joy, being none other than our old friend, Mr. James J. Hill.

In the year of grace 1889 Mr. Hill had been for ten years in the enjoyment of the wealth wherewith the good-natured and confiding Americans had so pleasantly endowed him. His path had fallen in goodly places; from an investment of nothing he and his fellow Canadians had reaped (in ways presently to be shown), profits of many millions. So sudden and so dazzling an ascent can hardly be paralleled in even our gracious annals of good fortune. But a dozen years back and he had been a lowly commission merchant in St. Paul, appraising pats of butter and baskets of eggs; and now stood he forth a financial Colossus with a great and populous region for what Mr. Higginson calls "his domain," in which, as he owned the highways he was practically ruler. And all made almost automatically by the mere revolving of a machine that rested neither day or night, grinding out profits. How poor by comparison seem the tales of Oriental enchantment and the Magic Lamp!

Naturally Mr. Hill thought well of this machine and was bent upon extending and enlarging it that it might coin yet more money for its fortunate owners. He had, therefore (as I mentioned in the last chapter), re-organized the original St. Paul, Minneapolis & Manitoba, under which name he and his fellow Canadians had secured the machine, and renamed it the Great Northern, a railroad having branches in many directions. One of these branches he determined to extend from St. Paul to the Pacific Coast.

There was already one line of railroad from St. Paul to the Pacific coast—the Northern Pacific, a name none too fragrant in our commercial history, for it had been the recipient of monster grants of the public land and had been plundered and wrecked and revived and plundered again, in the highest style of the art. Mr. Hill decided to build a line that would reach all the important places reached by the Northern Pacific and be so cheaply built and so lightly loaded with bonds, stocks, preferred stocks, debentures, refunding certificates, consolidated mortgages and other agreeable mementos of plunder that with it he should have the Northern Pacific at his mercy. That is to say, he meant that if it came to rate-cutting, he could cut the heart out of the Northern Pacific and possess himself of the carcass.

This benevolent purpose he carried out to the letter. Few railroads have been more cheaply built. To the engineers the instructions were to find the low levels, so that the grades on the line are usually less than one per cent.

And then the people along the route were invited to assist the enterprise by contributions from their own slender purses.

On what ground? On the ground that Mr. Hill was to free them from the deadly grip and devastating blight of railroad monopoly.

Happy thought! said the people. Let us be free from this terrible monster. So they gave of their substance and Mr. Hill built his railroad.

In due time he dawned thus upon the oppressed and weary citizens of the Spokane country, bringing glad tidings of great joy.

If you doubt that literally he dawned, go back to the newspaper files of the period and see.

It was February 9, 1892, when Mr. Hill came to Spokane town in his private car over the Northern Pacific railroad, and in an interview in the Spokane Review of February 10th, the good news was heralded to all. Mr. Hill was pushing his railroad westward, headed straight toward Spokane. He hoped it would reach Spokane, he most earnestly desired that it should. And, indeed, it would—if certain difficulties could be cleared away. You see the natural line of the railroad was north of the city. Mr. Hill desired with all his heart that the railroad should not pass by without entering, but to come in would involve a very great expense—that was the trouble, a very great expense.

I understand that even in those days, Mr. Hill had acquired something of the large, warm, patriarchal manner that has since become so justly famous, and we can readily imagine how impressive were these words that next fell from his lips.

"We come to give you people the lowest possible rates, which are absolutely necessary for the development of the country, and to do that, we must have a cheaply operated road. The rates you people are paying at the present time are in many cases absolutely prohibitive, and are very much higher than they ought to be. * * * I hear your coal costs you $8 per ton. It ought not to be more than half of that, and when my road gets in here, you will be supplied with fuel at not near that rate. * * * We propose, too, to give you people a rate on flour so low that the whole grain crop of the Palouse country and the Big Bend will be drawn here and converted into flour."

The heart of Spokane leaped with joy. No wonder!

In the midst of the loud acclaim, the mayor issued a proclamation, a grand mass meeting was called in the Auditorium, all classes of citizens packed the hall. Mr. Hill made a speech, declared by the Spokane Review to be "A Plain and Manly Statement of Facts." It was greeted with salvos of applause. Mr. Hill again expressed his ardent desire to bring the Great Northern into Spokane instead of carrying it along to the north. But there was that same difficulty in the way—the great expense. To build the line into Spokane would cost a million dollars, and the company could not really afford such an outlay.

"Some gentlemen whom I have met," said Mr. Hill (I quote from the report in the Spokane Review of February 12th), "have raised the point as to what would be our policy when our road is completed in regard to the present method of making tariff [rate discriminations]. I say frankly that our policy will be to back the country where the Great Northern goes through. You can make a distributing point of Spokane and compete with, if not surpass, other distributing centers in this community [Applause] and we should not feel that we are doing ourselves justice if we cannot bring goods here to sell at a competing point less than any city west or south of here." [Applause.]

Yet there was still the one sad fact about the expense. Even this, however, was not a condition wholly without hope. Mr. Hill had looked the situation over and he saw one way out. If Spokane would present the railroad with the right of way through the city the matter of expense would be overlooked. [Tremendous applause.]

A right of way? That all? Spokane went out to get it overnight. The newspapers, always foremost in good works, made fervent appeals, the best citizens took off their coats and rested not from the toil of gathering subscriptions; a great wave of enthusiasm swept over the community. Freedom was in sight, here came the herald thereof with the magic emblem upon his banners inscribed, and an editorial in the Spokane Review warned the citizens that whosoever should be backward or reluctant in this great crisis must look well to himself thereafter. "The occasion," said the Review, "calls for the supreme effort of encouragement. No man who at this critical juncture in the history of the city should fail to come forward with the most liberal tokens of assistance need ever afterwards to be considered a true friend of the city. The occasion is one when lack of generosity and public spirit will be little better than a crime."

Meanwhile Mr. Hill was not silent. In an interview published February 14th, he eloquently denounced the wicked practice of the railroads already in Spokane by which they discriminated against the city. Their invariable rule of making the rate to the Pacific coast plus the rate back, seemed to him not only evil but clearly illegal. He gently rebuked the people of Spokane for complaining to the Interstate Commerce Commission about such a matter. They should have gone at once to the courts, refused to pay the extortion and compelled a test case. "I don't think that a jury of twelve men," said Mr. Hill, "could have been found to decide that such a charge was legal."

As for the competition of water carriers, a fig for that! "We are not coming here to show fear of the water carriers," said Mr. Hill. "If we had been afraid of them we would not now be building our road to the coast."

At this bold declaration the last doubter in Spokane surrendered. Here was clearly the railroad Moses. Deliverance was at hand. When the poorest resident of the city read that statement he fished up another nickel and the well-to-do added from their hoards.

So the sum required was raised; $70,000 and the right of way, five miles long, straight through the city, were conferred upon Mr. Hill according to his desire; the Great Northern was built into and beyond Spokane. At last it reached the Pacific coast at Seattle, and the people of Spokane sat down to watch the resulting prosperity.

Somehow it did not come. For a time the Great Northern operated on a lower tariff rate than the other roads. Presently it abandoned this tariff and adopted precisely the rates and methods of the other roads. That is to say, it made the rate to Spokane the rate to the Pacific coast plus the rate back.

The rosy promises of Mr. Hill vanished into air—thin and hot, whereof they had been born.

Spokane had given of its money and bestowed the right of way five miles long through the heart of the city merely to add to the number of its oppressors—simply this and nothing more.

Sadly Mr. Hill's attention was called to the discrepancy between his unctuous promise and his arid performance. Alas! that great and good man had become afflicted with a malady that seems reserved for the great and good in his position. He had lapsus memoriæ in its worst form. As to everything connected with his visit to Spokane his mind seemed a blank.

But he kept the $70,000 and he kept the right of way. The malady did not affect his power to keep things; only his power to remember things.

Hence, the spoliation of Spokane and the Inland Empire goes merrily on today as at any time for the last twenty-five years.

I will give some examples of the rates actually charged that I may show just what these things mean to the Inland Empire. Incidentally you may get some impression of what similar things mean to you. You can see that if a grocer in Spokane is charged an abnormal freight rate on everything he sells he has no resource but to pass that rate along to the people that buy of him; so that, as a matter of fact, it is not the wholesaler of Spokane, nor the retailer, nor the manufacturer, that pays these extortionate rates, but always and invariably the consumer.

And similarly, you that do not live in Spokane but are subjected to the like extortionate freight rates, it is not the shipper that pays these rates, nor the wholesale merchant, nor the retail merchant, nor anyone in the world but just you, the consumer. You pay them all and each, of whatsoever kind and for whatsoever purpose levied. You pay whenever you purchase anything from apples to zinc. For every dollar of watered stock and needless bonds, you pay. Every time the merry railroad gentlemen cut what they pleasantly term "another watermelon," you pay for it. Everything you eat and everything you wear and everything you use in your house or your office or your shop has an extra price to pay for these watermelons and the like good things.

Bearing in mind these indisputable facts, you should find a peculiar interest in the table on another page showing exactly how the extra price was landed upon the people of one region. I hope before we get through to have some other tables showing how the extra price is landed upon people in other regions.

One item in this list deserves a word of comment. You may note that in one case, and one only, that of pig iron, the rate to Spokane is the same as the rate to the coast cities. The reason is instructive. Up to 1904 the freight rate on pig iron from Alabama to Spokane was $21.90 a ton, which was $6.80 a ton more than the rate from Alabama to the Pacific coast. Some Spokane men that needed pig iron discovered they could buy it in England, have it shipped as ballast in the wheat ships to Portland, Oregon, and thence by rail to Spokane at a total cost of $27.80 a ton, which included the price of the iron. Whereas to buy iron in Alabama, have it shipped direct to Spokane and pay the rates demanded by the railroad combination would make the cost of the iron $30.80 a ton. When this fact had been demonstrated the railroads secretly made a rate on iron of $13 a ton from Alabama to Spokane, the same as the rate from Alabama to Pacific coast points.

FREIGHT RATES TO SPOKANE AND TO THE PACIFIC COAST, 340 MILES FARTHER.

Commodity	Shipped From	Rate to Spokane	Rate to Coast a Pacific Point.
Agricultural implements.......	Chicago	1.65	1.25
" "	Mississippi river points	1.45	1.15
" "	New York & Boston	1.75	1.25
Baking powder	Chicago	1.64	1.10
Bath tubs, sheet steel.........	"	3.25	2.40
Bath tubs, cast iron..........	"	2.10	1.40
Belting	Eastern points	1.95	1.10
Belting (less than car load)...	Chicago	3.13	1.65
Belting link	"	1.73	.85
Bicycles	"	3.70	2.50
Books, blank, etc............	"	1.79	1.25
Boots and shoes	"	2.90	2.35
Boxes, paper	"	1.44	.90
Beef extract	"	2.18	1.40
Bolts, nuts, washers, etc......	Pittsburg district	1.28	.80
Canned corn	New York and Ohio	1.43	.95
Car wheels, mining...........	Chicago district	1.26	.85
Canned goods	Chicago	1.35	.95
Carpets	"	2.60	1.75
Coffee	"	1.38	.90
Cast-iron stoves, cooking, etc..	"	1.70	1.40
Clothing	"	2.35	1.50
Castings, plain	"	1.45	.75
Crockery	"	1.49	.95
Cotton piece goods...........	New York	1.85	1.00
Cottons, duck and denims.....	Chicago	1.75	.90
Dry goods, calicoes, etc.......	"	1.85	1.00
Earthenware	"	2.18	1.40
Fire escapes	"	1.70	1.25
Furnaces	"	1.91	1.40
Gas stoves	"	3.77	2.50
Glass, common window........	"	2.35	1.50

THE ROMANCE OF THE INLAND EMPIRE

Commodity	Shipped From	Rate to Spokane	Rate to a Pacific Coast Point.
Glassware	"	1.80	1.10
Granite ware	"	1.80	1.10
Hardware, saddlery	"	2.20	1.75
Horse blankets	New York	3.88	2.40
Horseshoe nails	Chicago	1.39	.85
Ink	"	1.81	1.00
Insulators	"	1.60	.75
Iron, structural	"	1.23	.75
Iron, bar	"	1.10	.75
Iron, bar (less than car load)	"	2.07	1.25
Iron, bridge	"	1.23	.75
Iron, pig (a ton)	Alabama	13.00	13.00
Lamps, incandescent	Chicago	3.20	2.00
Lamps, not electric	"	1.95	1.10
Lamps, glass	"	2.35	1.10
Linoleum	New York	1.72½	1.00
Leather	"	2.98	1.50
Lawn mowers	Chicago	2.10	1.25
Linseed oil	"	1.64	1.10
Mattresses, etc	"	1.79	1.10
Mining machinery	New York	1.68	1.40
Nails and wire	Chicago	1.10	.65
Nuts	"	2.31	1.30
Oilskin clothing	New York	2.45	1.60
Oilcloth, table	"	1.70	1.00
Paint, mixed	Chicago	1.21	.90
Picture moldings	"	1.85	1.00
Paper, corrugated	"	1.78	.85
Paper, building	"	1.19	.75
Paper, building	New York	1.29	.75
Paper bags	Chicago	1.40	1.00
Paper, wrapping	"	1.80	1.20
Paper, wrapping	New York	2.00	1.20
Pig iron	Chicago	1.00	.50
Pipe, corrugated	"	1.78	1.00
Pumps	Chicago	1.95	1.40
Refrigerators	"	2.20	1.35
Rubber boots and shoes	"	2.20	1.35
Rubber clothing	"	2.45	1.60
Rubber tires	"	1.95	1.10
Rubber tubing	"	2.05	1.20
Seeds	"	1.70	1.20
Sewing machines	"	2.25	1.40
Soap, toilet	"	1.23	.75
Soda, ash	"	1.00	.50
Spices	"	2.03	1.25
Steel safes	"	2.41	1.75
Steel plates	Pittsburg district	1.23	.75

Commodity	Shipped From	Rate to Spokane	Rate to a Pacific Coast Point.
Steel sheets	"	1.28	.80
Steel angles, beams, channels, etc.	"	1.23	.75
Shafting	"	1.23	.75
Toys	Chicago	2.20	1.35
Tobacco	"	2.91	1.50
Trunks and valises	"	3.05	2.20
Twine for harvesters	"	1.44	.90
Typewriters	"	5.96	3.00
Underwear and hosiery	New York	2.35	1.50
Wagons	Chicago	1.65	1.25
White lead	"	2.20	1.80
Wire and wire goods	"	2.35	1.50
Window-curtain poles	"	1.76	.90
Washing machines	"	2.10	1.40
Washing machines	New York	2.55	1.40
Window-shade cloth	"	1.85	1.00

In doing this they nullified, of course, their contention that they could not afford to haul freight to Spokane for the rate charged to the Pacific coast (340 miles farther), but that contention was from the beginning so manifestly ludicrous that it could always be nullified without difficulty.

Of course the natural query that arose was why, if the railroads could make the rate on pig iron the same to Spokane and to the Pacific coast (340 miles farther) they could not make a similar rate on other things. To this question no answer has ever been returned. But that is one of the good things about running a railroad. You do not have to answer questions. There is no power on earth to compel you to answer them; the Supreme Court of the United States has so decided.

SAMPLE RATES FROM THE TARIFF SHEETS PREPARED FOR MR. HILL'S DOMAIN.

ON LUMBER.

From Portland, Seattle, etc., to Spokane	$0.20
From Spokane to Portland, Seattle, etc.	.26
Portland to St. Paul, Minneapolis & Duluth, about 2,050 miles.	.40
Spokane to St. Paul, Minneapolis & Duluth, 1,500 to 1,700 miles	.40
Portland to Lewiston, 687 miles	.20
Spokane to Lewiston, 147 miles	.13

Lumber is hauled eastward from Portland 687 miles for twenty cents; it is hauled eastward from Spokane only 385 miles for twenty cents. Eastward from Seattle it is hauled 348 miles for twenty cents; eastward from Spokane it is hauled only 216 miles for twenty cents.

MISCELLANEOUS.

Wallace, Idaho, is 102 miles east of Spokane.

Rate on bar iron, Pittsburg to Spokane	$1.23
Local rate, Spokane to Wallace	.45
Total	$1.68
Rate on bar iron, Pittsburg to Portland	$0.75
Local rate, Portland to Wallace	.82
Total	$1.57

The haul is 350 miles farther than if shipped by way of Spokane. Can you beat this?

The local from Spokane to Wallace, 102 miles, is forty-five cents; the local from Portland to Wallace, 452 miles, is eighty-two cents.

This is the way Mr. Hill develops the Northwest and brings prosperity and plenty to the Inland Empire. Let us hope that the inhabitants of "Mr. Hill's domain" will not continue to be restless under these conditions nor show indifference to the favors bestowed upon them. Let them be calm and remember how Mr. Hill, as Mr. Higginson has so kindly reminded them, has improved their live stock and taught them how to farm. And shall such good deeds be without reward?

What actual effect did these rates have upon manufacturing and business in Spokane?

Good question. Let us see. Here is one concrete illustration: The Pacific Coast Pipe Company was organized at Spokane in the spring of 1900 and began to manufacture bored wooden pipe for water conductors and the like purposes. There was only one other such manufactory in "Mr. Hill's domain" and that was at Seattle. The rate on manufactured pipes was then forty-six cents a hundred pounds from Seattle to Spokane, plus the local rate from Spokane to any Eastern point if the shipment went beyond Spokane. This put the Spokane factory and the Seattle factory on something like an equal footing and the Spokane factory did well. After a time the Seattle factory, feeling the competition, called the attention of the railroads to this condition and the railroads immediately put manufactured wooden pipe under the classification of lumber. This reduced the rate from Seattle to Spokane from forty-six cents to twenty cents a hundredweight.

From the first the Spokane factory had been compelled (by reason of the railroad rates) to pay fifty cents more a hundredweight for the wire it used and twenty cents a hundred more for its raw material and had still managed to keep alive. It was now suddenly confronted with the fact that because of the change in classification the Seattle factory was able to sell pipe in Spokane for about half of the Spokane factory's price. The first intimation of this fact was the sudden discovery that the Seattle factory had far underbidden the Spokane factory on a contract in Spokane itself. The Spokane factory perceived the hopelessness of the situation and moved to a suburb of Seattle.

That is why, in spite of magnificent water power, manufacturing languishes in Spokane.

Spokane is abundantly supplied with pine and cedar lumber adapted for many purposes, but particularly window sash. With this advantage, and the water power, Spokane should be making windows for all the towns in "Mr. Hill's domain." As a matter of fact, it makes them for only the local trade, and not even for all of that. Railroad rates enable the coast factories to overwhelm the trade in the Inland Empire. Thus the rate on window glass from Pittsburg to Spokane is $1.38½ a hundredweight. This kills the Spokane manufacturer.

A great lumber and manufacturing company from the East planned to build a $75,000 sash factory in Spokane if it could get the same rate on glass that was paid to Seattle (340 miles farther). No such concession could be obtained from the railroads in "Mr. Hill's domain" and the lumber company moved to another region. The railroads allow the Pacific coast cities to ship sash at lumber rates. This enables the coast manufacturers to lay down manufactured sash in Spokane for freight charges of $1.10 against a rate of $1.38½ charged to Spokane for the glass alone. The only thing that has kept the Spokane factories alive is the local demand for special sizes in sash. The coast factories supply only regular sizes.

"Above all, the highways of the nation must be kept open to all upon equal terms," roared President Theodore Roosevelt in his annual message of 1904. The people of the Inland Empire like to recall those words: in the light of their experience with the highways of the nation (and the highwaymen) they find the irony quite piquant. Because, by means of the methods I have described, the four railroads take from the city of Spokane every year at least a million dollars in excessive freight charges.

Singularly enough the railroad that has seemed to be most active and zealous in defeating the efforts of the citizens to secure relief is the Great Northern—once hailed by them as their savior and friend.

In the course of the pleas of the Great Northern much is made of the capitalization of the railroad and the impossibility of granting any rate concessions and paying interest on that capitalization. It appears that the capital stock of the Great Northern is $210,000,000 and that there is a funded indebtedness (bonds) of $126,397,909, making a total capitalization of $336,397,909. It is for the sake of maintaining interest and dividends on this capitalization that the rates are defended. I purpose in my next chapter to show just what that capitalization means and where it came from. And I shall show it in a way not before shown to you. And I think you will be astonished with the showing.

As for example, in passing: What is the total capitalization of the Great Northern railroad on which we must keep up the rates to provide interest and dividends? $336,396,909. And how much have Mr. Hill and his friends drawn from the enterprise, exclusive of interest, dividends, and the like emoluments? $407,000,000. And how much did they invest in the enterprise? Not a cent. How does that appeal to you as a really interesting fact?

So stands this most remarkable story of the railroads and the Inland Empire. And yet even now you have not all of it. Still more significant than anything I have told here is the marked hesitation that has been displayed in dealing with the case.

The whole situation has been laid bare before the Interstate Commerce Committee of the United States Senate and the Committee, realizing what was involved, persistently dodged any decision. Writers have offered it to magazines and newspapers and the astute editors have perceived what impended therein and steered away from such a vortex. Efforts have been made to interest in the case various public men and they have fled incontinently from the thought.

There was too much involved; the thing was too tremendous; it meant too much.

The whole American system of railroad rate making was fatally attacked in that one case.

In a decision made public on March 3, 1909, the Interstate Commerce Commission upheld the position taken in these pages and the plaint of the wronged people of Spokane by declaring the rates I have given here to be "unjust and unreasonable" and ordering the railroads to reduce such rates (in the great majority of instances adduced in the test case) to the basis of the rates to Seattle.

Three years later that ruling was still ineffective; one court after another had taken a hand at blocking it; the railroads, including those managed by the paternal Mr. Hill, were still engaged in levying the forbidden toll upon "his domain"; and the people of Spokane were holding indignation meetings and raising public subscriptions to protest at the delay.

That is one reason why this story is of vital interest to us now. The analysis of the Spokane rates and the frustrated hopes of the plundered Spokane people lead to the same great lesson, which is that the railroads of the United States are a power superior to the government, that they levy and collect from every community whatever toll they please and that every attempt to restrain them or control them ends in the same ridiculous failure.

But suppose this long drawn out case to be settled; suppose by a stretch of the imagination that the railroads could be brought to obey the ruling of the Interstate Commerce Commission.

Who or what is to compensate the people of the Spokane country for the huge injury these rates have inflicted upon them all these years? Who is to assure them that upon some other excuse equally "unjust and unreasonable" they shall not again, perhaps tomorrow, be subjected to a similar injury?

Who is to make any such assurance to hundreds of other American communities?

For is the Spokane region the only one to which rates are made in this manner?

Not by many. The basic principle employed in this case of such charges as the traffic will bear is the universal rule.

Meantime you and I, we pay the extortionate rates in everything we buy, and meantime these same extortionate rates pile up to make the fortunes that are produced from an investment of nothing.

In other words, the money mill that we have described here keeps on grinding beyond any present power to stop or control it, our labor is thrown into the hopper and our dollars are the grist, cheerfully borne away by combinations like that of the four Canadians.

And thus do we develop the Northwest—also other regions. Brethren, how would it do to still for a time the resounding platitude concerning wealth "honestly acquired," and the trite old formulas about the romance of the railroad, and come down to contemplate facts as they are?

CHAPTER III.

THE GREATEST MELON PATCH IN THE WORLD.

Now and then, at rare intervals, an American community, oppressed in the manner of the Inland Empire, wearies of the oppression and ventures upon revolt.

That makes a story even more interesting than the oppression itself—possibly for the sake of the novelty.

Patience is the badge of all our tribe. It is one of the cardinal virtues much extolled by the old writers. Therefore, with some touch of patriotic pride, I believe we are accustomed to refer to the marvelous and perdurable American patience that makes Job under his boils seem by comparison but an irascible neurotic. Very likely, too, our virtue is the more admirable in us that we can at any time end our troubles; for this brings our endurance to the level of voluntary sacrifice and self-immolation, a merit not to be overlooked.

That is one reason why I wish to tell in detail the story of the revolt of Spokane before the Interstate Commerce Commission.

Now, this grand old body has existed for twenty-five years, most of the time in a state of coma.

In former days it roused but seldom, making at long intervals a noise like one awake and then relapsing into sweet repose.

This is not so important as you might think, because even when it did wake up, the courts nullified its actions, so it might as well have been asleep as awake.

Latterly, because of the appearance of a restless and aweless disposition on the part of the public, it has insisted upon trying to do things, courts or no courts.

One of its seasons of dangerous activity was when it heard the case of the Inland Empire.

The reason it woke up then was because the case developed such extraordinary features and was the occasion of such an amazing revelation, beyond all precedent in railroad history, that even a Government commission under a law designed to produce atrophy was obliged to give heed thereto.

This is news to you. Although in a thousand ways it is of very great importance, so great that no presidential campaign nor change of administration nor succession to the speakership could mean so much, very little of it has been reported in your daily newspaper, scarcely any of it has been sent out by the Associated Press. You might profitably put in a few hours asking why not. Only I know you will do nothing of the kind. You never do.

The cause of the Inland Empire against the railroads that had so long throttled and despoiled it was undertaken by the revolting citizens of Spokane. "Before the Interstate Commerce Commission, the City of Spokane, Spokane Chamber of Commerce, Spokane Jobbers' Association and the County of Spokane versus the Northern Pacific Railway Company, Great Northern Railway Company, the Union Pacific Railroad Company, Oregon Railroad and Navigation Company, Spokane Falls & Northern Railway Company." So the case was termed. It turned on the conditions related in the foregoing chapter. That is, the railroads had for years oppressed the Spokane region by making the freight rate from the East to Spokane equal to the rate from the East to the Pacific coast (340 miles farther) plus the rate back from the Pacific Coast to Spokane.

This the wearied citizens said was unjust and unfair.

In its final form that has special interest for us, the case came to a first hearing in June, 1906. Naturally, the defendant railroads combined, and having at issue the vital

THE GREATEST MELON PATCH IN THE WORLD 59

question whether they can at all times in their own domain make such rates as they see fit to make, they were represented by able, learned, skillful, adroit, experienced corporation lawyers. You know what that means.

Of the counsel for the revolting serfs of the Inland Empire, there were also very able men, Mr. H. M. Stephens, Mr. J. M. Geraghty, Mr. A. M. Winston, Mr. R. M. Barnhart of Spokane, and Mr. Brooks Adams of Boston.

Much of Mr. Brooks Adams' life has been spent in studies of the railroad problem. He has convictions on the subject. I am told that because of his convictions he served without compensation in the Spokane case. I do not know how this is and admit that it seems too good to be true. Yet it may be. Mr. Adams comes of that kind of a family. He is a grandson of John Quincy Adams and a son of that Charles Francis Adams whose services as Minister to England in our Civil War were so monumental.

When the hearings came on, the railroads defended their rates to Spokane on two chief grounds.

First, there was the phantom ship seen at long intervals off Cape Horn. That is to say, they pleaded water competition. Sometimes a man could ship something by water from New York to San Francisco. Therefore they had a right to gouge what they pleased out of Spokane.

Second, they said that the value and capitalization of the railroads were such that if rates to the Spokane region were reduced the railroads would not be able to earn a just and reasonable profit; such a profit as the courts had decided a railroad was entitled to make.

Kindly note that this was on the basis of the value and capitalization of the roads.

"These defendants, in order to show the reasonableness of the total revenues drawn by them from the public, valued the entire property employed by the corporations in the public service, and then, deducting the cost of operation, taxes and depreciation from their receipts, calculated the balance as a species of rental upon the sum total which their schedules showed."[1]

This plea struck squarely into Mr. Adams' convictions. I suppose it must have seemed to him basic and vital to the whole vast national transportation problem. Anyway, he advised that the dear old Cape Horn hooker be allowed to beat and bang her stormy way and the issue be joined on this great point of value and capitalization.

As applied to this particular case the issue meant whether the railroads could afford to loosen their grasp on Spokane's throat; but the total question involved was almost infinitely greater than that.

Facts as to the existing rate discriminations and the effect thereof were amply testified to. The railroads submitted much testimony as to value and capital. We may learn with gratification that conspicuous in the vanguard of the forces fighting for the right to charge at will was our old friend, the Great Northern. The broken-backed St. Paul & Pacific, of which Jesse P. Farley had been appointed receiver in 1873; the remade St. Paul & Pacific that in 1879 Mr. Hill and his friends had for a merry song secured from the Dutch bondholders; the St. Paul, Minneapolis & Manitoba mint that American generosity had conferred on the Canadian brotherhood; the money-making machine from which had come so huge a fortune—behold it now neatly disguised and come to court on this pleasant occasion, protesting that on any reduction of its rates to Spokane it would be unable to earn "a just and reasonable income" on its value and capital.

What was its capital at that time?

According to the company's statement, $250,120,989.39.

---

[1] No. 870 Interstate Commerce Commission, City of Spokane et al. versus Northern Pacific Railway et al. Supplemental brief for complainants, page 1. Brooks Adams of Counsel for Complainants.

And what was the value of the property?

An expert summoned by the railroad put the value at $415,000,000. On this the annual income, after the necessary deductions for depreciation, left for profit no more than a pitiable 3.65 per cent. Could the Commission have the heart to reduce the revenue of an enterprise that was making only 3.65 per cent? Think of the widows and orphans!

All this was very ably supported. Detailed estimates were submitted showing the cost of construction; bridges, trestles, ties, and spikes were considered; labor and the cost of transporting it. Some very ugly discrepancies between different testimonies at different times were neatly skated over; also some highly suggestive facts about the methods of bookkeeping; and a total reproduction cost of $62,570 a mile was shown.

So now we go back to Receiver Farley and recall that he built and equipped 112 miles of this railroad at an average of $9,500 a mile. How does that agree with the testimony? I do not know. But it is not the only difficulty. The State Railroad Commission of South Dakota found that many miles of railroad in that State had been built for $8,000 a mile and even less. In hunting over the records of this case I have found many instances where railroads have been built and equipped for $12,000 a mile. According to repeated assertion and even sworn testimony in other cases the Great Northern was cheaply built; its grades were lower than those of any other transcontinental line.

I do not pretend to explain the discrepancy. But I know that discrepancies are no novelty in railroad testimony, and if you could get an Interstate Commerce Commissioner to tell what he has heard from the witness stand you would be amazed.

Next, terminals, stations, gifts of public lands, right of way, and other possessions were put in at startling figures, including, if you will believe me, the right of way and other donations bestowed by the people of Spokane. That their presents, secured and given with such a pathetic outburst of public feeling, should now be used as a club against them must have struck many Spokane citizens into cynical laughter. And upon all this value so heaped up Mr. Hill's Company desired to obtain "a just and reasonable profit" by making such rates as it might be pleased to make.

Included in the lands thus valued were certain areas that had been taken away from the Indians that the Government might bestow more riches upon the railroad. I do not know of any fact better worth the philosopher's attention—or the patriot's either, supposing such there be. For how do you imagine any such gift was brought about?

Tables were presented by the railroad company showing the losses it would suffer if the Spokane rates should be reduced. These tables were ably prepared and calculated to convince any person not initiated about such manipulations. Much testimony was heard on the railroad side. Some of it was erroneous, and erroneous in a very astonishing way; but we need not bother about that; as before observed it is no novelty in such hearings. Altogether the case was very strong; no doubt it was the strongest for the railroads ever made in this country.

This was the difficulty that confronted Mr. Adams. He felt perfectly certain that the showing made for the railroad company was wrong; all his investigations and studies in the railroad problem taught him it was wrong. Somewhere in the company's argument existed a fatal flaw, but no one had ever demonstrated the flaw. Universal custom had decreed the taking of a railroad company's statement at its face value. Thoughtful men knew well enough that the face value was usually fictitious and that the whole American railroad business was rotten with fraud and lying.

But no one had ever analyzed and destroyed an ably structured statement such as this.

Mr. Adams now brought into the case Mr. Frederick O. Downes, a Boston attorney with an extraordinary gift for financial analysis and research, in which he had long been engaged with great insurance companies. Mr. Downes inserted his probe at the beginning of Mr. Hill's railroad career and for many weeks patiently followed its trail down to the day of the hearing.

What he discovered is to the outsider the most amazing and significant revelation ever made about the American railroad.

Mr. Downes put his finger directly upon the chief nerve in the railroad problem. For the first time he revealed the real nature of the railroad business as conducted in our broad, happy land.

You have always believed that business to be the carrying of freight and passengers. To the real purpose of a modern railroad, freight and passenger traffic is but a necessary blind. The real business is to issue, to manipulate, and to possess railroad securities.

Other persons have asserted this; Mr. Downes proved it. He did his work thoroughly and finally. Henceforth we shall not be able to utter very successfully the sonorous platitude and the familiar formula when dealing with the railroad problem. Mr. Downes brought things from aerial flight to plain cold earth.

Let us see how, for now we stand at the center of the whole subject. Here is one reason why you pay too much for everything you buy; here is why your cost of living goes up while your wages are stationary; here is why railroad travel in the United States is so notoriously unsafe; here is why we have grade crossings and single tracks, why they kill and maim so many persons; why the New York Central is able to maintain Death Avenue in the heart of the metropolis of the nation, why the railroads have desired and have been able to debauch legislatures, to corrupt politicians, to maintain bosses, and to own newspapers; here is why they are able to defeat or to nullify every attempt to restrain them, why the Interstate Commerce Law is a joke, the Elkins Bill a farce, the Hepburn Bill a pleasantry, the Commerce Court a barricade. Here is why the railroads hire writers and manipulate magazines and own editors. It is all here, the grand story; miss not a word, because herein lies not only what affects day by day your pocket-book and your comfort, but what affects your country as a republic and your position therein as a free citizen.

We return to the days of Mr. Receiver Farley and the compact that he swore he made with the four Canadians to secure the old St. Paul & Pacific.

Mr. Farley was the receiver, trustee and guardian of that property. He swore that largely because of his assistance the four Canadians were enabled to obtain it from the Dutch bondholders. They got it without expending a cent of their own for it and issued upon it $8,000,000 of new bonds with which they paid the purchase price. How much was that? As told in the first chapter, $4,380,000. That would leave the syndicate $3,420,000 (after other expenses) as net profit on the bond deal. As a matter of fact the real profit was doubtless larger[2] and probably approximated

---

[2] See Steenerson versus Great Northern Railway Company 69 Minnesota, 372, wherein Judge Canty says in his opinion:

"Of the lines of railroad here in question, 565 miles were built for and owned by other railroad companies prior to the foreclosure sales of 1879. At one of these sales the promoters of the St. Paul, Minneapolis & Manitoba Railway Company bid off a part of the property; [for $1,500,000, as shown in the court records at St. Paul] and the company itself, after it was organized, bid in the rest of said property. These properties, the franchise connected with the same, and a large land grant, earned and to be earned, were bid off for the aggregate sum of $3,600,000, subject to a prior lien of $486,000. The promoters transferred to the new company the part bid in by them, and the properties were immediately bonded by the new company for $16,000,000 and it issued to the promoters its stock to the amount of $15,000,000."

$4,000,000. Besides which the syndicate had secured 565 miles of completed railroad and 2,580,606 acres of fertile land. No wonder Mr. Farley sued and some of the bondholders cried aloud in agony.

Mr. Hill and his associates next proceeded to issue the $15,000,000 of stock which they divided among themselves, and $8,000,000 of second-mortgage bonds.

We have therefore at the start of these operations $31,000,000 of new capitalization, of which $15,000,000 went straight to Mr. Hill and his associates without the payment of a cent therefor. Of the remaining $16,000,000, being two issues of bonds, the first issue, $8,000,000, was paid for out of the lands granted from the public domain by the Congress of the United States; and as for the second $8,000,000 issued ostensibly for improvements and extensions, there is no record of how much, if any, of the proceeds was permanently invested in the railroad.

The first balance sheet of the company, June 30, 1880, showed discrepancies of $550,955 in the assets and of $992,367 in the liabilities.

I make bold to beg for what follows the honor of your close attention through all its details, because it is essential to a clear understanding of the most important question with which this generation will have to deal.

In the dialect of Wall Street the dividing of a good thing by the insiders is called "cutting a watermelon."

Here then were the first watermelons from what was to be the most prolific garden of the kind in the world: Specimen No. 1, about $4,000,000 profit on the first mortgage bonds; No. 2, the railroad and the land grants; No. 3, $15,000,000 of stock. All from an investment of nothing.

And leaving still to be considered the unascertained profits on the second-mortgage bonds.

I doubt if imagination has conceived anything more romantic.

But—and here is the great point not to be overlooked—these operations had placed on the road a capitalization of $31,000,000 of which only $8,000,000 was anybody's money risked in the venture, while at least $19,000,000 of it reposed with the promoters and their associates, chief among whom were the four Canadians, James J. Hill, George Stephen, now Lord Mount Stephen; Donald A. Smith, now Lord Strathcona; and Norman W. Kittson, deceased. On this, as upon the rest of the capitalization, the property was thenceforth to furnish dividends and interest obtained from the public; you and me.

On June 8, 1882, this sum was increased by the issue of $5,000,000 of additional stock at par to the stockholders. The market price was 140. Value, $7,000,000; price, $5,000,000. Melon No. 4, $2,000,000; capital stock now $36,000,000; total of melons to date, $21,000,000.

On April 13, 1883, there came to the syndicate melon No. 5, a choice, luscious, early spring variety. The company issued $10,000,000 of six per cent bonds—to the stockholders at ten cents on the dollar. Size of melon, $9,000,000.

This was indeed precious fruitage. It brought the capitalization to $46,000,000, the total in melons to Mr. Hill and his associates to $30,000,000, and added to the interest charges that the public must pay $600,000 a year.

No wonder the people of the Spokane region felt elated when years afterwards they learned of this delightful fact. They could see where some of their money had gone, and surely nothing in the world is pleasanter, or, I may add, more rare.

At the close of 1884 the total capitalization was $51,368,000, and millions had been charged off into operating expenses or the purchase of securities or in extensions and improvements. Three years later the capitalization was

$66,298,977, and $3,400,000 of the earnings had been quietly set aside to fructify the melons of the future.[3]

The garden produce of the next year, 1888, came to table amid loud applause. President Hill announced the issue of $8,000,000 of collateral trust five per cent bonds to be secured by the deposit of $11,750,000 of the securities of other railroads acquired by the company—principally out of surplus earnings. In other words, these were "stock bonds," an excellent device to conceal stock watering. The whole issue went to Mr. Hill and his associates at seventy-five cents on the dollar. Market value, par; melon, $2,000,000; added capitalization, $8,000,000; additional interest charge for the public, $400,000 a year. Why should the spirit of mortal be proud? Total capitalization to date, $80,985,000; total melons, $32,000,000.

All this time the stock of the company was paying six and seven per cent.

It appears that there were still left in the hands of the company about $10,000,000 of the securities of other companies purchased with surplus earnings not used in dividends. This surplus proving irksome, in 1889 the Great Northern Railway Company was organized as a holding company to absorb these surplus securities. Preferred stock in the Great Northern was issued to the stockholders in the old company (St. Paul, Minneapolis & Manitoba) at fifty cents on the dollar. The other fifty cents was supposed to be provided for by transferring to the new company the accumulated stock assets of the old. What this really meant was that the surplus earnings, invested from time to time in the securities of other companies, had formed another watermelon (about $10,000,000), now to

---

[3] "It would be difficult to devise a scheme better intended to confuse and to conceal than that employed in the development and operation of the Great Northern Railway System."—Interstate Commerce Commission, Report and Order in City of Spokane versus Northern Pacific Railway Company et al., page 405.

be cut. It had also great advantages because without chance of publicity it brought the securities into the capital, and was a neat and effective device generally.

The new company, having chiefly the same stockholders as the old, leased the lines of the old company at an annual rental of six per cent on the capital stock, which, as we have seen, was chiefly water. If you will think for a moment you will perceive how all these operations provided for the distribution of enormous profits without paying on any stock a larger apparent dividend than seven per cent. The real dividends on the real stock were in the year of grace 1890 twenty-four and seventy one hundredths per cent, and in 1892 twenty-eight and thirty-two one hundredths per cent, but ostensibly they were only seven per cent, and these were the measures that disguised them.

As soon as the Great Northern was well organized there were issued $15,000,000 of collateral trust bonds secured by a deposit of £3,000,000 of a previous "Pacific Coast extension" bond issue of the St. Paul, Minneapolis & Manitoba. These bonds were issued to stockholders at 72½ cents on the dollar. Being worth, we may believe, par, here was melon No. 8 of $4,125,000 and an increase in capitalization (on which the public must pay dividends and interest) of $15,000,000.

The next melon was small but tasty—$5,000,000 of stock, issued in 1893 to stockholders at par; market value, 140; melon, $2,000,000.

The company had now completed and was operating its line to the Pacific coast, the chief cost thereof having been paid out of the accumulated earnings of the old St. Paul, Minneapolis & Manitoba, being in effect another melon. "Watermelons," by the way, as a term applied to these things, is not scientific. The scientific name is "secret reserves," which sounds much more respectable, I am sure. "Secret reserves" exist in the operation of almost every

American railroad. Nobody knows about them but the gentlemen on the inside. When they are ripe they are cut up, usually in the form of new stock or bond issue. Lately the question has been raised whether "secret reserves" are honest. This, no doubt, will cause pain to Mr. Hill and Mr. Higginson.

But to return to our muttons, or, perhaps I should say, our melons (a figure of speech that Mr. Hill will appreciate). Having put its road through to the coast, the Great Northern in 1895 (hard-times year) earned a five per cent dividend on all its stock, paid the "rental" of six per cent on the original $15,000,000 of watered stock in the St. Paul, Minneapolis & Manitoba, $540,000 interest on $9,000,000 of watered bonds, $500,000 interest on $10,000,000 of watered stock exchanged for securities taken over from the St. Paul, Minneapolis & Manitoba Company, and had a surplus.

Tribute was good in the Inland Empire that year.

It was the year when the people of Spokane, having waited vainly for the low rates and consequent prosperity promised by Mr. Hill, were thinking wearily of the $70,000 and the right of way they had bestowed upon him.

It was also the year in which the plea was first made that Mr. Hill could not afford to keep his promises to the people of Spokane.

Suppose we take a look at that.

What was the share of Mr. Hill's railroad in the annual loot for the Spokane country?

Total: about $800,000; three roads; share of Mr. Hill's road, $266,000—a year.

Good. And what interest did Mr. Hill and his associates draw that year merely from the various watermelons they had cut? $1,940,000.

Therefore if they had deducted the Spokane loot from the watermelon interest, there would still have remained that year $1,674,000 of watermelon interest. Mr. Hill's share of this fund was something like $300,000 a year. With proper economy a man can live on $300,000 a year, especially if he have other great sources of income. No, you may say, if you like, that Mr. Hill did not care to keep his promises to Spokane or had forgotten them; it is rather difficult to say that he could not afford to keep them.

The Great Northern now proceeded to redeem the $15,000,000 four per cent collateral trust bonds, heretofore mentioned as melon No. 8, by exchanging them for seven per cent stock. The insiders, who held the four per cent bonds, had paid on them at the rate of 72½ cents on the dollar—a fine melon. There was now issued $25,000,000 of the new stock, and for their portions above the equivalent of their bond holdings the insiders paid 60 cents on the dollar. The other 40 cents were juggled for them behind more "secret reserves" of stock assets; that is to say, stocks purchased with diverted earnings. This was in fact the finest growth so far produced in our melon patch. Thus, the market value of the seven per cent stock was 180. The bonds were worth about par, let us say. Bonds worth $15,000,000 were exchanged for stock worth $45,000,000; melon, $30,000,000.

On the bonds the annual interest charges to the public were $600,000; on the new stock the annual interest charges to the public were $1,750,000; difference to the public $1,150,000—a year. But if we will grow fancy melons, we must pay fancy prices for them.

In October, 1898, the melon cutters issued $25,000,000 of Great Northern stock which they exchanged (in their own safes) for $20,000,000 of St. Paul, Minneapolis & Manitoba stock. The Great Northern stock was worth 192. The happy gentlemen gave a share of St. Paul, Minneapolis & Manitoba and received a share and a quarter of Great

THE GREATEST MELON PATCH IN THE WORLD 71

Northern. Actual value of what they received, 240; price paid, nothing; melon, the whole thing.

Think of it. In 1879 the happy gentlemen had voted themselves $15,000,000 of St. Paul, Minneapolis & Manitoba stock for which they paid not a cent. On this stock they had received every year after 1881 dividends of not less than six per cent; and now for this investment of nothing they received securities worth $36,000,000.

About this time the capital stock of the Great Northern had become $75,000,000. Not more than $35,000,000 of this could be supposed to represent actual investment; $40,000,000 represented watermelons, great and small, on which the public was industriously paying the dividends and interest.

Of the total capital, 53 33-100 per cent was water.

On water and all, the enterprise was paying six per cent a year; on the capital paid in, 12 8-100 per cent a year.

Meanwhile the garden ceased not to produce goodly fruit.

The next year, 1899, the Head Gardener brought in a fine specimen from the vines—an additional issue of $15,000,000 Great Northern stock to stockholders at par; market value, 190; melon, $13,500,000.

The next year's crop was an issue at par to stockholders of $9,000,000 of additional stock; market value, 175; melon, $6,750,000. Not bad for an off year.

The next year's product was a lovely thing—an issue of $25,000,000 of additional stock to stockholders at 80; market price, 203; melon, $30,750,000.

For the next three years the gardeners were busy in preparing the soil for future crops by charging off profits into operating expenses and by capitalizing earnings.

In 1905 the results of these labors were apparent in a mammoth melon of the choice early-seedling variety. Twenty-five million dollars of additional stock was issued to stockholders at par; market value, 364; melon, $41,000,000.

The next year saw the issue of $60,000,000 of additional

stock at par to stockholders and worth 240; melon, $84,000,000. Stevenson speaks somewhere of the Arabian Nights' extravaganza of American business. These operations seem to have been its delirium.

But even these with all other exploits were soon to be surpassed.

In all these years the company had not ceased to accumulate (chiefly from its earnings and "secret reserves") property of various kinds; railroads, coal mines, iron mines, lands, docks, and so on. These were as a rule, held nominally by companies having different names, the Great Northern merely owning the stock. Of these properties most of the railroads were reserved for future manipulation. All the others were now reorganized and absorbed into one company, and in that company stockholders of the Great Northern were presented with certificates of equitable interest.

The greatest of the properties was a vast area of iron-ore land in the Mesaba country of Minnesota. It had cost the Great Northern stockholders nothing, having been paid for out of earnings or acquired from land grants, or in other inexpensive ways—showing the great advantage of having a good profit-and-loss surplus and a healthy "secret reserve."

Of the certificates in the new company there were issued to stockholders 1,500,000. They then had a market value of 90; melon (up to that time), $135,000,000.

But this is a mere fraction of the aggregate profit.

The company had a contract to furnish ore to the United States Steel Corporation. The terms reveal a staggering prospect of wealth. Experts report the ore covered by the certificates at between 400,000,000 and 600,000,000 tons. Mr. Hill believes it to be still more.

If it is 600,000,000 tons, the yield to the holders of these certificates will be $1,186,400,000.

THE GREATEST MELON PATCH IN THE WORLD 73

Nothing equaling or approaching this colossal gain has been known in the commercial history of the world. And with such almost inconceivable wealth assured in addition to the great wealth already reaped, the Great Northern Railroad refused to give up its share in the loot of Spokane, $266,000 a year.

But as to the great wealth already reaped, we are not yet through with that.

I said in the beginning that Mr. Hill and his associates had taken from the enterprise, aside from dividends, interest and other emoluments, the sum of $407,000,000. Let us recapitulate and see how this total is reached.

Four hundred and seven million dollars' worth of watermelons in twenty-seven years. That eclipses all records.

Counting interest on straight bonds and interest on straight stock, with the watermelons, the Great Northern stock paid in 1906 152 46-100 per cent.

At the same time there had been capitalized $100,000,000 of earnings.

Yet all this, overpowering as it seems, is but a prelude to the whole story. Four hundred and seven million dollars and all these dividend and interest charges are only a part of the profits made by the men that in 1879 secured for nothing the St. Paul & Pacific railroad and by their associates in these delightful enterprises.

In 1896 the Great Northern bought for $4,133,456 control of the Northern Pacific Railroad and with it an absolute control and domination of the traffic and rates of the Northwest. The Northern Pacific stock for which $4,133,456 was then paid was now a par value of $25,834,100 and a market value still greater.

In 1905 the same interests bought for the Great Northern and Northern Pacific a control of the Chicago, Burlington & Quincy Railroad, giving in payment therefor the promises to pay of the Chicago, Burlington & Quincy, principal and interest guaranteed by the purchasing roads. These bonds are to be paid in twenty years from the surplus earnings of the Chicago, Burlington & Quincy. The Great Northern and the Northern Pacific will then own the great Burlington system without the expenditure of a dollar. If the nation does not interfere, what a melon will be here, my countrymen!

In 1908 the same interests bought control of the great Colorado & Southern system.

All of these purchases were (or are to be) paid for out of the profits of the enterprise that began when, with or without the assistance of Jesse P. Farley, court officer and receiver, our Canadian friends agreed to get possession of the St. Paul & Pacific without paying for it.

Taking everything together, the value of the Great Northern Railroad as given by Mr. Hill's witnesses on the stand, the various securities owned, the present value of the Northern Pacific and Chicago, Burlington & Quincy holdings, the value of the ore lands based upon a reasonable calculation of product, the present total extent of this property (excluding the Colorado & Southern) is one billion eight hundred and forty-six million nine hundred and fifty-two thousand five hundred and fifty-three dollars.

From this is to be subtracted the total actual investment, including the Northern Pacific and the Chicago, Burlington & Quincy, but excluding the Colorado & Southern, $320,935,932.

This leaves the total actual profits (achieved and in sight) of this syndicate one billion five hundred and twenty-six million sixteen thousand six hundred and twenty-one dollars.

Before this stupendous fact there is no appropriate comment.

In his first brief Mr. Adams had indicated some of these conditions. Having now the indubitable proof of them for

THE GREATEST MELON PATCH IN THE WORLD 75

the first time laid bare, Mr. Adams, produced in his second brief a memorable argument. Would that every American citizen could read it. I know not where else in such compass is anything so clear, so comprehensive, so strong and yet so calmly and reasonably phrased.

Mr. Adams seemed to show that he was not only a great lawyer, but a student marvelously well versed in men and history. He went first to the roots of things and argued for these doctrines.

1.—That a representative government exercises its functions as a trustee for the public and cannot divest itself of its trust.

2.—It can and does employ a railroad company as an agent to build and administer a highway, but the agent cannot lawfully exercise sovereign power except as an agent.

3.—Railroad rates are a form of taxes, levied to maintain the highways and compensate those that operate them, but all taxes are an exercise of sovereign power which our government holds as a trustee for the public. Therefore railroad rates must always be subject to the decision and supervision of government.

4.—There can be no such thing as a private highway. All highways are public. The railroads do not own the highways they operate, but rather administer them as agents of the government which merely executes a public trust.

He then took up the contention of the railroads in the Spokane case that they could not lower the rates to Spokane and still derive a just and reasonable compensation. He cited the foregoing discoveries. He showed that whereas the Great Northern had indicated an annual profit of only 3.65 per cent on its valuation, the real profit of the enterprise was in 1906 162 46-100 per cent, and for many years had varied between seven per cent and 240 per cent a year. He showed that aside from dividends and interest the actual profits had been almost as much as the highest total valuation of the property itself as asserted by Mr. Hill's witnesses.

To this great plea no adequate refutation was attempted. We may well believe that none was possible.

No such probing of the depths of railroad management had ever been made in this country. For nineteen months the Interstate Commerce Commission considered the case. Then it rendered a decision, based chiefly upon the question of valuation, in favor of the complainants, the people of Spokane, and against the railroads.

I emphasize the base of the decision as the question of valuation. I would have you note that the commissioners did not pass upon Mr. Adams' powerful thesis concerning railroad sovereignty. I take it they did not care to handle that stick of dynamite. But their concurrence in his doctrine of valuation was sufficiently revolutionary without anything else.

Because if the courts should ever uphold the decision of the Commission there must needs be a new and unprecedented basis of railroad rates in this country. The companies might as well tear up their tariff sheets.

Throughout the Southwest, to give but one example, exactly the principle that has governed the Spokane rates has likewise governed the rates to many an inland community. Water competition to Galveston has been at least as valid an exercise for extortion as water competition to Seattle ever was.

If now such excuses are not to avail in the face of these sobering revelations about actual profits, actual values, and "secret reserves," great changes must be made in many directions.

Other and greater results will follow. The good old basis of "what traffic will bear" (the crux of the present theory of railroad management) will be sadly shaken. The produce of the watermelon patch will lose some of its deserved popularity. The inevitable results of tolerating "private public highways" will be made clear to every intelligence. The value of railroads will no longer be accepted at whatever figures head gardeners may choose to put upon them, but the Downes probe will be applied to lay bare the monster profits to the insiders of such financial mosaics as the Erie and the Reading, the Wabash and the Rock Island, so that we can see for ourselves, as the people of Spokane are enabled to see, how large a percentage of our butcher bills and grocer bills, gas bills and coal bills, tailor bills and rent bills, shoe bills and furniture bills, goes day after day to make up the interest on the watermelons that have luxuriated upon almost every railroad in America. For this is what the railroad business in America really is.

From control of our highways a few men gather a monster secret tribute, and this tribute they use secretly to extend their control of the highways and gather more tribute.

In the end they become more powerful than any government, more powerful than the people. Intrenched in their huge accumulation of tribute, every dollar of which spells power, they make the future tribute what they will.

From your minds now lay aside all prejudice, all doctrine, all romance, all of the misrepresentation with which a controlled press has surrounded this subject. Consider what these figures really mean that have been set forth in the foregoing pages. Here, then, is the plain question:

Is it humanly possible that these things shall continue if we are to have a republican form of government?

One other thing:

Eminent beneficiaries of the system of concealing and dividing enormous railroad profits continually assert that the issuing of watered stock is "none of the public's business."

If that be true, then, as clearly shown in the experience of the people of Spokane, the prices you pay for the commodities you daily consume, for food, clothing and shelter, are none of your business, and you have, in fact, no business except to furnish the tribute extorted by these watered stock issues and to hold your peace.

You have never seen a table of railroad statistics like the table below.

You should study it well. Bear in mind that it represents only the Great Northern Railroad, which was organized in 1890, and had practically the same stockholders as the St. Paul, Minneapolis & Manitoba. On the securities of the St. Paul, Minneapolis & Manitoba there were still profits reaped besides these. Moreover, kindly observe that this table takes no note of certain profits earned on purchased securities of other roads, nor of earnings charged to operating expenses and improvements; and also remember that all these profits have been made from the public on an investment of nothing. Then I am sure you will greatly enjoy the reading of the table:

ACTUAL PROFITS OF THE GREAT NORTHERN RAILROAD.

Year.	Amount of Great Northern stock.	Dividends on stocks.	Interest on undervalued bonds.*	Watermelons or "benefits."	Total Returns.	Per cent.
1890...$	20,000,000	$ 200,000	$ 540,000	$ 4,200,000	$ 4,940,000	24.70
1891...	20,000,000	450,000	540,000	....	990,000	4.95
1892...	20,000,000	1,000,000	540,000	4,125,000	5,665,000	28.32
1893...	20,000,000	1,000,000	540,000	2,000,000	3,540,000	17.70
1894...	25,000,000	1,187,500	540,000	....	1,727,500	6.91
1895...	25,000,000	1,250,000	540,000	....	1,790,000	7.16
1896...	25,000,000	1,250,000	540,000	....	1,790,000	7.16
1897...	25,000,000	1,250,000	540,000	....	1,790,000	7.16
1898...	25,000,000	1,500,000	540,000	58,000,000	60,040,000	240.14
1899...	90,000,000	3,851,033	540,000	20,250,000	24,641,033	27.37
1900...	99,000,000	6,408,777	540,000	....	6,948,777	7.02
1901...	99,000,000	6,897,369	540,000	30,750,000	38,187,369	38.57
1902...	125,000,000	8,225,920	540,000	....	8,765,920	7.01
1903...	125,000,000	8,673,973	540,000	....	9,213,973	7.37
1904...	125,000,000	8,683,925	540,000	....	9,223,925	7.37
1905...	125,000,000	8,693,860	540,000	41,000,000	50,233,860	40.18
1906...	150,000,000	9,148,520	540,000	219,000,000	228,688,520	152.46
		$69,670,877	$9,180,000	$379,325,000	$458,175,877	

How does this showing appeal to you in the way of "just and reasonable profits?"

---
* See Page 68.

And before the Interstate Commerce Commission the Great Northern tried to show that it made only 3.65 per cent a year.

To this astounding demonstration from the records the attention of all reactionary editors, cave-dwelling reviewers, troglodyte critics, and the champions of the corporations is respectfully invited. I earnestly hope each of them will feel free to attack it in any way that occurs to him—quite free, in fact.

TABLE OF THE FAMOUS JAMES J. HILL "WATERMELONS."

Year.	Security Issued.	What the treasury of the railroad got.	What Mr. Hill and his associates got as extra profits.
1879	St. Paul, Minneapolis & Manitoba stock, original pure water		$ 15,000,000
1882	St. Paul, Minneapolis & Manitoba stock at par market value 140	$ 5,000,000	2,000,000
1883	St. Paul, Minneapolis & Manitoba bonds at 10 cents on the dollar, par 100	1,000,000	9,000,000
1888	St. Paul, Minneapolis & Manitoba bonds at 75, par 100	6,000,000	2,000,000
(Reorganization Into the Great Northern as a Holding Company.)			
1890	Great Northern stocks at 50, market 71	10,000,000	4,200,000
1892	Great Northern bonds at 72½, par 100	10,875,000	4,125,000
1893	Great Northern stock at 100, market 140	5,000,000	2,000,000
1898	Great Northern stock at 60, market 180	15,000,000	30,000,000
1898	Great Northern stock in exchange for St. Paul, Minneapolis & Manitoba, market 192	....	28,000,000
1899	Great Northern stock at 100, market 190	15,000,000	13,500,000
1899	Great Northern stock at 100, market 175	9,000,000	6,750,000
1901	Great Northern stock at 80, market 203	20,000,000	30,750,000
1905	Great Northern stock at 100, market 264	25,000,000	41,000,000
1906	Great Northern stock at 100, market 240 and	60,000,000	84,000,000
1906	Ore certificates at 90	....	135,000,000
	Totals	$181,875,000	*$407,325,000

*This table, which, except for the comments, is taken from Mr. Downes' report to Mr. Adams, does not include the net profit on the original bond issue of 1879.

CHAPTER IV.

THE ROMANCE OF DEATH AVENUE.

Glory be to the Canadian brotherhood, reapers thus in our pleasant fields of $407,000,000 profits tangible and $1,526,016,621 profits tangible and prospective; glory be to the profits, glory be to the pomp and majesty the profits support, glory to us that patiently supply the profits.

Yet not too much glory. Because—a word in your ear: the Canadians were but imitators; no more. Simple was their device for huge fortune-making and devoid of the least originality. On the confiding Americans they had but practiced the games by which often and again the confiding Americans had been separated from their substance.

So say the records. In fact, if we except only the narrative of Mr. Receiver Farley, reciting strange, sinister things about a most illegal, not to say criminal, compact, everything that was done in the case of the old St. Paul & Pacific, the St. Paul, Minneapolis & Manitoba and the Great Northern, has been done in the case of almost every American railroad. It is being done now. For some space of time it will continue to be done; and so, incidentally, will the people.

If doubt linger as to the perfect accuracy of these statements let us betake ourselves to the records of the most famous of American fortunes intimately connected with one of the best known and most confidently advertised of American railroads. And to this inquiry all phases of human interest incite us. It has romance, for this is the fortune that has occasioned international marriages, repaired dear old Blenheim Castle, refreshed debilitated dukes, warmed ancient Hungarian palaces and cheered the drooping spirits of money lenders in London and of croupiers in Monte Carlo. Also it appeals to our commercial and patriotic instincts, because this is the enterprise widely heralded as "America's greatest railroad" and few institutions have exerted upon our affairs a more profound influence.

Altogether, as you will agree, here is a grand subject for our investigation.

And lest you think that anything we shall deduce may originate in partiality or mere assertion, I take pains to assure you that all our proceedings shall be founded upon official reports and sworn testimony before investigating committees.

We go back now to the first chapter of railroad history in America and note that a business continuing in extortion had its origin in fraud. Thus:

Before 1853 ten separate railroad companies operated, or were assumed to operate, pieces of the track now forming one continuous line between Albany and Buffalo.

Like the other railroads in the State of New York these links had been built, if built at all, with public funds. State, counties and municipalities had granted, all told, $45,000,000 to aid in the building of railroads. This paid for all, or practically all, the cost of construction, and of the grants (which were in the shape of loans) only $10,000,000 has been paid back. The remaining $35,000,000 of public money has been fraudulently withheld by the companies. If you entertain a question that a railroad is purely and simply a public highway you might reflect carefully upon these facts. They are important to you.

Some of the ten companies between Albany and Buffalo financed thus from the public treasury had chiefly a paper existence, and one, the Syracuse & Utica, was merely a name.

In 1853 by the inevitable process of consolidation and unification, which is evolutionary and goes on forever and irresistibly, these ten pieces of junk had been consolidated into one called the New York Central. To show how old are the methods we have been considering I may point out that in effecting this consolidation each of the ten railroads was entered with fictitious stock. Some of those that had chiefly a paper existence were put in with the heaviest (fictitious) capitalization and when all was done, on the top of all this water there was added $8,894,500 of still more water in the shape of a stock issue. Strictly considering all these elements, the water in the first capitalization of the New York Central was not less than three-fourths of the whole.

From the beginning, therefore, this was no arid region. Vanderbilt? You ask. Oh, no. This was years before that genius had appeared on the scene. No Vanderbilt, no James J. Hill, no E. H. Harriman engineered these transactions. They were carried on by a group of obscure financiers now lost to fame—from which we should be reminded how simple is the process and how ordinary the mentality it requires. Anybody that can hire a printing press can issue watered stock; anybody that can lie can sell it; anybody that can bribe can be protected in the making of it; and whenever it is issued it becomes an enduring tax upon the public; you and me.

Similar consolidations reduced the various railroad companies between New York City and Albany to one, called the Hudson River Railroad. In both the true secret of fortune making seemed to be well understood. Thus in 1865 the capital stock of the New York Central had become $24,136,661, of which $5,000,000 had been issued against surplus earnings, which is merely a handy way of watering. Besides there were $6,200,000 of bonds convertible into stock, which may be regarded as additional water. Three years later still further issues had brought the capitalization to $28,795,000 of which, strictly speaking, more than three-quarters was water.

On watered stock and all the New York Central paid dividends of six per cent, in 1854, 1855, 1856, 1857; seven per cent in 1858 and 1859; eight per cent in each year from 1859 to 1865 and nine per cent in 1866 and 1867.

In 1867 this same railroad, making then nine per cent dividends, petitioned the legislature for permission to increase its passenger rates on the ground that at the existing rates it could not earn "a just and reasonable profit." Observe how old is that good round phrase; also how well founded. The petition was promptly granted. Evidently legislative benevolence to railroads is a very ancient custom.

Meanwhile the Hudson River Railroad had a capital stock of $6,962,971 (liberally watered) on which it was paying nine per cent dividends.

In 1869 the Hudson River Railroad cut a fine melon. It doubled its stock, one-half the increase being water. The new stock was issued to stockholders at fifty cents on the dollar, an arrangement subsequently copied by Mr. Hill. With the cash the company bought St. John's Park, New York City, and destroyed the most beautiful pleasure ground in America. Total capital $13,900,000, more than half water.

In both roads Commodore Vanderbilt had become the controlling influence. He was now to give a startling exhibition of his powers as a manipulator and sleight-of-hand performer with railroad properties.

Late on the night of December 19, 1868, the directors of the New York Central met secretly at his house. There they voted first on the outstanding stock of the railroad a cash dividend equal to seven and two-tenths per cent. Then they voted to each stockholder free additional stock to the extent of eighty per cent of his holdings at the time.

"Interest certificates" to provide for this huge graft and to be exchanged later for stock had been printed and prepared in advance. They were signed on the spot and each director annexed his share of the loot.

What Commodore Vanderbilt got was the beginning of the Vanderbilt fortune, created thus with the stroke of a pen.

Some news of this remarkable performance seems to have leaked out the next day, which was Sunday. Before daylight Monday morning an injunction was served upon the treasurer of the company restraining him from issuing the "interest certificates" which stood in lieu of stock. It came too late. They were already issued.

Even Wall Street gasped and revolted at this bold exploit. The ostensible excuse for the enormous melon was that the company had large surplus earnings, many improvements and great real estate investments to be capitalized and this was the way to capitalize them. The leading financial journal of that day pointed out that these assertions were utterly false. There could be no surplus because the company had repeatedly borrowed money to pay dividends. The total surplus earnings in fourteen years had been only $5,000,000 and these had been already capitalized. There were no improvements and no great real estate investments. The whole story, therefore, was merely an example of the sheer fraud and iron-faced lying that have always attended the railroad business in the United States. The men on the inside had merely lied to the public while they rifled the public's pockets.

Yet the money obtained in this way was not all of the melons that graced the festive board on this occasion. Mr. Vanderbilt had quietly organized a little pool composed chiefly of members of his own family. He deposited in London $7,000,000 of New York Central stock as security for a loan wherewith to work his purposes. He then drove down the price of the stock from one hundred and thirty-five to eighty-four. This shook out the small holders and he picked up what they dropped, his total purchases being made at an average of ninety. When all the timid ones had fled he held his secret meeting, declared the cash dividend of seven and two-tenths per cent and the stock dividend of eighty per cent, grabbed his certificates and locked them up in his safe.

Up bounded the stock like a balloon.

By these operations he made first $4,200,000 profit on the $7,000,000 of stock he had deposited for collateral; he had with a printing press almost doubled his fortune; and he now held all the stock the timid ones dropped in the decline he himself had caused.

Remember these things when next you admire the repaired Blenheim Castle or the rejuvenated dukes, because from these sources came both styles of rehabilitation; also many other grand things.

Commodore Vanderbilt by no means escaped without public scorn and wrath.

"Either," declared a prominent Wall Street journal, "the New York Central has had a much larger surplus income than appeared from its annual reports and the present dividend fairly represents it, or the representations of surplus earnings are fictitious and the dividend is unwarranted." In either case one would think the operation about on a par with safe-blowing or second-story work.

But expressions of public resentment availed not to check the melon-cutting. They never do.

All things being now prepared, Head Gardener Vanderbilt brought in the next fruit, being the consolidation of the Hudson River and the New York Central railroads, planned before the secret meeting at his house.

The manner in which this scandalous deal was carried out is worth your attention; particularly as you have paid for it ever since.

First, a new company was formed, the New York Central and Hudson River, with capital stock of $45,000,000, being four hundred and fifty thousand shares of one hundred dollars each. Of this the stockholders of the New York Central received $28,972,000 and the stockholders of the Hudson River $16,028,000. So far, good. But this left the $22,500,000 of "interest certificates," the flood of water that has been issued at the secret meeting. These were now provided for. The directors of the new company had been authorized to issue additional stock. They issued enough to enable the "interest certificates" to be exchanged into stock at par.

When this had been done it appeared that the stockholders of the Hudson River had really received $29,651,800 for their $13,900,000 of stock in the old company, and for their $28,795,000 the stockholders of the New York Central had received $59,605,650. Total capitalization of the new company $89,257,450. Water upon water and then more water.

The authorization of the new issue by which this result was achieved was so worded that while ostensibly it meant one thing, another and a very different meaning could be drawn from it. So great was this inconsistency that ever since thoughtful men have questioned the validity of the issue, and wondered what the courts would do about it if it should be brought to their attention.

Of the huge accumulation of water in the $89,257,450 of capitalization more than $50,000,000 consisted of securities that were largely in the nature of gifts of Cornelius Vanderbilt to himself and his family.

On this fictitious capitalization, amounting to a sum that seems to the reflective mind not less than colossal, the public has ever since continued to pay five, six and seven per cent a year.

To such a sordid and repulsive story nothing was lacking but rotten bookkeeping, and this was presently supplied. The water in the $89,257,450 of new capitalization included $44,428,000 of "consolidation certificates." For twenty-five years the annual reports of the Company were obliged to juggle with this item. Therefore every year $31,157,904 of the $44,428,000 was shoved into the "cost of construction" table along with buildings, bridges and the like. The remainder must have been divided among the other departments—"oil account," maybe, or "coal" or "stationery."

Such are the difficulties (and dangers) pertaining to this branch of horticultural effort.

Meantime, the watermelon was by no means the only produce that added millions to the fortunes of the insiders. There were the fast freight line and the express company, both fertile in illegitimate profits.

The fast freight line largely disappeared after a legislative committee had turned upon it a certain light of investigation (in which it presented a very unwholesome appearance), but for many years it had been operated with great success. This was the manner of it. The gentlemen in control of the New York Central and allied railroads organized a fast freight company with themselves as the sole stockholders. Then they made a contract between themselves as the fast freight company and themselves as directors of the New York Central by which the fast freight cars were carried with greater speed than other cars and on terms exceedingly and unfairly advantageous to the fast freight company. Then they charged the public additional rates for carrying commodities in these cars and raked off the profits, which were enormous.

If a shipper wished to have his goods forwarded with any reasonable celerity, he must ship by one of these fast freight lines, and pay the toll to the insiders. Otherwise his shipment would be subject to delay. So-called "Red Lines,"

"Blue Lines," "White Lines," gave an appearance of competition to this nefarious traffic. As a matter of fact all were owned by the same insiders and all represented swindles on the public and on the small stockholders of the railroads.

Millions were gained in this way—for the benefit of Blenheim and other dear old castles, and the refreshing of the dukes.

Another profitable device was the express contract, which, rather strangely, still survives in spite of public opinion. Cars of the express companies were hauled by the railroads at low rates, enabling the express companies which are owned exclusively by the railroad insiders, to reap great profits. The Vanderbilt family owned some years ago, thirty thousand shares of American Express stock. In the Merchant's Despatch Transportation Company, another favorite concern, the same family owned twenty-four thousand of the thirty thousand shares. This singular institution, the exact utility of which was never disclosed, was not long ago earning forty per cent annual dividends on stock only one-fourth of which had been paid for, and earning these returns chiefly by means of the favorable contracts with the New York Central lines. This seems to be better than many watermelons, because it goes on forever.

Similar observations apply to the relations between the New York Central railroad and the old Wagner Sleeping Car Company, a concern owned almost entirely by the Vanderbilts. A committee of the legislature once looked into the arrangement between the railroad and this company and made some exceedingly pertinent comments thereon, but nothing ever came of its findings. The Wagner Company made for its owners ten per cent a year, chiefly because of the contract that its owners had made with themselves as directors of the New York Central. In 1900, the

THE ROMANCE OF DEATH AVENUE 89

Wagner Company was merged with the Pullman on very favorable terms to the Vanderbilts, who became large stockholders in the amalgamated company. In 1907, the statement was made that the company, since the consolidation, had made annual dividends of thirty per cent a year in stock and cash.

But all such items suggest only a part of the sources of the wealth that remade Blenheim. Included in the same generous fountain are such things as the Albany bridge and the Spuyten Duyvil & Port Morris railroad.

The small steel bridge across the Hudson River at Albany was for many years owned by a separate company, of which the Vanderbilt family were the chief stockholders, and that sturdy and famous champion of commercial idealism, Chauncey M. Depew, was president. This company had a contract with the New York Central (which used the bridge as an approach to Albany station) by which the bridge company collected approximately ten cents for every passenger carried across the bridge, with other tolls for freight cars. The profits under this arrangement were goodly. As a matter of most obvious fact the railroad company should have built and owned the bridge, but the other company was interposed as a convenient form of "benefit." About four years ago, this scandal, after festering twenty-five years or so, came to a head in the New York legislature and the bridge company disappeared.

The Spuyten Duyvil & Port Morris railroad was part of the main line of the old Hudson River railroad. It was less than six miles long and owned by Commodore Vanderbilt. He leased it at a highly remunerative rental, first to the Hudson River, and then to his consolidated company. Three years ago the New York Central, for reasons of public policy, bought the interest of the Vanderbilt heirs in this simple money making machine, but even this occasion was utilized for further financial jugglery, and the essence of the old Spuyten Duyvil & Port Morris still goes on drawing illegitimate profits.

Many suggestive facts were revealed by the forgotten investigating committee to which I have referred. For instance, the committee learned that peculiar relations existed between the New York Central and the Standard Oil Company, that a member of the Vanderbilt family had been made a large stockholder in the oil company, that the railroad company gave to the oil company very heavy rebates. The committee also learned that for years the insiders had made great sums of money by the grossest discriminations in freight rates. Among the curious and coincident revelations was the fact that the railroad insiders had aided to build the great fortune of A. T. Stewart, celebrated as the most successful merchant of his time in New York, and that his fortune had not been the product of any phenomenal ability on Stewart's part, but chiefly resulted from a system of freight rebates arranged by and participated in by the gentlemen that managed the New York Central's affairs. Ability! As a matter of fact, the ability required to make money in this way is less than the ability required to play successfully with marked cards or loaded dice or to bet on a foreknown result.

Returning to the chronicle of New York Central finance, we find that in 1873 more bonds were issued to lay two additional tracks from Albany to Buffalo, and the same year the New York and Harlem railroad was leased, whereby the New York Central obtained possession of the Grand Central terminal in New York City, and twenty thousand shares of Harlem stock that never had been issued. This was a good day's work.

In 1877 Commodore Vanderbilt died and was succeeded by his son, William H., the originator of the two most famous phrases in railroad history—"all the traffic will bear," and "the public be damned." Two years later, the world had a chance to learn how much the various secret money-making operations had meant to the Vanderbilt fortune. William H. Vanderbilt sold $35,000,000 of New York Central stock at $130 a share, and remarked that he still held more than half of his holdings. Never has money been more easily made. The original cash investment in the enterprise had been supplied from public funds that were never returned, the total capital stock was now $89,257,450, mostly representing water and watermelons, and extracting from the public five to eight per cent a year. As before observed, blessed be horticulture.

The financial policy of the road was now firmly established. Year by year it piled up surplus earnings and concealed and absorbed them through capitalized "improvements" and investments. Year by year it extended itself by purchasing outlying or competing systems, making each purchase the occasion for more water and more profit for the insiders. Once, to be sure, in the case of the West Shore Railroad, competition forced it into the purchase of a huge unprofitable property constituting a drain on the rest of the enterprise; but in the main the money-making machine grew steadily, and as steadily increased the burden of the public that supported it. In 1887 and 1888, the company absorbed more than $5,000,000 of surplus earnings "in improvements." In 1890 it issued $15,000,000 of four per cent debenture bonds, a great part of which was subsequently redeemed out of surplus earnings. The next year it absorbed the Rome, Watertown & Ogdensburg Railroad, liberally watered the stock for the benefit of the insiders and then guaranteed five per cent on the stock so watered—held by the same insiders. In 1893 the capital stock was flooded up to $100,000,000, the increase being issued to stockholders at par. And so on.

Some of these operations represented melons to the insiders.

Much grander melons were to come.

The gentlemen on the inside had long owned controlling interests in the Lake Shore & Michigan Southern, and the Michigan Central Railroads—interests secured with the surplus and by-profits of the New York Central.

They now issued $100,000,000 of New York Central bonds, and with them ostensibly "bought" the $50,000,000 of Lake Shore stock.

That is, they themselves owning the Lake Shore stock, exchanged each share of it for two New York Central bonds having the same par value as the stock. This fine, ripe melon added $50,000,000 to the capitalization (and to the burden that the public must bear), and gave to the fortunes of the insiders a magnificent addition for which they had paid not a cent.

At the same time they exchanged $18,738,000 of Michigan Central stock for $21,550,000 of New York Central bonds—a neat little melon of $2,812,000, likewise planted upon the public patience.

One trifling circumstance had long stood in the way of this operation. It was illegal. Therefore the gentlemen on the inside had the law changed. About ten words inserted by the obedient legislature in a statute of the State of New York did the business. One authority has placed the cost of this addition at $500,000. Ten words, $500,000; $50,000 a word. This is the highest rate ever paid for writing and should dispose of the sneer that great wealth is indifferent to literature.

Meanwhile the good old game went on with undiminished ardor, the absorbing of outlying roads by watering stock already overflowing, and the capitalizing or concealing of earnings. In 1898, the management took care of $1,345,948 of surplus earnings by charging them to "extraordinary expenses and additions to property"—not specified. In 1899 the financial Moses struck the rocks again and out gushed $15,000,000 of new stock, issued to stockholders at par; market value, 137; melon, $5,550,000. In 1900 the management sopped up $1,691,060, of surplus earnings as "extraordinary expenses" (unexplained) and $2,000,000 in a "special improvements fund"—possibly having an ethical purpose, none other being specified. Some of the railroads and securities purchased with surplus earnings, cost a pretty sum ($23,000,000 in one year) and yet the enterprise earned five per cent dividends on the stock, the annual deficit on the West Shore bonds and the rest of the fancy financiering. It was a community both patient and rich that was worked for these things.

Every time a new property was bought, there was more water, and between water issues ripened the luscious melon. Thus, in 1902, $35,000,000 of additional stock was authorized, one-half to be held in the directors' discretion, and the other half issued to stockholders at 125. The market price was 163, and the melon $6,650,000. In the four years ending with 1903, there had been absorbed into the capitalization $7,000,000 of surplus earnings, disguised under the heads of "betterments," "extensions," and so on, all constituting water. In 1904 the company charged off to operating expenses $3,196,452 of additions and replacements, and set aside $1,500,000 of another "special improvement fund" (also possibly ethical). These are but samples of the goodly fruitage.

The company now went into the trolley field and used millions of surplus earnings in the purchase of various trolley lines. Additional capitalizations seem to have reached the balance sheet under the head of "extraordinary expenditures"—which they certainly were. In 1905 the directors issued the remaining $17,500,000 of stock to stockholders at par, market 150; melon $8,750,000. As an example of what the management was doing meanwhile with the subsidiary lines, I may mention that it capitalized this year more than $7,000,000 of the surplus earnings of the Lake Shore besides the 12 per cent that the Lake Shore regularly earned on its stock.

I give one other sweet sample. It is the year 1907 in which the New York Central put $2,800,000 of its surplus earnings into a "special improvement fund," charged off $1,308,260 more as operating expenses, bought 5,748 shares of Boston & Albany stock, paid 6 per cent dividends on its own stock, milked all of the connecting, subsidiary, trolley and other lines into which it had converted its surplus earnings, and convinced Charles Evans Hughes, then governor of New York, now a Supreme Court justice of the United States, that it could not afford to carry passengers at two cents a mile. The legislature had passed an act reducing fares to the two-cent basis, and the governor vetoed it.

We must suppose Governor Hughes never to have studied a New York Central balance sheet. I urge him to get one. He will enjoy reading it.

In the year 1907, the capital stock was $178,632,000, the funded debt $230,414,845, the total capitalization $409,946,845, of which $175,814,990 was water or capitalized earnings. On this $175,000,000 the interest charges to the public are something like $8,750,000 a year. The total receipts from passenger traffic in 1907 were $29,837,859.02. It is to pay interest on this fictitious capitalization that the passenger rates are based upon three cents, instead of two.

But bearing well in mind the decision of the Interstate Commerce Commission in the Spokane case, here arise two questions—pivotal, inevitable, to be thrust more and more into our lives.

The Commission entertained the contention that a railroad may not base freight rates upon a fictitious valuation.

If it may not base freight rates thereon, how can it base passenger rates thereon?

If it may not base rates thereon may it pay dividends thereon?

To these questions I should be charmed to receive answers from the reactionary mind.

In the year following the conversion of Governor Hughes to the three-cent theory, there was taken from the railroads owned or controlled by the New York Central, $5,331,384 of surplus earnings and converted into "special improvement funds," while $12,595,440 of new equipment and new construction was charged off as "expenses." In that year alone, almost $18,000,000 of surplus earnings was concealed. This is more than one-half of the total passenger receipts.

I should be most happy to have the comments of the reactionary and three-cent champions on these significant facts.

In addition, the New York Central holds $153,700,000 of the stocks of other railroads, purchased out of surplus earnings. On these its income in 1907 was $10,078,754.29. No wonder Governor Hughes stood firm for a company in such a poverty-stricken condition.

```
Capital stock, $178,632,000.
Water in original stocks, lowest estimates:
  Old New York Central.................$13,894,560
  Old Hudson River.........................  6,480,985
  Consolidation, 1869 ....................... 44,428,000
                                             ----------
                                             $64,802,545
```

Actual capitalization (most liberal estimate), $113,828,455.

This seems so romantic.

The net earnings in 1907 were $22,565,725.67, or twenty per cent on the utmost sum that can be regarded as actual capitalization. Yet Governor Hughes vetoed the two-cent fare bill.

In view of that fact, who is it that pays for the water in the stock?

There is also in the funded capital (with other water) $45,289,200 of water from the Lake Shore deal, and $2,522,145 from the Michigan Central deal, $47,811,345 in all. Besides which $63,200,000 of surplus earnings have been capitalized. Altogether the water and the capitalized earnings amount to $175,814,990.

Dear old Blenheim!

In mitigation of such showings as these in the tables below it is urged that some of the water has since become real value, and is therefore justified.

No. None of it is justified. For this reason:

There are only two possible views of a railroad. Either it is sovereign, with powers equal or superior to government and not to be regulated or restrained. Or it is an agent of the government, employed to maintain a highway and taking as compensation for its services "a just and reasonable profit."

Then, as an agent of the government, which in turn is nothing but a trustee for the public, all its earnings in excess of "a just and reasonable profit," should be returned to the public in the shape of reduced rates.

By such methods as are here described, such earnings have not been returned at all, but have been concealed, juggled, manipulated and finally swept, through the device of watered stock, year after year, into the coffers of the insiders.

Such are some of the results of the private ownership of public highways. Others exist that affect you and me in our citizenship and freedom as gravely as these effect us in our pocketbooks and household expenses.

Of such results I can indicate here no more than one, and that by but one example taken at random from a catalogue without end.

In the city of New York, the metropolis of Western civilization, with more than four million inhabitants, a steam railroad is operated for miles through crowded streets and on the street level.

For miles, from St. John's Park (Freight station) on the lower west side of New York through one crowded street after another, crossing at grade important busy thoroughfares like Canal, Christopher, Fourteenth, Twenty-third and Forty-second streets, through the densely populated region of the upper west side to the head of Manhattan Island, runs this private public highway owned by the same New York Central Railroad Company, of watered stock and shady financial history.

In popular speech the street it thus traverses has earned another and more fearful name. It is called Death Avenue.

Along this private public highway, trains that earn the dividends on this watered stock and produce these rich watermelons roll all day, obstructing traffic, killing or maiming people. Most of the street crossings are wholly unguarded; a few are watched by infirm or superannuated flagmen.

One of these trains has killed more people than any other train in the world. Kindly note that it is a passenger train not operated to carry passengers. It is operated to hold one of the franchises that produce melons and enable the watered stocks to reap dividends.

Since 1897 the validity of that franchise has been more than doubtful, but no public officer has moved to test the question. And on the last day of the session of 1909 of the New York legislature, the railroad lobby rushed through an act making this doubtful franchise valid and perpetual—including the right to kill people. Mayor McClellan of New York City, to whom the bill was referred, vetoed the measure, but meantime the company's trains continue running through Death Avenue.

A fraction of the water in the New York Central capitalization, of the amount on which you and I annually pay an unjust and improper tribute, would suffice to elevate the track and put an end to Death Avenue.

So terrible have been the Death Avenue casualties, especially among children, that many parents in that neighborhood have refused to allow their children to go to school because to go to school the child must cross these tracks, and up and down these tracks all day in the heart of the metropolis, thunder the flying trains—franchise savers and freight trains.

To date, the number of persons recorded as having been killed by the New York Central Railroad Company in Death Avenue, is nearly 400. This is not a complete total. Also, the maimed numbered hundreds; nobody knows how many.

Against this frightful slaughter-house, the people of the region traversed have carried on for twenty-seven years a pathetically fruitless agitation. They have petitioned the legislature, they have besieged commissions, they have sent men to Albany, they have maintained associations, pleaded with public officers, introduced bills, signed protests, held mass meetings, deluged the mails with complaints; and the net effects is that the situation has only grown worse.

How they have been defeated you can readily understand if you know anything about the vast and sinister control that the railroad companies exercise over legislative bodies.

In 1906, the outraged citizens felt that they could endure no more. In a memorable uprising they elected to the senate a man that they believed could not be bribed, bought, humbugged, influenced, nor bullied.

He introduced a bill to compel the New York Central to cease slaughtering people in Death Avenue. It was about the one hundredth bill of that kind. The railroad lobby had succeeded in strangling the others in committee. This man would not let his bill be strangled. He got it through.

It provided that on or before May 1, 1908, the New York Central Railroad Company should contract with the City of New York for the elevating of the tracks in Death Avenue. If no such contract were made by May 1, 1908, the city should seize and condemn the tracks.

The act was passed and became part of the law of the sovereign State of New York. May 1, 1908, came and went. The New York Central made no contract with the City to elevate the tracks. The City did not seize and condemn the tracks. The tracks are just where they were when they were put down. On them the trains rush to and fro killing and maiming people. Not the slightest attention has been paid to the law. It remains on the statute book a monument to our methods in dealing with this problem, and when the suggestion was made to certain officers of the New York Central Railroad Company that the City might seize and condemn those tracks, the officers defied the City to do anything of the kind.

Law and order, you know. We must have law and order about everything but the corporations.

But is there no reason why masses of people are allowed thus to protest, petition and beg in vain for relief from a most barbarous and intolerable condition? Certainly. An excellent reason. Let me indicate it to you.

Seth Low Hascamp, seven years old, living at No. 544 West Forty-fourth Street, was a pet of his neighborhood and a favorite with his schoolmates. On October 22, 1908, on his way to school he crossed Death Avenue. A franchise-saving train was flying down the tracks. It caught Seth and tore him to pieces. When they picked up the little mangled limbs, men found that this boy had been clad only in a blouse, overalls, and a pair of shoes. His parents were poor.

It was a tragedy commonplace enough; he was the one hundred and fiftieth or one hundred and sixtieth child that had gone that way, on that deadly avenue: and yet his funeral was the occasion of one of the strangest spectacles ever seen in New York. Behind the cheap hearse and poor little coffin marched five hundred school children, the dead boy's companions and playmates. They marched in solemn silence on their own suggestion, behind that hearse, as a spontaneous protest against his death, and because they had loved him and because they felt he had been cruelly murdered and they had no other way to protest against his murder. They marched by the church and parish house of St. Ambrose and the good fathers came out and stood with bared heads while the silent children passed. They marched by the school in which the boy had been a pupil and the flag was at half mast and the teachers stood at the windows and cried. Men lined the sidewalks to watch the procession and some had tears in their eyes and some cursed. It was only a little boy, but everybody had loved him and he had been cut down as a needless sacrifice to the system that makes of public highways a private graft.

And now for your reason. He had been poor, his parents were poor, all the children that marched in that procession were poor, all the people that dwell in that region are poor, all the people that have been cut to pieces by the franchise savers were poor, all the people that have petitioned and pleaded so many years in vain, were poor. There is your reason. How do you like it?

You think I am bitter and unfair about this because you read these things with your eyes but not with your understanding. I do, therefore, beseech you to reflect upon one certain fact. If they had been rich they could have met bribery with bribery, lobby with lobby, influence with influence, wrong with wrong. True, is it not? Being but poor they must submit to the monstrous perversion of justice and law-making that always and inevitably attends the gathering of wealth by illegitimate means—of which the history of the New York Central Railroad Company affords these conspicuous examples.

Private public highways! We are the only nation in this wide world that has ever tolerated any such monstrous and insane doctrine. The price we pay for tolerating it is expressed to us on one side in augmented cost of living and on the other in such stories of lawless tyranny and wrong as this of Death Avenue.

Brethren, is not the price too high? For when all is said and done, what do we get for surrendering the rights that other peoples hold to be inalienable? Or what is it to us that Blenheim Castle should be repaired or partnerships like the Canadian brotherhood should be made suddenly rich?

TABLE OF SOME OF THE SURPLUS EARNINGS OF THE NEW YORK CENTRAL THAT HAS BEEN CAPITALIZED.

1890	Earnings in debentures	$10,000,000
1900-1907	"Special improvement funds"	16,600,000
1902-1907	Equipment charged off to operating expenses	20,600,000
1898-1900 1905	Charged off as extraordinary expenses	7,400,000
1903	Charged off as additions, improvements, etc.	3,200,000
1887-1888	Enlarging terminals	5,400,000
		$63,200,000

FIFTEEN YEARS OF THIS MELON PATCH—GOOD THINGS SECURED IN NEW YORK CENTRAL INSIDERS.

1893	3% on $10,000,000 stock issue	$ 300,000
1899	37% on $15,000,000 stock issue	5,550,000
1902	38% on $17,500,000 stock issue	6,650,000
1905	50% on $17,500,000 stock issue	8,750,000
1906	40% on $29,839,000 stock issue	11,935,600
	Total melons of fifteen years	$33,185,600

CHAPTER V.

ROMANTIC DAYS IN EARLY CALIFORNIA.

The large, bland, unctuous man in the witness chair was with a visible effort maintaining his habitual poise and air of benevolent tolerance while the chief inquisitor of the government's commission pounded at him with sharp questions.

One after another there had been produced before him receipts signed with his name, showing that he had drawn from the railroad company of which he was president great sums of money for purposes wholly unexplained. The state legislature had been in session, he had been in the capital city, he had made mysterious drafts upon the company's treasury. With uneasy shiftings and a face like the must of wine, he had heard repeated questions as to the nature of these drafts. Sometimes he had answered that he could not remember; sometimes his lawyers, paid by the railroad company and watching like hawks, had commanded him to silence. One of these drafts was for $171,000, two were for $83,000 each, one was for $111,000, another for $91,000, one for $52,000, many were for smaller sums, $20,000, $46,000, and so on. The chairman asked ironically whether the witness were so much in the habit of carrying $100,000 in his trousers pocket that he could not remember the circumstance. To this the witness made no response, except to show on his swollen neck and face a deeper shade of purple.

A half hour passed thus. Finally, in the midst of a tense and painful silence (for the witness had been governor of his state, was then a United States Senator, and was the most eminent citizen of California), the inquisitor said:

"As to any of the sums referred to, were any of these payments made for the purpose of influencing legislation?"

Before answer could be made, the watchful counsel cut in:

"For the reasons already stated," said he, "the witness declines to answer."

"For reasons above stated," parroted the witness, obviously relieved, "I decline to answer."

The three members of the commission conferred, and then Governor Pattison, who had been asking the questions, arose and abruptly announced:

"The hearing is adjourned until tomorrow at ten o'clock."

The spectators began to file out of the room in the Palace Hotel, San Francisco, where the commission was holding its sessions. Putting on their hats, the commissioners moved briskly toward the door. A reporter approached Governor Pattison.

"May I ask where you are going?" says he.

"Going? We are going down to the Federal Court."

"Ah, yes," says the reporter. "And may I ask what for?"

"To get an order compelling Governor Stanford here to answer the question I put to him."

"Ah!" said the reporter. "It is a pleasant day for a walk. Yes—you will enjoy it. I think, if I may, I will walk along with you. I can show you the sights."

They went down to the Federal building. Little time was lost. Justice Stephen J. Field and Justice Sawyer promptly decided that Governor Stanford need not answer the question he had been asked, nor apparently any other questions that were disagreeable to him. It was a lovely day, but contrary to the reporter's prediction, the commissioners did not seem to enjoy their excursion.

The next morning the hearing was resumed. **Governor** Stanford did not answer the question. So far as the National Pacific Railroad Commission of 1887 was concerned —that august body appointed by the President of the United States and clothed with dignity and such extraordinary authority—the question was never answered.

And yet it was a question upon which rested a matter of grave concern to the government of these United States, and of direct personal interest to every citizen therein. The Central Pacific Railroad owed to the treasury of the United States more than $50,000,000, being an original loan, and the interest thereon.

Of this sum the company was endeavoring to cheat the government. In violation of its explicit contract and agreement, it had declined to meet the payment of the interest long overdue. Essentially its attitude was that the laws of the nation and the practice of good faith, incumbent upon all others, were not valid upon itself.

The first question, therefore, was whether a corporation practically created by the government could defy its creator and maintain in respect to itself a condition of anarchy.

Ostensibly the first plea of the company was that it was too poor to pay—a plea that the government and the commission and the entire nation knew perfectly well to be a lie. It was, moreover, a lie having in it a certain touch of impudence that aggravated the company's myriad other offenses, for it was annually refuted in all men's eyes by the company's own reports. The business of the commission was to put that lie on record, and to expose something of the vast diversion of the company's funds from the paying of its just debts to the making of great fortunes and to other purposes far more detestable.

What did Governor Stanford, at Sacramento, draw the money for? And how did it happen that the books of the company offered no explanation of the transactions? Legitimate business enterprises do not pay out money without adequate bookkeeping, nor without the material for an audit, should one be required.

How did it happen that these sinister entries were among hundreds similarly unsupported and unexplained?

How came it that millions upon millions of dollars had thus vanished from the coffers of this company?

That, the recipient of the most lavish and extravagant bounty from the nation, it had returned upon its benefactor a contemptuous disregard of all legal obligations, seizing the bounty for private aggrandizement and using one unwarranted privilege to get another?

That its management, from the first secret, predatory, and dishonest, had been able to do as it pleased under all kinds of administrations? How did all this come about?

We shall do very well to go into this story because now we can begin to see clearly what it means and will mean for us. This is no chapter of ancient history that we can notice or neglect as we please. Here is something started that as surely as the earth revolves will, before long, bring us up with a round turn, jostle us out of our national complacency, and compel us against our wills to revolutionize our national practices.

The men that built the Central Pacific and drew from it their gigantic fortunes, are dead; but the system they founded goes on; and now day by day we pay for it all; for the system, the fortunes, the diverted funds, the dishonest contracts, the burned books, the broken laws, the pelf and plunder, the unpaid debts, the whole great structure of fraud —every day something is taken from each of us to pay for it.

We pay heavily today and we shall pay more heavily tomorrow. We shall keep on paying much today and more tomorrow so long as the system endures.

We shall not elude it; it is not to be turned, regulated, nor checked.

It is not any matter of theories, doctrine, nor the well trained hobby horse. It is simply a matter of cold fact that will soon be thrust upon our attention in a way not to be ignored, for it will come to us in our rent bills, butcher bills and grocery bills, telling daily of increase.

How in this particular instance this great force, no doubt the greatest that ever existed among men, was organized and started on its way is a very marvelous story. From a long and humble study of its records, I come with the conviction that, considering the century in which it occurred, it belongs among the most amazing histories of human activities, to be ranked with empire building and conquests. I shall not tell it well, but even badly told, it should seem something to think much about.

How an enterprise purporting to be for the public good came to usurp all the functions of government; to rule great states, not nominally nor spasmodically, but as a definite and minutely organized system of society; how it inflicted upon one of those states a very great and irreparable injury; how it corrupted all grades of public service from town constabulary to national legislators; how it was stained with crimes ranging from petty larceny to manslaughter; how laws and constitution were nullified; how a fertile empire was deprived of much of its incomparable resources; how a system enabled one small combination of men to reach their hands into a storehouse of natural wealth and help themselves; how they maintained a political oligarchy as autocratic as that of old Venice and far greedier; how they abolished government by majorities and established government by a corporation; and how for these achievements also we pay and must pay cent per cent and many times over—that is the story.

All elements of interest are here: human, economic, moral, philosophic.

Take first the men that created this gigantic instrument of evil—what a study! Good men, in their way, not bad; each a perfect expression of a certain system and a certain ideal; each, no doubt, with a code and standard of morals to which he believed himself to adhere; each highly respected and, according to the existing system, respectable; all following out logically the tuition of their times; not much different from other men, no worse and no better; like other men the product of conditions; brought up to accept without one question the essential morality of the dollar hunt; trained to it, eager for it, snuffing it like hounds on the trail. And then being endowed with the opportunity of wealth, making of it (in accordance with their training and the accepted system) this misuse for which the next generation pays such a price!

A curious and fascinating study! And typical, too. Whatever we may say, however hard, after the national fashion, we may chase the scapegoat, the fact remains that this one American railroad enterprise is fundamentally not very different from other railroad enterprises. Something of the price we are paying for this we pay for the others. Only here it happens that we can see with startling clearness every step and its consequences to us; we can make the actors repeat all the scenes; we can see the deed and the result. And that rarely happens.

We should note something else. The men of this story began very poor and very obscure. All had been penniless adventurers starting in life with no wealth but their hands and their wills. They rose to eminence, almost inconceivable wealth, and colossal power.

Achievements of this order have long been held up to us as the most admirable; our young men have been pointed to them as to the chief and highest aims of life; the winners in this race have had praise and honor.

We have not often an opportunity to see exactly how great fortunes are quickly gathered and how this exalted goal of ours is won. Then this is a very unusual chance; we should not neglect it. We can see now what this fortune-getting really is and what it means for the rest of us, for the physical and moral stamina of the nation—for instance, national honor and political safety.

All is here, turned up for your instruction, link by link; not told by me, the poor story teller; told in the records and in the towering facts.

All through I must remind you hourly that the course of these fortunes from your pockets to the pockets of these four men is clearer than day; you can actually see the hands passing to and fro, transferring your means; not once but all the time, today, tomorrow, and always, so long as we keep the system, taking your money. Because, as you may see here, these fortunes are not fortunes alone; once established at the public expense, they cease not day and night to draw the means of life from those that need it and to amass it upon those that need it not.

So. And the scene being made ready, let us bring in the characters of the story.

Of the four men that founded the Central Pacific system, one stands out conspicuous. The rest are rather commonplace types; you can find men like them anywhere about the country now. We grow them in herds, and until fortune in their own despite puts much money into their purses, we think lightly of them, they being money grubbers and among the dullest of God's creatures.

But Huntington was different: there was always something tigerish and irrational in his ravenous pursuit of money that made him interesting. He was always on the scent; he struck and clawed at money as men long starving would strike and claw to get food, gorging and making strange sounds.

The others got money for what money would buy for them: power, position, ease, enjoyment, travel, luxury, and applause. This man got it for its own sake, piling it up behind him as he reached out his long arms for more, using the power of one million only to secure another; cold, shrewd, relentless, getting money and defending his hoard with a kind of snarling ferocity—a most extraordinary figure!

About him the whole story revolves—Collis Potter Huntington; he dominated all.

We can easily see now why he selected the others. One was a man of details, systems, and accounts; one was a smooth, adroit politician, able to throw over any transaction, however questionable, a glamor of respectability and statesmanship; one was a good builder and a born commander of men.

But Huntington himself was at all times chief, because he was so made, I suppose—a big man physically, six feet in height, broad shouldered, with muscles so strong that he could lift a barrel of flour by the chines and set it upon his shoulder; a frame like a grizzly bear, incapable of fatigue, delighting in labor as other men delight in ease, delighting in his strength and the use of it, abounding in health, and full of the love of combat.

Mentally he seems to have been the incarnation of the idea of gain, and particularly the chilliest aspect of that idea that has been called a product of New England. To trade with men and to outwit them; to make them think he meant one thing when he meant another; to mine and undermine; to add always to his store; to take in much, to pay out little; this was the substance of his philosophy. His earliest activities were devoted to its practice; there was something insatiable, even beyond American precedent, in his avid pursuit. Nothing could withstand him: "methought if the great wall of China were to arise across his path, he would attack it with his nails."

He had almost no schooling and needed none; schoolhouse education would have been a handicap to him. In his habits he was generally exemplary; a man without a vice, without a weakness, without tolerance for vice or weakness in others; rugged, abstemious, and looking upon luxury as a kind of crime. To him life was very simple. It was to work without ceasing and to regard as essentially right whatever was necessary to secure money, and essentially wrong whatever wasted money.

In this he was perfectly sincere and perfectly honest. He could not conceive that there could be anything wrong about getting money, through business or through the developing of an enterprise of the kind that with easy consciences we have called "legitimate." It was wrong to break into a safe, to pick a pocket, or to forge a note of hand; it was not wrong to manipulate stock deals nor to cheat the government nor to "influence" a legislature if conditions made "influence" necessary.

He had no sense of humor, which was, no doubt, a fortunate omission in his make-up; and with a kind of naive sincerity he believed that a man's right to anything consisted in his ability to keep it from other men—a recrudescence of jungle creed that should interest all students of reversionary types.

He was an ill man to cross. Once he left Washington, traveled by rail to the Missouri River, thence by stage coach more than a thousand miles in peril of Indians, floods, and the roads, for the pleasure of orally expressing his opinion of a contractor struggling in the mountains to lay a piece of track. For some hours the sound of his big, harsh voice rang through the canons, conveying objurgations; having relieved his system of which, he instantly wheeled about, and traversed plains and mountains straight to Washington.

As he grew in wealth he grew in contempt of weaker men until he was a kind of modern imperator, quelling and dominating with his look and his presence and to the last years of his life accustomed to unquestioned sway.

He was born October 22, 1821, in the hamlet of Harwinton, Litchfield County, Connecticut, a region where in his time the struggle for life was hard and primitive. His father was so penurious that he was called a miser, a name that, considering the time and place, seems of peculiar significance; but his mother possessed unusual gifts and exalted character. At fourteen he turned out to shift for himself, first for a year as a farmer's boy on a wage of $7 a month and board and clothes. Characteristically, he saved from his meager income $84 and had it when he returned.

"Why, that's all the money you received for the whole year's work," said somebody to whom he showed his hoard.

"Exactly," said Huntington, "that's the reason I didn't have any more." [1]

Even then, it was as if the strong jaws and great teeth gripped money and would not be unclosed upon it. All his days he never received wages and never made a profit without laying by something, pinching himself to save, and toiling for money with a kind of fanatical desperation. Thrift, thrift, the much bepraised virtue! No man ever had more of it.

From the farm he entered a country store as clerk; then to New York City whence he peddled watch findings, walking or driving over much of the United States, a young Yankee peddler sharpening his wits against many minds and learning to surpass them in cunning.

In the South once, he saw a chance for profit in what is called, I believe, "note shaving." He bought for a very low price a lot of doubtful notes that a man had taken in ex-

---

[1] Bancroft's "Life of C. P. Huntington," p. 13.

change for patent clocks, and went out and collected the money and kept it.

After some years, he made his way to Oneonta, Otsego County, New York, where his brother Solon had a store. He was there as his brother's partner when, in 1849, the news came of the gold discoveries in California. At once he determined to join the rush to the new country; not to dig gold, for he was never so much of a fool, but to trade with the new population in the gold fields, and at high prices sell it what it must have.

He had $1,200 he had saved from his business ventures; with that he started for California by way of the Isthmus of Panama. There he was delayed three months, waiting for a vessel to take him north on the Pacific side. He wasted no time. His first exploit was to transport his fellow passengers on the river Chagres (this was before the days of the Panama Railroad) and his next to enter actively into trade with the natives and the halted emigrants. In these operations he walked twenty times across the Isthmus, bought and sold a trading schooner, and made $4,000.

A sailing vessel took him to San Francisco, whence he pushed on to Sacramento, then of 12,000 inhabitants, and a place of great importance because, being near the gold fields, it was a headquarters for the miners. He had a capital of $5,000, most of which he had invested in hardware and miners' supplies. A tent was his first wareroom; in it he began to sell goods and to make money, added other tents until he had five, and then got him a store. Anything that people must have and he could buy for little and sell for much was in his line. Once he cornered the shovel market (rare stroke in a mining region!) and made the miners pay dearly for shovels; once he bought old bars of steel at one cent a pound, and when quartz mining came in and men must have steel, sold his purchase (with which he had filled his back yard), getting for most of it $1 a pound.

Men called him "Old Huntington," when he was not thirty, because he was always serious, always full of business, always intent upon the money for which he hungered and thirsted.

After some years, he took into partnership his near neighbor, Mark Hopkins, a native of Henderson, New York, an older man, methodical and exact. Hopkins kept the accounts and the stock in good condition; Huntington sold the goods.

The firm prospered; Huntington & Hopkins became a name well known. For the head of the house, men in Sacramento had a peculiar respect after his achievement with the shovels and the bar steel; a town full of traders and speculators saw here a master of chance and one that looked far ahead.

Indeed, he did seem for a time to be prescient, spying out needs long in advance and supplying them at the top of the market; and yet to one primal necessity, then most apparent to all about him, he was indifferent until it came to force fortune into his hand—a fact that would prove (if any proof were necessary) the fortuitous nature of achievement, how little there is in the assertion of superior intelligence, and how little control men have over the opportunities of success.

All this time the attraction of the gold fields was drawing every year great hordes of emigrants to California.

You know all that story, how almost over night San Francisco, from a lonely station by an empty bay, grew to be a metropolis; how the mountains were gashed by armies of miners; how sudden camps filled the wastes; how towns supplanted the camps; how, in the face of appalling difficulties, more and more men and women were leaving the eastern states for California.

By three ways they could risk their lives to reach it: They could undergo the voyage around Cape Horn, 17,000 miles, at all times a passage of frightful hardships and in the Antarctic winter season offering scarcely two chances in five of security; they could go down to the Isthmus and make their way across Panama or Nicaragua, thence going North on the Pacific as they could find shipping; or by wagons they could attempt the overland journey, threading unknown plains, hideous deserts, and the snows of two mountain ranges.

No other chapter of our history is so picturesque as this; for all its brilliant literature it seems imperfectly celebrated. For the first thousand miles of the overland journey, the way was among hostile Indians; if the emigrants escaped these, they were exposed to death from starvation or thirst on the deserts, or to freezing among the mountains. From the Missouri River until their slow wagons lumbered down the last slopes into the smiling Sacramento valley, hardly one mile of their passage was without its separate peril.

Yet in one year (so it is said), 30,000 persons left the eastern states and faced the horrors of that journey of 2,500 miles, unequalled in all the migrations of men. Sometimes they were a year or more upon the way; so often in their ignorance or inexperience they met with disaster that the plains, at the beginning untracked, came to have defined trails marked in white bones of oxen and of men.

At St. Louis, Jefferson City, St. Joseph, Atchison, Leavenworth, finally at Omaha in Civil War days, the travelers would gather with their wagons and for better protection form themselves into companies, well armed, being at last taught caution by so many reports of tragedies. At the first sign of Indian attack, the wagons would be swept into a circle for a fortification, the women and children in the center, the men crouching behind the wagon boxes with their rifles. Thus beleaguered they would endure a siege sometimes of hours, sometimes of days, very likely to be overwhelmed at last by the number of the savages, or by thirst if they were caught far from water.

Even if they beat off their mortal foes they might be lost in the alkali desert and wander miserably until they perished; or be trapped by the snow in the mountains. The name of a beautiful lake in the Sierras preserves one such terrible story from among many that are forgotten. There in the pass the Donner party from Illinois, sixty persons, was overtaken by the Sierra winter, and after such terrible sufferings as have since literally filled a book of its mishaps, only a few of its members escaped starvation.[2]

Naturally, as the traffic increased, the routes became better recognized and something like system began to appear. Emigrants for Oregon and the North and sometimes men for the gold fields went up the Missouri River in steamboats to the head of navigation and followed thence the old Lewis and Clark trail, shortening the overland journey.

Lines of stagecoaches were established, and at last came men like John Butterfield and Ben Halliday, organizing the business of travel. Butterfield chose the southern and easiest route; from St. Louis by way of El Paso he turned, as it were, the flank of the mountain ranges, and his coaches went bowling through to San Francisco in twenty-one days.

Meantime the railroads were creeping westward and all men that could think saw the great transcontinental line close at hand and inevitable from the sheer force of so great a necessity. It was a very old project; before the discovery of gold, before California was an American possession, men had advocated it. I find a curious record of a public meeting held in Dubuque, Iowa, as far back as 1838, at which a civil engineer named John Plumbe spoke for a railroad to the Pacific and showed how it could be built—the first of many such meetings.

---

[2] This is the story that suggested "Gabriel Conroy" to Bret Harte.

Thomas H. Benton devoted much of his life to ardent support of this cause. A Pacific railroad convention[3] was held at St. Louis in 1849; Stephen A. Douglas presided. Two years later, a Pacific railroad bill was introduced in the United States Senate. In 1853, Congress appropriated $150,000 for a preliminary survey and $190,000 the next year for additional surveying work. Both the Republican and Democratic conventions of 1856 demanded the railroad and by that time the legislatures of eighteen states had indorsed it.

In California many railroads had already been built on paper and one or two had a physical existence, all looking toward the transcontinental route. One of the tangible kind was actually opened in 1856 from Sacramento to Folsom.

The San Francisco and Marysville dates from 1857, and the Western Pacific, which undertook to build from San Jose, fifty miles south of San Francisco, to Sacramento, is almost as old. These are names with which we shall have to deal hereafter.

Most of the materials for railroad building were brought at great expense around Cape Horn in sailing vessels; yet despite the cost that this entailed, all the roads honestly constructed and operated, became at once profitable.

As to the transcontinental line, most men thought it would come by the southern and easy route, where Butterfield's coaches rolled over moderate grades and the level alkali desert. We know now that this was the opinion of Colonel Thomas A. Scott, of the Pennsylvania, one of the world's ablest railroad constructors. In this direction several lines

---

[3] At another Pacific Railroad convention held at Philadelphia in 1850, Joel B. Sutherland advocated a national railroad, and as if by inspiration pointed out the evils that would result from private ownership. "No man living," he concluded, "ought to have the power of building this road vested in him and his heirs —nor should any company have that grant made to it." This man seems to have been a prophet.

were already heading from the East. Enterprises and plans were not lacking; what really was needed was capital, for want of which, and for no other reason, California was still without the transcontinental railroad when the new decade began.

Sacramento, thriving with the growth of the state and already a metropolis, hoped for a northerly route, but admitted the barrier of the Sierras. Theodore D. Judah, a very able civil engineer, who had directed the construction of the best California railroad, was the first to attack this notion. He seems to have had his original impetus from Daniel W. Strong, an old pioneer of Dutch Flat, who from his own observations was convinced that more than one way was open through the mountains. In the course of twenty lonely excursions among the canons, Judah found what seemed to his trained eye a perfectly feasible route to the East by the way of Dutch Flat and the Truckee. He had in Sacramento a friend, James Bailey, a jeweler, to whom he explained his conclusions and measurements, and in the spring of 1861, with Bailey's co-operation, he called, at the St. Charles Hotel, a meeting of merchants, who listened apparently without much enthusiasm to his appeal that they should subscribe funds for a definite survey and secure the transcontinental line for Sacramento.

Bailey, warmly indorsing the project, introduced Judah to Huntington and Hopkins. They studied Judah's scheme and were convinced by him that is was practicable. Huntington brought in Leland Stanford, of the Sacramento firm of Stanford Brothers, a rising politician, and Republican leader, and Charles Crocker, at that time a dry goods merchant but with experience in developing coal mines and directing construction work.

These and others organized on June 28, 1861, the Central Pacific Railroad Company of California, capital stock $8,500,000. Stanford was President; Huntington, Vice-President; Hopkins, Treasurer; Bailey, Secretary; and Judah, Engineer. Stanford, Huntington, Hopkins, Crocker, and Judah took 150 shares each. The par value of each share was $100. There were a few other subscribers, among them Strong, the two Lambards and Samuel Brannan, of Sacramento. Ten per cent of the subscriptions was paid in cash; this gave to the company a working capital sufficient for its first movements, which were not in railroad building but in lobbying.

Huntington and his three friends were the real directors of the enterprise. None of them was of more than very moderate wealth even for that day; the four being worth together not a quarter of a million dollars.[4] The only cash they ever invested in their enterprise was represented by their stock subscriptions. Even their payments on this account are extremely doubtful, and so far as can now be ascertained, never exceeded the first ten per cent.

With the money thus secured, Huntington and Judah went to Washington, where they planned and carried out a wonderful campaign against Congress. Of Mr. Huntington's tactics there we shall have to say much hereafter; all we need now to observe is that, considering the times, the amount of loot secured, and the terms, the achievement

---

[4] According to the sworn statement made by each of the four and accompanying the memorial to Congress asking for subsidies, Leland Stanford and his brother were worth, in 1862, $32,950; Charles Crocker was worth $25,000; Mark Hopkins was worth $9,700; C. P. Huntington, $7,222; and the firm of Huntington & Hopkins, $34,115; total, $108,987. Some years later, before a committee of Congress, Mr. Huntington testified that in 1862 each of the firm was worth several hundred thousand dollars and the total wealth of the four at that time was about $1,000,000. Unluckily, such discrepancies under oath are common in testimony about railroads. In Sacramento, it is said that each of the four put in cash and credit to about $100,000 and strained his credit to do that; but in the suit of Robinson versus the Central Pacific the assertion was directly made that Messrs. Stanford, Huntington, Hopkins, and Crocker never paid for their stock and their total investment in the enterprise was nothing.

stands unequaled in the history of lobbying. It is not at all wonderful that Congress was induced to grant aid to a Pacific railroad; Congress had been ready for years to grant such aid, and now the exigencies of the Civil War had made the railroad an imperative necessity. What is wonderful is that Congress, discarding many better and fairer plans, should have made with these four adventurers a contract that bestowed upon them such vast and unjustified advantages. About this, men will marvel so long as they read the story.

The bill passed both houses and was signed July 1, 1862. In substance and effect the government built the road with public funds, made of it a present to the four gentlemen, and loaded them besides with great fortunes.

The wording was, of course, somewhat different. First, there was given to the Central Pacific Railroad Company every alternate section of public land designated by the odd numbers to the amount of five alternate sections for each mile of the railroad, and on each side of it. You will not understand this unless you are familiar with the mystery of railroad grants, so I will translate it for you. A section, as I have explained in a previous chapter, is 640 acres. The bill set apart a strip of land twenty miles wide, ten miles on each side of the track for the whole distance, and then gave to the company half of the land in that twenty-mile strip, or 6,400 acres of the people's land for every mile of railroad. This land was worth, at the lowest possible estimate, $15,000,000.

The bill then provided that as soon as the company should complete forty miles of track the government should issue to it bonds of the United States of $1,000 each, bearing 6 per cent interest, for each mile of railroad constructed, as follows:

For every mile in valley or level land, $16,000 in bonds.
For every mile in the foothills, $32,000 in bonds.

For every mile in the mountains, $48,000 a mile.

On the route planned by the Central Pacific, the value of this subsidy was $27,500,000. Total gift from the government so far, $42,500,000.

Meantime Leland Stanford, President of the Central Pacific, had been elected Governor of California, and under his care the legislature passed many bills for the company's benefit, most of them allowing the towns and counties to contribute to the company's coffer, which they promptly did. San Francisco gave $400,000; Placer County, $250,000; Sacramento County, $300,000, all in subscriptions to the stock; and the state of California gave a liberal donation.

With all these and still other resources in hand, the company saw that it was in a condition to begin actual operations, and on January 8, 1863, with much ceremony, ground for the new line was broken at Sacramento, the legislature being present in a body and Governor Stanford digging the first shovelful of earth. Contracts for the first eighteen miles were let to nine different persons. Beyond that and so far as the 138th mile, Mr. Crocker was the sole contractor. Thirty-one miles of track had been laid up to September, 1864.

Although the grants to the company under the Act of July 1, 1862, had been so amazingly liberal, Mr. Huntington was not satisfied with them, and believed that still more could be extracted from a government so generous with the people's money. Partly in conjunction with the interests back of the Union Pacific, he planned a new raid on Congress. The Union Pacific had been authorized to build west from the Missouri River to meet the Central Pacific, and had received similar grants. Mr. Huntington particularly wished to have the act of 1862 enlarged about the bond gift. As it stood it read thus:

"*The issue of said bonds and delivery to the company shall* ipso facto *constitute a first mortgage on the whole line of the railroad and telegraph, together with the rolling stock, fixtures, and property of every kind and description, and in consideration of which said bonds may be issued."*

Mr. Huntington maneuvered so well and, in his own apt phrase, "explained things" so successfully to congressmen that he got a new act passed in July, 1864, drawn apparently in every respect to his will. It changed the first mortgage of the government bonds into a second mortgage, and allowed the company to issue its own first mortgage bonds to the same amount as the government bonds. It also changed the land grant. The strip of donated land on each side of the track was now made forty miles wide instead of twenty, and the number of acres bestowed upon the company increased from 6,400 to 12,800 for every mile constructed. In the old act mineral land in the donated tracts had been exempted. Mr. Huntington had that changed so that mineral lands containing coal and iron were included in the gift to the company, the reason being that much good coal lay along the route. Bonds of both kinds were also allowed to be issued in advance of construction.

Land grant value now was $30,000,000.

The new law virtually made the government guarantee the company's first mortgage bonds, and the company now began to issue such bonds and to sell them. Mr. Huntington went to Boston and sold a great many at par and interest; and some at a premium.

Mr. Crocker pressed on with the building, Mr. Huntington buying the material in New York and shipping it around the Horn. He was a shrewd and successful buyer; of some of his exploits in that line Bancroft, his fervent biographer, says they should be judged by the exigencies of business, rather than by the code of ethics[5]—a comment that will strike the present-day reader of these annals as extremely

---

[6] Bancroft's "Life of C. P. Huntington," p. 49.

well merited. One of the achievements thus defended by casuistry was to trick the rail manufacturers into furnishing 60,000 tons of rails at abnormally low rates, and another to trick a ship broker into supplying twenty-three vessels.

As fast as the road was built, it was opened and began to do business and to make money. For the construction from the eighteenth to the 138th mile, Mr. Crocker received a little more than $10,000,000 in bonds and stocks, besides the cash that was advanced to him. This liberal reward, averaging more than $82,000 a mile for work in regions presenting no great difficulty, he did not keep, but for a peculiar reason, to be explained hereafter, bestowed upon others. After the 138th mile, another contractor assumed the work and carried it to completion.

The strange and interesting details of this part of the story are to be told in a succeeding chapter, but to give some notion now of what went on, I may say that the company charged the government at the mountain rate, $48,000 a mile, for building on thirty miles of level or nearly level ground near Sacramento, and at the foothill rate, $32,000 a mile, for many miles of level building in the valley east of the Sierras. This is the origin of the familiar saying in California that the Central Pacific was the strongest corporation in the world because it had moved the Sierra Nevada Mountains thirty miles. It not only made these charges, but collected for them, although Mr. Judah, the engineer, refused to assent to the transaction.

Meantime, most of the other stockholders than the four congenial gentlemen of Sacramento had been frozen out, and in the process the interests of Bailey and Judah,[6] who were the real projectors of the road, were callously sacri-

---

[6] Theodore D. Judah died in 1863 on his way to Washington. He left some very interesting letters, which subsequently threw light upon certain phases of the early history of the road when it was investigated by the Pacific Railroad Commission.

ficed. Mr. Huntington's proposal was that they should buy or sell. As they had no money to buy with, the alternative was like a pistol at their heads. Still they hesitated. To encourage decision, Mr. Huntington rode one day along the entire line and stopped all work, a privilege he had retained under the contract. Menaced with the failure of the enterprise, the outsiders were driven to sell, and Huntington, Hopkins, Stanford and Crocker secured the ownership, which they retained uninterruptedly for sixteen years.

They increased the capital stock first to $20,000,000, and finally to $100,000,000, of which $62,000,000 was issued.

This, by a clever device that I shall describe later, they divided among themselves without paying for it one cent. They had in sight:

Stock (issued up to 1873)	$ 62,000,000
Land	30,000,000
Government bonds	27,500,000
Their own guaranteed bonds	27,500,000
Donations, about	2,000,000
Total	$149,000,000

And their railroad was steadily pushing eastward.

Only one prospect clouded their felicity.

The Union Pacific Railroad, backed by a band of speculators as greedy but not nearly so fortunate, was now (with government money) building its line westward from Omaha. For three or four hundred miles its way led through a country flat as a board, close to water, and in sandy soil easily dug. It, therefore, progressed with great rapidity, sometimes laying as much as ten miles of track in a day.

The act of 1864 had authorized the Central Pacific to build eastward to a junction with the Union Pacific, wherever that might be. At first the four partners had assumed that this junction would be far to the eastward, allowing them goodly mileage and many fat bonds, but the swift advance of the Union Pacific began to annoy them, and by 1867 they were thoroughly alarmed. The Union Pacific was approaching the mountains. If it should thread them first, the Central Pacific would lose the fattest part of its contract with the government; also the best of the joint haul when the roads should be united.

There ensued the maddest chapter in all railroad history. The two roads entered into a race, tearing into the work before them regardless of any question of cost, working day and night with relay gangs. On the line of the Central Pacific 12,000 men dug, blasted, tunneled, and graded, urged to greater haste by the incessant goading of the overseers. To add to the mileage, and therefore to the compensation, much of the railroad had been laid out on the plan of a corkscrew or a ram's horn; but this could not now be remedied, and the builders followed the line, pressing on without a moment's halt.

This was where the so-called difficulties of the work arose. Nothing about the grades was particularly difficult if the work had been normally done, the steepest gradient being 116 feet to the mile, which had already been equaled by the Baltimore and Ohio. But the insane haste made the task arduous and often dangerous. The builders did not wait for a completed road, but sent gangs of men far in advance, sometimes forty miles, hauling with wagons all the material, as well as supplies for the men. Often the wagon roads had first to be cut through the forest. Camps were built and rebuilt in a vast solitude as the lines of attack moved on; even water had to be hauled forty miles.

It was the wild romance of railroading. Winter came on, the terrible Sierra winter with its phenomenal snowfalls, but to the world's amazement the work never stopped. In the tunnels the men worked securely; otherwise they toiled on in the canons where there was less of snowfall, and great fires constantly burning kept them from freezing.

In the dead of winter, rails, machinery, cars, even locomotives in pieces, were dragged hundreds of miles on wagons, traversing roads heavy and badly made, threatened with imminent disaster from the snowslides and the storms.

The problem of the commissariat for the working army was often acute; stores must be brought up and deposited far in advance of the line.[7] Over the snow the builders hauled to the ill-omened Donner lake the materials for forty miles of track, three locomotives, and forty cars, besides all the stores for so many men, the region being destitute of human habitation or of any supplies save fuel. At that time the end of the continuous track was fifty miles away.

Of human life the builders were equally prodigal. Men froze or slipped down the steep canon to their death, other men took their places, and the work went on.

More than one squad a foreman saw as they clung to the hillside, above them the white mountain heads, below them the canon down 300 feet, perhaps more, deep snow at the bottom, snow above and about them, while they dug and blasted into the frozen earth. Then there would be a shout, a rumbling sound that the watchers knew too well, the impending field of snow would rush down the mountain, a great cloud of snow dust would arise with a sullen roar, and when the air was clear, peering down the canon they would see a wide spreading of tumbled snow on the white expanse and maybe a man's arm sinking, or a pickax, and the squad was gone.

In the spring when the snow melted they might find the bodies; or the freshet might carry them off to beat them to pieces on the bowlders. It was but fifteen or twenty Chinamen gone. What mattered?

Once there were two white men standing side by side in a cutting. So they were seen one instant; the next, an ava-

---

[7] Governor Stanford's testimony before the Pacific Railroad Commission.

lanche poured into the cutting and hid them from view. Weeks afterwards the cutting was dug out; the men still stood there erect, leaning on their shovels, dead—two grisly monuments to the mileage race of the Union and Central Pacific.

In April, 1869, they were almost within sight of the enemy's lines. Before them was Ogden, the goal of the race, in the great valley between the Rocky and Sierra Nevada ranges. In the fury of competition both companies far overshot the mark. The Union Pacific had its graders one hundred miles west of Ogden; the Central Pacific had its advance line forty miles beyond its track layers. Only the iron actually put into position counted in the race.

On the last day, ten miles of track were laid; on April 28th, they struck the Union Pacific line fifty-three miles west of Ogden; and May 10th, they drove the golden spike that cemented the two roads. The Union Pacific had won by fifty-three miles. Subsequently, the Central Pacific bought of the Union Pacific, at a high price, the over lapping road[a] and charged this and its own superfluous building and all the other lunacies of the race into the capital on which we now have the pleasure of paying interest. But the road was built, and the four promoters of Sacramento had a mileage sufficient to justify their bond issues. They now sat down to figure the cost and to pass it to the public in a needless and increasing burden that the public has patiently borne ever since.

The world rang with the exploit; the country rejoiced; California was superbly happy. That May day she hailed as her deliverance; she was now truly of the country, bound to it with more than iron cords. The new communication, reducing her distance by three-fourths, brought her into the house of states; all would now be well with her. So her

---
[a] Pacific Railroad Commission Report.

people said. And yet, so tangled and contradictory are the affairs of men, there was at the same time laid upon her a heavy and bitter curse that to this day she has never been able to shake off.

The rapid building of the Central Pacific through the mountains was for the times a great exploit. Naturally it has since been far surpassed as an achievement of engineering and construction. Abating nothing of admiration for the physical performance, it is time now to reflect that it was also a monstrous triumph of greed, fraud, and corruption; that it might have been had at a fraction of its cost to the public; and that it might very easily have been a blessing instead of a blight to that rich country of which it was ecstatically miscalled the Gateway.

For the Gate was quickly closed and before it appeared the grim figure of Collis Potter Huntington, one hand holding the key and the other stretched out taking toll. The physical figure of Huntington is no longer there, but the Gateway remains closed and before it are his successors, still busily taking toll.

How much—do you think?

From the day the Gate was erected and closed, down to the present year, first Mr. Huntington and his associates and then their successors have taken and divided more than $700,000,000 in unjust tolls, all from the people of the United States, who so kindly erected the Gate across their own highway.

With that sum, the people could have built ten railroads from the Missouri River to the Pacific.

And they need have had no closed Gateway and no toll takers fattening upon an enforced and arbitrary tribute.

CHAPTER VI.

UNCLE MARK PACKS UP THE BOOKS.

John Miller came, a young man, from Virginia to California, in 1870, and found employment with the California Pacific Railroad as clerk and ticket agent at the South Vallejo station. He was capable and industrious; and capable railroad men were few in California.

A year later when some men in the railroad way at Sacramento wanted an efficient accountant, they learned of Miller, sent for him, looked him over, and thought he would do; so he went up to Sacramento and entered upon his new job, which was better than his old one had been. It was with the Contract and Finance Company, of which a kindly old man known as Uncle Mark Hopkins was the president. The office was right over Huntington & Hopkins' hardware store in K Street, and across the hall were the offices of the Central Pacific Railroad, of which Uncle Mark Hopkins was treasurer and director.

Young Mr. Miller's task was to assist the paymaster of the Contract and Finance Company, and to keep books—not the main books of the concern, for these were always kept by William E. Brown, the company's secretary, but certain other books that he called auxiliary books.

To build and keep in repair the lines of the Central Pacific and of railroads with other names, was the business of the Contract and Finance Company, but the books that young Mr. Miller kept did not contain a complete record of these matters; they related only to minor phases of the work in hand.

Young Mr. Miller was observant as well as studious, and when, some months after he entered the office, he observed

Mr. Brown to be employed diligently upon the main books of the concern, the nature of this employment aroused your Mr. Miller's curiosity. He took occasion when Mr. Brown was absent to examine the books that Mr. Brown kept, and found them to contain matter of much interest.

In fact, the more he examined them, the more interested he became. They were books that recorded the building and repairing of railroad lines for the Central Pacific—what the work actually cost, and what had been paid for it[1]—and might, therefore, be deemed to be among the most juiceless and unattractive volumes in the world; but young Mr. Miller found them remarkably diverting.

Finally, he became so much interested that, like the careful student he was, he made from day to day a series of abstracts and memoranda of the matter wherewith he was being entertained, and these he took home, perhaps for more deliberate enjoyment in quiet hours.

He did not let Mr. Brown nor anyone else know of the literary treasures he had found, but just read and made abstracts and copies and put them away.

I am not to suppose that he knew Charles Reade's "Hard Cash," that he was familiar with the character of Young Skinner therein, nor that suspicion—evil sprite!—had been aroused in his breast by Reade's somewhat cruel jest about man as a cooking animal, being a cooker of books, but unconsciously he came to enact rather closely a vivid passage in a sensational novel, the while he furnished a significant chapter in railroad history.

Of a sudden, one day in September, 1873, Mr. Brown entered the office and hailed young Mr. Miller with glad tidings.

"The Contract and Finance Company has elected you to the office of secretary," said Mr. Brown. "I have resigned

---

[1] Pacific Railroad Commission Report, testimony of Miller.

and am going to Europe. And now here is a set of new books for you to go to work with."

Young Mr. Miller was duly gratified. He took possession of the nice new books and observed that they had already been opened in Mr. Brown's handwriting,[2] each account starting with a balance apparently carried over from the old books.

About noon he went forth, as was his habit, to his midday repast, leaving Mr. Brown in the office with the old books and with the new. When, an hour later, he returned he found Mr. Brown there and the new books there, but the old books had disappeared, nor did young Mr. Miller ever see them again.

So far as the world knows, only two other persons had that pleasure.

Some time after Mr. Miller had departed in search of luncheon, in came, for no particular purpose, young Mr. Yost. Mr. Yost was private secretary to Mr. Leland Stanford, who was President of the Central Pacific and one of the owners of the Contract and Finance Company. Mr. Yost saw the old books. He saw them in the hands of Uncle Mark Hopkins. And Uncle Mark, with his coat off, was busily at work packing those books into boxes and fastening the boxes with screws.[3]

The next day Mr. Brown started for Europe. Thereafter all trace of the old books was lost; also all trace of the books of Charles Crocker and Company, the contracting firm to which the Contract and Finance Company was the successor.

By some persons the loss was grievously mourned, these being chiefly persons that had certain lawsuits and needed the books for evidence. But their grief availed them noth-

---

[2] *Pacific Railroad Commission Report*, testimony of Miller. pp. 2880-92.
[3] *Ibid.*, testimony of D. Z. Yost, p. 2717.

ing, even when it led them to cause the arrest of the most eminent officers of the Central Pacific and when, in a dirty, common police court, these gentlemen were compelled to declare their ignorance about the books that never were found. According to a current belief in California, these books now repose at the bottom of the River Seine, which is in France; and that seems a very strange place indeed— for books to repose in.

For about a year young Mr. Miller discharged the duties of secretary to the Contract and Finance Company, being also made secretary to the Western Development Company, another very nice company with much the same owners and exactly the same purposes.

Some suspicion then arose that his books and accounts were not in the admirable and apple-pie order to be expected of first-class accountants and really nice companies, and Mr. J. O'B. Gunn, auditor of the Central Pacific, made quiet observation of these matters. On his oral[4] report, young Mr. Miller was arrested and indicted, charged with embezzlement. We are not to conclude off hand that he had been corrupted by evil example, which is ever in wait for youth, but only that he had grown careless, maybe, or something of that kind.

He was not at once prosecuted, possibly because of his youth or good looks. Instead, certain negotiations began, lasting for a month, in which young Mr. Miller was every day in consultation with the highest officers of the Central Pacific,[5] who were also, by a curious coincidence, the highest officers of the Contract and Finance Company and its sole owners.

After a time, Mr. Miller's wife called upon former Judge N. Greene Curtis (who had once defended a man for the

---

[4] Pacific Railroad Commission Report, testimony of Gunn, p. 3003.
[5] *Ibid.*, testimony of Miller, p. 2888.

Central Pacific) and engaged him as her husband's counsel. To him Mr. Miller delivered all his memoranda and abstracts.

The trial of Mr. Miller took place in San Francisco, whither meantime the officers of all the companies here mentioned had been removed. All the witnesses against him were officers and employees of the Central Pacific.[6]

It appears that the prosecution was afflicted with a curious languor, resulting perhaps from the climate, which is known to be at times enervating. At the close of the trial, young Mr. Miller was acquitted. From the courtroom former Judge Curtis went straightway to his room in the Cosmopolitan Hotel, took all the abstracts and memoranda that Mr. Miller had given to him, and put them into the grate, where they were presently consumed[7] in a cheerful blaze.

These abstracts and memoranda were of the actual cost of the work done by the Contract and Finance Company, and the actual amounts received therefor.[8]

Young Mr. Miller, thus happily cleared from blame, disappeared from the public view. The next heard of him was as a prosperous farmer and owner of a fine ranch in the Sacramento Valley, and as a buyer of coal lands.[9] As previously he had been an accountant on a moderate salary, followed by a year of idleness and (presumably) heavy legal expenses, this affluence occasioned some remark. Mr. Miller farmed on, nevertheless, and so, by a figure of speech, did the Contract and Finance Company, the Western Development Company and the Central Pacific Company.

All this, it will be admitted, is of itself a strange and entertaining little narrative. And now to fit it into its true

---

[6] *Ibid.*
[7] Pacific Railroad Commission Report, testimony of Curtis, p. 3033.
[8] *Ibid.*, testimony of Miller, p. 2880.
[9] *Ibid.*, p. 2891.

UNCLE MARK PACKS UP THE BOOKS

place in Southern Pacific history, where, properly viewed, I am sure you will greatly admire it.

The contracting firm of Charles Crocker and Company was composed of Mr. Charles Crocker and, according to his testimony, of nobody else. Previously, he had been a dry goods merchant in the Plaza at Sacramento and then, in 1861, one of the organizers and first directors of the Central Pacific. He was the contractor that built for that road its first few miles. The dual capacity of director and contractor (by which, of course, a man must as director vote contracts to himself as contractor) seems to have aroused criticism among the captious and unsympathetic, and the next few miles were done by many contractors in small bits. When the undesirable persons had been frozen from the enterprise and the four of Sacramento had the thing in their own hands, Mr. Crocker resigned from the directorate, where he was succeeded by his brother, and took the contract for the rest of the road from the thirty-first mile to a point near the state boundary, or one hundred and thirty-eight miles from Sacramento.

This contract disappeared with the books that, in 1873, young Mr. Yost saw Mr. Hopkins pack into boxes.

So far as can now be ascertained, it must have been of extremely loose terms. No lump sum was named. Mr. Crocker, composing the firm of Charles Crocker and Company, built the railroad, and the Central Pacific Company paid his bills, whatever they were and without question. This seems to have been the substance of the arrangement. It will be admitted to have been most unusual.

As the firm composed of one man went along it needed money, which was supplied to it (or to him, as you prefer) by the Central Pacific Railroad Company, consisting of himself and three others, from the proceeds of bonds that had been granted by the government.

He was supplied also with the bonds themselves, and with the company's stock. He said afterwards that for the first eighteen miles he received $250,000 in cash, $50,000 in stock, and $100,000 in bonds.[10]

It is interesting to note that for at least eleven of these miles the Central Pacific Company received from the government $528,000, which was more than enough to build the whole eighteen.

For some of the miles Charles Crocker and Company secured as much as $300,000 or even $400,000[11] a mile. For excavating earth they, he, or it, received from 40 cents to $1.50 a yard, and for excavating rock as much as $10 a yard.[12]

In 1867, the one-man firm completed the one hundred and thirty-eighth mile, and the remainder of the work was transferred to the Contract and Finance Company, of which young Mr. Miller was subsequently the secretary.

I said in my last chapter that for a very peculiar reason, Mr. Crocker did not retain the stocks and bonds he received for his work in constructing the railroad. The peculiar reason was that he turned over all these securities, amounting to more than $10,000,000,[13] to his successor, the Contract and Finance Company, which immediately distributed them among its stockholders.

And who were they?

Messrs. Leland Stanford, C. P. Huntington, Mark Hopkins, and Charles Crocker.

---

[10] Pacific Railroad Commission Report, testimony of Charles Crocker, p. 3640.

[11] *Ibid.*, p. 3645.

[12] *Ibid.*, p. 3649.

QUESTION: If I should recall it to your mind, would you remember that the higher priced excavation was very much larger in number of yards entered on your estimate from which you received your payments, than the ordinary earth?

ANSWER: I do not remember about it.

[13] Pacific Railroad Commission Report, p. 3649.

UNCLE MARK PACKS UP THE BOOKS

It is time we should take a look at this extraordinary concern, for the part it played in the affairs of our railroad, as well as its relations to public interests now, are of vital importance.

The Central Pacific Railroad Company was organized under the constitution and laws of California, which forbid the stock of a railroad company to be issued, except for cash or its equivalent. Not less than ten per cent must be paid for when the railroad is organized, and the rest by installments—in cash or its equivalent.

Also these laws forbid a railroad to issue bonds in excess of its stock.[14]

As fast as the railroad was constructed, it was receiving $48,000 a mile from the government, and it was also authorized to issue its own bonds for the like amount, but it could not do this in excess of its stock issue.

Observe, therefore, that it was obliged to issue stock before it could issue its bonds, and for the stock issued it was obliged to pay in cash or its equivalent.

Now, bills of a contractor for work done in constructing a railroad are to that railroad clearly the equivalent of cash.

The company had started with $8,500,000 of capital stock. As the work went on this was increased to $20,000,000 and finally reached $100,000,000, issued from time to time as required. In 1873, the amount issued was $62,608,800.

Naturally, the four gentlemen conducting the enterprise desired to get possession of this stock (which carried with it control of the road) and to get it without paying for it. One way to that desirable result was through a contracting agency that would present bills for its work (these bills being the equivalent of cash), accept in payment thereof the stocks and bonds of the company, and subsequently return these securities, less the actual expenses, to the four

---

[14] See section 456 of the Civil Code.

gentlemen. The greater its bills the more stock would thus be sent upon the circuit. All that was needed for the perfection of this device was a good handy pretext for the final distribution of the accumulated securities among the four gentlemen.

A firm composed of one person could not very well perform this function, but to a corporation it was easy, because a corporation can always distribute its assets among its stockholders. If the Central Pacific stock composed the assets of such a corporation and the stockholders among whom they were to be distributed were the four gentlemen, how lovely that would be!

To suppose that these conclusions so obvious to you and me escaped the attention of the four wise gentlemen of Sacramento were to wrong their intellectual acumen; only, since Uncle Mark Hopkins' exploit as a book packer, the details of their operations are obscure.

Still, you may care to note that in December, 1867, the Contract and Finance Company was organized with a capital of $5,000,000—not one cent of which was ever paid for—by three dummy organizers[15] who subsequently transferred their stock to Messrs. Stanford, Huntington, Hopkins, and Crocker, and that this company received Mr. Crocker's $10,000,000 of securities and properly distributed them,[16] where they would do the most good—to Messrs. Stanford, Huntington, Hopkins, and Crocker.

The Contract and Finance Company proceeded with the construction work from the one hundred and thirty-eighth mile to the junction with the Union Pacific, fifty-three miles west of Ogden.

Of the extravagant expenditures caused by the insane race for mileage with the Union Pacific, we have already

---

[15] Pacific Railroad Commission Report, testimony of William E. Brown, p. 2895.
[16] *Ibid.*, testimony of Charles Crocker Brown, and others.

spoken. How much other unjustified expense appeared on the books will never be known.

When the Pacific Railroad Commission tried to ascertain the facts, its expert engineer presented to it a statement that the entire line of the Central Pacific from Sacramento to five miles west of Ogden, 690 miles, cost to construct, $32,589,117.93.

Adding the $2,130,000 paid to the Union Pacific for the overlapped parts, this makes the total construction cost $34,719,117.93, or $50,317 a mile.[17]

How much of this, again, is real, nobody knows, but if we accept it as veritable, there was to offset it:

United States Government bonds	$27,500,000.00
Central Pacific bonds practically guaranteed by the government	27,500,000.00
Land grant[18]	30,000,000.00
Assistance voted by California counties	1,000,000.00
	$86,000,000.00
Less alleged cost of construction	34,719,147.93
And depreciation of currency[19]	7,000,000.00
Balance	$44,280,882.07

In other words, they built the road for about one-half of the government subsidy, and pocketed the rest.

Other goodly profits pertained to these matters, and on top of all, the Central Pacific Railroad Company delivered to Charles Crocker and Company, and the Contract and

---

[17] William E. Brown, Secretary of the Contract and Finance Company, testified (see p. 2897 of the Pacific Railroad Commission Report), that his company got $86,000 a mile for construction.

[18] Before the Forty-eighth Congress, Representative Barclay Henley showed that the whole road could have been constructed for its land grant alone.

[19] Pacific Railroad Commission Report, testimony of Stanford, p. 2465.

Finance Company, $62,000,000[20] of Central Pacific stock, and this treasure trove was divided as assets among the stockholders of the Contract and Finance Company.

And who were they?

Messrs. Stanford, Huntington, Hopkins and Crocker, who were also the chief owners of the Central Pacific, who never paid a cent for their Contract and Finance stock, and who by this device secured also $62,000,000 of Central Pacific stock without paying a cent for that.[21]

On this stock, so obtained, were declared in the next seven years dividends amounting to $12,000,000—all obtained from the contributions of the public.

When these matters came many years afterwards to be reviewed, Governor Stanford tried to show that when the construction work was done, the Contract and Finance Company owed a great deal of money—several million dollars,[22] in fact.

This statement led to a remarkable revelation. When William E. Brown, former secretary of the Contract and Finance Company, was asked about the matter, he said that

---

[20] Up to 1873, when the last division of stock took place. The progress of these operations may be seen readily from the following table of the capital stock of the Central Pacific Railroad Company:

Year	Amount
1866	$ 8,580,600
1867	14,923,400
1868	24,679,900
1869	40,168,100
1870	51,079,200
1871	59,644,000
1872	59,644,000
1873	62,608,800

[21] QUESTION: Then it was substantially, that the builders of the road under the contract should take all the bonds whatever character they were, as you have stated, and the amount of stock to authorize you to issue those bonds under your own first mortgage?

ANSWER: Yes, sir. Pacific Railroad Commission Report, testimony of Leland Stanford, p. 2646.

[22] *Ibid.*, Stanford's testimony, p. 2669.

UNCLE MARK PACKS UP THE BOOKS 139

at the end of the construction period, the Contract and Finance Company owed (unquestionably to Messrs. Stanford, Huntington, Hopkins, and Crocker) $1,636,000, against which it held the notes of the Central Pacific Company for $6,000,000, and that in payment of the $6,000,000 of notes the Central Pacific (owned by the same men) delivered $7,000,000 of land grant bonds;[23] so that instead of being a debtor when it completed its work, the Contract and Finance Company was a peculiarly happy kind of a creditor.

And what became of those $7,000,000 of bonds exchanged for $6,000,000 of notes held against $1,636,000 of debt?

Why, all went by the assets route to the pockets of the same wise and fortunate four, Messrs. Stanford, Huntington, Hopkins and Crocker.[24]

Subsequently, all these assets with the $62,000,000 of stock obtained for nothing and all the other perquisites, "melons," good things, grafts, "rake-offs," and clever deals, were merged into one of the most valuable railroad stocks in the world, *on which to this day we are paying the colossal interest charges.*

But in estimating the immediate profits of the Big Four we must not, to be sure, overlook the fact that for a part of the time of construction, currency was much depreciated and its depreciation added heavily to the cost of everything

---

[23] Pacific Railroad Commission Report, Brown's testimony, p. 2682.
[24] "It is found that Messrs. Stanford, Huntington, Hopkins and Crocker received over $142,000,000 in cash and securities through the Contract and Finance Company, Western Development Company, and Pacific Improvement Company, and dividends of the Central Pacific. In addition to this sum of $142,000,000 they also made large profits in the operation of fifteen or more companies which were directly or remotely sapping the revenues of the Central Pacific Company."
Pacific Railroad Commission Report, p. 143.

that was bought. But the real building work was done after the end of the war when currency was rising in value—and the first mortgages were gold!

Moreover, to offset the loss on currency were some items usually neglected in these considerations.

Thus, the road was operated as fast as it was built as part of a continental rail and stage line, and from this operation there accumulated, by 1869, above all expense and interest charges, close upon $3,000,000 of net profits.

Also, to head off a rival line building eastward to Placerville, the wise and happy four built a connecting wagon road from Dutch Flat through the Carson Valley (charged to Central Pacific construction account), and this road gathered for them at trifling expense tolls estimated at $3,000,000[25]—an enterprise that had the further advantage of ruining the rival railroad so that it fell by its own collapse into the Central Pacific's possession.[26]

No sooner was the first transcontinental railroad line opened, the gateway established, and the toll taker at work, than the four thus pleasantly endowed began to establish other gates to take further toll. They had started with next to nothing apiece, and now, after nine years, they shared a stupendous fortune that was, indeed, much more than wealth in hand since it was an infallible and unceasing machine for gathering more and still more wealth.

As they constructed the Central Pacific, it stopped at Sacramento, ninety miles east of San Francisco, with which the Sacramento river connected it, as did also the Western Pacific, another and earlier railroad project, liberally aided with government grants as an incipient transcontinental route. The main line of the Western Pacific had its western terminus at San Jose, fifty miles south of San Francisco, but

---

[25] By Daniel W. Strong, who was a Dutch Flat pioneer and one of the original founders of the Central Pacific.
[26] Bancroft's "History of California," p. 553.

it had a branch to Oakland on San Francisco Bay and opposite the city.

In 1867 the contractors that had undertaken to build the Western Pacific became "embarrassed," and the Contract and Finance Company completed the road and took all of the stock, issued and unissued, all the bonds and all of the land grants not previously allotted to the first contractors, delivering the whole to the Central Pacific, composed of Messrs. Stanford, Huntington, Hopkins, and Crocker. The land grants were exceedingly rich and the possession of the road thus cheaply secured carried the Central Pacific from Sacramento to San Francisco Bay and gave it an invaluable terminus.[27]

Another rival road, the California Pacific, had been projected to build over the Beckwith pass through the Sierras to an Eastern connection. In 1869 it was completing its line from Vallejo to Sacramento by a shorter and better route than the Western Pacific. The Central Pacific tried hard to keep the California Pacific from entering Sacramento, and at one time a pitched battle between the armed forces of the two companies was imminent; but while the contestants were waiting for a court decision, the California Pacific stole a march and got into the city.[28] This was in 1870.

Being thus defeated, the Central Pacific had recourse to strategy. In 1871, it agreed to buy the California Pacific for $1,579,000. It had previously secured a contract for the

---

[27] The true nature of this transaction is now not likely to be disclosed, but the reason for the first contractors' troubles seems to have aroused some suspicion. In Robinson versus the Central Pacific, filed in San Francisco in 1876, very damaging allegations are made concerning the matter, the substance thereof being that the Central Pacific unfairly obtained $2,000,000 of Western Pacific bonds and about $3,000,000 of other valuable properties. It is certain that the Western Pacific cost the Central Pacific little and was an immensely profitable acquisition.

[28] Bancroft's "History of California," Vol. vii.

Contract and Finance Company to build and repair certain sections of the California Pacific line. When this work was done, the Contract and Finance Company presented a bill for $1,600,000, which neatly offset the purchase price[29] and left a margin. Some bonds were used as counters in this unique deal, but the substance of it was that the happy four got the California Pacific practically for nothing.

The subtle influences, political and business, that were back of these operations were never revealed.

The happy four now went through the formality of leasing the California Pacific to themselves for $550,000 a year, afterwards increased to $600,000. The par value of the stock was $12,000,000, having an actual value of less than $3,000,000, secured for practically nothing, and charged up to the public at $550,000 a year.

Twenty-four years later the sworn value of this property was $1,404,935 and all that time $550,000 to $600,000 on its account had been extracted annually from the public by the four of Sacramento.

In those years the road had paid in rentals alone, $13,600,000—almost exactly ten times its value. For all of which the public has paid. Moreover, this rental was charged to operating expenses, the public was required to make the road profitable above such expenses,[30] and freight and passenger rates were and are based upon the reasonableness of such profits!

Subsidiary properties gathered with the California Pacific, included the San Francisco and North Pacific and the San Francisco and Humboldt Bay Railroads, with a nominal capital of $17,200,000; and having these roads in its possession, the Central held San Francisco and, indeed, all California in its grip, and could charge what it pleased.

---

[29] *Ibid.*, p. 584.
[30] As to the general policy of these leases, see Pacific Railroad Commission.

This was always Mr. Huntington's idea, to maintain at whatever cost, an absolute monopoly of the traffic; to allow the public no chance to escape; and to control the state through the control of the primal necessity of transportation. For many years he devoted to this object more attention than to all other objects together, until he was obsessed by it.

Now he looked out upon the field and saw his supremacy might be threatened from two directions. On the north, the Northern Pacific was slowly advancing from St. Paul; on the south, he was menaced afar by the Texas Pacific and others. He determined to fortify both approaches.

He saw that from the south, where the easy routes were, he faced most danger. Therefore, as soon as the Central Pacific was completed, he and his three friends organized the Southern Pacific Railroad to build southward and seize the southern gate of California.

Here comes in once more our old friend the Contract and Finance Company.

The grand secret of making fortunes, Mr. Huntington had discovered was to manipulate evidences of debt.

If you could bond a railroad enterprise, then do its work at extravagant or fictitious prices, then take its bonds in payment and its stock as a bonus, you had the public in debt to you and could always make the public pay interest on that debt, to your own great emolument.

That is what he meant when he said a few years before his death, "I made my money by going into debt"—a neat bit of word-play, since the debt he went into was always debt on which he contrived the public should pay the interest to him.

To this end, the Contract and Finance Company was a perfect instrument; it was, in fact, even now at work in more than one direction.

The Central Pacific owners had made with themselves, as the Contract and Finance Company, a most remarkable contract by which the Contract and Finance Company undertook all the Central Pacific's repairs and maintenance, charged 10 per cent profit thereon, and used the Central Pacific's tools, shops, and plants in the work.

This, for a simple little piece of money making by-play, seems hard to be excelled.

Having the same owners, the Southern Pacific now contracted with itself as the Contract and Finance Company for the building of the new line, and again the terms of arrangement were most peculiar—and profitable.

For its immediate uses the Contract and Finance Company received through its owners cash, bonds, coupons, and other valuable things from the Central Pacific's earnings and treasury, and paid interest thereon, some times as much as 12 per cent a year.[31] It repeatedly raided the Central Pacific's sinking fund or other surpluses, obtaining once $3,000,000 and once $5,000,000, although these funds did not belong to the Central Pacific, but to the government and the people of the United States.

With funds so secured much railroad line was built. On lines so constructed bonds were issued, and stock. Bonds and stock so issued, were delivered to the Contract and Finance Company in payment of construction work done at abnormal prices. Finally, as assets of this company, the bonds and stock were distributed among its stockholders, who were the four happy gentlemen of Sacramento.

In other words, the earnings of the Central Pacific, secured by charges upon the public, built the Southern Pacific, and the Southern Pacific bonds, stock and land grants were "velvet," [32] for the four happy gentlemen of Sacramento.

---

[31] Pacific Railroad Commission Report, testimony of W. E. Brown, p. 2908.
[32] Pacific Railroad Commission Report, pp. 2984, 2665, 2678, and particularly the testimony of Stanford at p. 2665 and of C. F. Crocker at p. 2999.

Not a cent of the stock got upon the market; it all went as fast as the presses issued it, into the coffers of the four. Beautiful!

The Contract and Finance Company did not long survive in these goodly matters. In 1875, its four owners took the very unusual step of disincorporating it, which enabled its affairs to be wound up and its books destroyed.

In its stead was organized the Western Development Company—same ownership (with the addition of David D. Colton), same purposes,[33] and $5,000,000 of capital, of which not a dollar was paid in.

It succeeded to the contracts of the Contract and Finance Company, including the Southern Pacific work. How well it fared on its way through fertile fields we may judge from the fact that on September 4, 1877, two years after it started, it distributed among its stockholders the following assets it had accumulated in its peculiar ministrations:

Southern Pacific stock	$13,500,000
Southern Pacific bonds	6,300,000
Amador Branch bonds	675,000
Berkeley Branch bonds	100,000
Los Angeles Branch bonds	13,500
Amador Branch stock	674,000
Berkeley Branch stock	100,000
Total for this sitting	$21,362,500

---

[33] By Commissioner Littler—Is it not true that the Western Development Company is an instrument by which Messrs. Stanford, Huntington, Crocker, and Hopkins performed work and furnished materials to the Central Pacific Railroad Company and that they, as officers of the Central Pacific Railroad Company, furnished the Western Development Company with funds belonging to the Central Pacific Company and charged a profit of 10 per cent on all work done and materials furnished, which profit they appropriated to their own use?

ANSWER: I do not call that a true statement. * * * I do not understand that they used the Western Development Company as officers of the Central Pacific but in their individual capacity.
— Pacific Railroad Commission Report, testimony of F. S. Douty, p. 2695. Quoted here also as a specimen of the ideas of business ethics that seemed to permeate this interesting company.

Fair—for a day's work!

The contract with the Contract and Finance Company, and later with the Western Development Company, was to construct and equip the whole line of railroad for $40,000 a mile in first mortgage bonds "and the balance in capital stock"—whatever that might mean, since the actual cost of construction could not have exceeded $25,000 a mile[34] for most of the distance.

For this the fat land grants from the federal government alone would have more than sufficed, and the rich donations from local sources were chiefly additions to the profits of the four. The state of California gave thirty acres of land at Mission Bay, San Francisco, a very valuable endowment. The city of San Francisco gave $1,000,000; other cities, counties, and towns gave $1,002,000.

Congress, at Mr. Huntington's instigation, had bestowed upon the enterprise half the land in a strip forty miles wide along its entire line, or 12,800 acres for every mile constructed. Much of this land was exceedingly rich, but if it were worth no more than the government's price to settlers, $2.50 an acre, the whole would have been worth $29,824,000; while at the excessive rate of $40,000 a mile, the whole line from San Francisco to the southeastern boundary of the state, including the branches, would have cost to build only $37,000,000.

This was an arrangement that constituted a great triumph of Mr. Huntington's ability in the lobby, but it was to have overlooked-for and bloody consequences.

The Western Development Company lasted three years, when it followed the Contract and Finance Company into the limbo of things better forgotten, and was succeeded by

---

[34] In a region of no greater difficulties Receiver Farley, of the St. Paul and Pacific, was at this time building and equipping a railroad on $10,000 a mile. In 1877, Jay Gould told Mr. Huntington that he built a branch of the Union Pacific for $9,500 a mile.

the Pacific Improvement Company, same owners (except one), same purposes, same capital, same absence of payments therefor. This company, inheriting the contracts of the Western Development Company, carried the building of the Southern Pacific to the state boundary at the Colorado River, and thence across Arizona and New Mexico, where had been organized by the same owners the Southern Pacific Railroad Company of Arizona and the Southern Pacific Railroad Company of New Mexico.

The Southern Pacific of Arizona had an authorized capital of $20,000,000 (none of which was paid in[35]), and bonds of $10,000,000. The Southern Pacific of New Mexico had similarly a capital stock of $10,000,000 (none of which was paid in), and bonds of $5,000,000.

The Pacific Improvement Company built for the Arizona road 384.17 miles, and for the New Mexico road 107.25 miles. The contract called for $25,000 a mile in bonds and practically all the stock.[36]

When completed, the road was leased by its owners to themselves as the Central Pacific, on extravagant terms from which the Central Pacific made great profits and drove its stock toward par.

The Southern Pacific stock, secured for nothing in this deal, is now worth 137.[37] The Pacific Improvement Company likewise seems to have done a prosperous trade in its line. At a meeting held April 11, 1882, as shown

---

[35] Pacific Railroad Commission Report, testimony of F. S. Douty, p. 2708.

[36] Ibid.

[37] These leases worked both ways for their profit. "They constructed 1,171 miles of adjunct lines at a cost of $27,216,931.01. On account of that construction, in addition to a small cash payment, they issued bonds to themselves to the amount of $33,722,000 and stock to the amount of $49,005,800, making a total issue of $82,727,-800, of which $55,531,554, represented inflation. Then as directors of the Central Pacific they took leases of their own lines for the Central Pacific for $3,490,828.81 per annum, which was at the rate of nearly 13 per cent." Pacific Railroad Commission Report, p. 143.

by its minute book, it distributed among its stockholders these securities that it had gathered in its own sweet way:

Southern Pacific of Arizona stock	$19,994,800
Southern Pacific of Arizona bonds	2,572,000
Southern Pacific of New Mexico stocks	6,688,800
Southern Pacific of New Mexico bonds	4,180,000
Monterey Railroad Company stock	284,000
Monterey Railroad Company bonds	248,000
Total at this sitting	$33,967,600

I find also that, in 1894, it transferred to the land department of the Central Pacific Railroad property worth something like $20,000,000, including more than 125,000 acres of rich land and 125 town sites on the line of the Southern Pacific of California. From which I infer that in the midst of other and exacting cares the thrifty owners had not overlooked the profit that lies in knowing where the stations are to be placed when you lay out a railroad.

But to return to earlier history. While the Southern Pacific was reaping bonds and things as it moved eastward, Mr. Henry Villard, in control of the Northern Pacific, was rapidly pushing westward. His main object was Portland, but men easily foresaw that he would wish to build a branch southward toward San Francisco.

The Central Pacific undertook to check him by building north a line called the California and Oregon Railroad and by forming an amalgamation called the Northern, both constructed in the same way by the Western Development Company or by the Pacific Improvement Company, on terms that filled the coffers of the four gentlemen and piled up capitalization and interest thereon.

I cannot do more than give some bare idea of these operations by citing a few instances from many, for to relate all the myriad sources of profit would fill a great volume. There was one piece of road 103 miles long from Delta, California, to the state line, belonging nominally to the California and Oregon branch of the Central Pacific's happy family and constructed by the Pacific Improvement Company. On this the price charged for construction was $4,500,000 in bonds and 50,000 shares of stock, together worth in the market $8,340,000. The actual cost of construction was $3,505,609; the net profit, representing also an unnecessary addition to the debt load that we must pay, was $4,834,391.

To own a construction company, a railroad company, and a good reliable printing press, is better than to own a mint. Nothing can limit your fortune but the extent of your greed.

In the same manner, these gentlemen organized the South Pacific Coast Railroad Company, with a line eighty miles long, on which the bonded indebtedness was $5,500,000 and the stock $6,000,000. The bonds alone represented almost $70,000 a mile. All of the bonds and all of the stock were taken by the Pacific Improvement Company for building the road, and, in 1886, the Pacific Improvement Company passed along all of these securities to the Southern Pacific, whose owners had gone through the formality of leasing their property to themselves on an arrangement that left the rental and the interest on the bonds and dividends on the stock (if any dividends were paid) all to be dug out of the road by means of freight and passenger rates.

Similar processes were followed with the Northern and with the Northern California. The Northern was an accretion of ten smaller roads, most of them with overlapping leases. It managed to pile up a stock issue of $9,182,000, with bonds at the rate of $30,000 a mile for 386 miles, its total mileage. In the end this conglomerate with all its leases was leased to the Southern Pacific and its stock exchanged for Southern Pacific stock in the hands of the toll taker, and the whole thing dumped on us—who pay.

Year after year, the interests of these men spread in many directions. They went into banking, politics, legislation, land-owning, navigation, and newspapers and, with particularly unfortunate results to the public, they went into street railroads. They increased their investments and power and turned the profits made from one greedy enterprise into power to secure more greedy enterprises and gain more profits and more power.

Sometimes they used their power as a bandit uses his pistol and sometimes as a confidence man uses his skill, yet on calm review it appears that at no time were they more than the successful exponents of the legitimatized spirit of their age, nor doing aught that was not sanctioned by the system the age had accepted.

Of their greater exploits we shall have to speak at length hereafter, but for your refreshing meanwhile, here is a little example of the bandit or highwayman style of business.

We go back first to the stage coach days. When John Butterfield's twenty-one day stage from St. Louis via El Paso to San Francisco had been well established, the business grew too great for an individual and a company took charge of it. The Civil War drove the stages from the easy southern route to a road across the center of the country, beginning at Omaha.

With this change the company was re-organized, and under its new name, Wells Fargo and Company, with Louis McLane of New York as its manager, soon became an institution in the West, operating a great express and banking business as well as stage coaches. When the Central Pacific was completed, Wells Fargo and Company entered into an arrangement to carry on express operations over the railroad.

The next year, however, 1870, the Wells Fargo people were dismayed to learn that Messrs. Stanford, Huntington, Hopkins and Crocker, with Mr. Lloyd Tevis, had organized the Pacific Express Company and purposed to compete for the express carrying trade. Competition with the men that owned the railroad and could do what they pleased with rates was no competition at all, but merely a game of stand and deliver.

The Pacific Express Company went no farther than to print some stationery and open an office, when Wells Fargo and Company surrendered. For a gift of one-third of the capital stock of Wells Fargo and Company, the Pacific Express Company agreed to go out of business.

One-third of the Wells Fargo stock was $3,333,333.33, thus acquired for the cost of a bunch of stationery. This seems fairly good business.

Afterwards the new stockholders put up one-third of $500,000 to develop the banking end of the Wells Fargo concern. Still later, $1,250,000 of Wells Fargo stock was issued to the Central and Southern Pacific[38] (Stanford, Huntington, Hopkins, and Crocker) in return for a new traffic arrangement, and the whole great business of the express company passed into the hands of the railroad, where it remained until the beginning of 1910. Then a new organization brought forth fresh melons, more water and more tribute from the nation.

These I cite as examples of the great profits. But the thrift of the fortunate gentlemen despised not the day of small things, also.

They built for $40,000 a bridge over the Colorado River, and owning it themselves, they leased it to the Southern Pacific, which they controlled, at $12,000 a year, and this they charged into the railroad's operating expenses and made a basis for rates.

---

[38] Pacific Railroad Commission Report, testimony of Lloyd Tevis, p. 3123.

They bought the steamer Solano, worth $100,000,[39] and, owning it themselves, they leased it to the Northern Railroad, which they controlled, at $90,000 a year, and they charged the $90,000 into that railroad's operation expenses and made it likewise a basis for rates.

Whenever they executed a neat bit of graft it was always charged either into capital or into operating expenses or into both, and wherever it was charged there it remains, and as you will see in another chapter, we pay for it.

All this time at the old original Central Pacific gateway the takings had been goodly and incessant. As soon as the cars began to run over the Sierra Nevada, the surplus earnings began to accumulate. At first these seem to have been used to build other lines, but by September, 1873, the business was so good that, in addition to the money slipped over to side enterprises, there was plainly enough for a dividend. From that time and with the exceptions of 1878 and 1879, the dividends ranged from 6 to 10 per cent a year until 1884.

Then the dividends stopped. In that year, 1884, the stock was worth 80 and more, and for the first time its owners parted with it. They sold the bulk of their holdings to an English syndicate under a remarkable arrangement that left the original holders still in control of the property. After that the road ceased to be profitable. Only Central Pacific stock was sold to the English. The original holders retained their stock in the Southern Pacific, which might now, of course, be deemed to be a rival line to the Central Pacific —from whose earnings it had been built.[40]

After ten years had passed without dividends the English stockholders sent over Sir Rivers Wilson, subsequently President of the Grand Trunk, to see what could be done

---

[39] Sworn statement of A. N. Towne, General Manager of the Southern Pacific.

[40] Congressional Record, 48th Cong., First Session, p. 4821.

UNCLE MARK PACKS UP THE BOOKS

with the property. To Sir Rivers Wilson a promise was made and faithfully kept that the English stockholders should have one per cent a year until "satisfactory arrangements" could be obtained for the "adjustment" of the company's debt to the government, and thereafter two per cent.[41] Adjustment is, I believe, the term in use for such things, but the sense in which it is employed therein cannot be its ordinary signification.[42] Before this arrangement was concluded, Wilson is said to have made a report on conditions as he found them, and this report is said to have been known to the officers of the Southern Pacific Railroad Company, and is also said to have contained some extremely plain language of a kind that would have been very interesting indeed to the American public if it had made its way into the press.

The market price of the stock declined until it reached 7½. Subsequently it was understood that the English investors had disposed of their holdings at the bottom figures, and in 1899, the public learned that the stock had found its way back to its original holders.

I trust that the essence of this transaction is sufficiently clear without further elaboration.

But to return to our chronology.

---

[41] The Southern Pacific Company versus The Board of Railroad Commissioners of California, Defendant's answer, Paragraph 4.

[42] For the attitude of the Company toward this just debt, see Pacific Railroad Commission Report; p. 2398, statement of A. A. Cohen; p. 2544, statement of A. N. Towne; p. 3408, statement of Creed Haymond, p. 3387, statement of J. C. Stubbs; and Governor Pattison's report.

Here is a list of the dividends paid before the unfortunate English came into the road:

Dividend No.	Date.	Rate.	Amount Paid.
1	September 13, 1873	3	$1,628,265
2	August 4, 1874	5	2,713,775
3	April 1, 1875	6	3,256,530
4	October 1, 1875	4	2,171,020
5	April 3, 1876	4	2,171,020
6	October 2, 1876	4	2,171,020
7	April 2, 1877	4	2,171,020
8	October 1, 1877	4	2,171,020
9	February 1, 1880	3	1,628,265
10	August 1, 1880	3	1,778,265
11	February 1, 1881	3	1,778,265
12	August 1, 1881	3	1,778,265
13	February 1, 1882	3	1,778,265
14	August 1, 1882	3	1,778,265
15	February 1, 1883	3	1,778,265
16	August 1, 1883	3	1,778,265
17	January 15, 1884	3	1,778,265
			$34,308,055

The marvelous career in Congress of Mr. Huntington and the Southern Pacific I must leave to another article, but perhaps we may do well to pause here at 1884 and observe how the four gentlemen had fared.

They started in 1861 with a total wealth among them, according to their sworn statements, of $108,987.

In twenty-three years they had won $34,308,055 in dividends on their original enterprise, had enjoyed the almost incalculable profits arising from mechanical million-making contrivances such as the Contract and Finance Company and the Western Development Company, and they and their heirs and associates controlled 5,906 miles of railroad with total capital stocks of $219,000,000 and bonds of $235,000,000, a total capitalization of $454,000,000.

The companies they had founded dominated the affairs of ten states and territories, and over a great part of this region exercised an absolute rule not comparable to anything ever known under the guise of free government and to be equaled only by going back to the days of great conquerors like Tamerlane and Alexander.

In California it is not too much to say that the will of the railroad company had superseded all law, all government, all authority, and thereafter the people were in an anomalous condition where an irresponsible and self-created power ruled their affairs.

The railroad monopoly had become supreme. No man could win position, distinction, or office, without its sanction; too often, men found that they could not do business nor make a living if they antagonized this great power.

The rates it charged for transportation were always arbitrary, and being perpetuated as "vested rights," remain to this day as curiosities in the history of transportation. The accepted basis of its rate-making was found in the famous quotation:

"What the traffic will bear."

But it was in reality a dual foundation. What the traffic would bear was one reason for making abnormal rates; what would punish the railroad's enemies or reward its servile friends was another. The control of the highways, as Hannibal and the old Romans knew very well, was a greater power than any government, armies, laws, majorities, or constitutions. The four of Sacramento held absolute control of the Western highways, and out of it they made vast fortunes and established an empire.

Aside from this, if the fortunes made in the way I have described could have remained merely fortunes, segregated and enjoyed by their owners, we could read of them and wonder and pass on. But the truth is that the making of these fortunes, created out of debt and based in reality upon the power to tax the public, was the origin of a great and steadily growing evil, now become more menacing than any problem any nation has ever dealt with.

Look back and see. When, in 1880-81, the Southern Pacific was completed across New Mexico, and leased to the Central Pacific, Mr. Huntington, always the controlling spirit, saw his way to colossal strides in railroad combinations. Tom Scott had failed to build his Texas Pacific to California and was out of the way. No other rival need be feared in the South.

Mr. Huntington and his friends organized the Southern Development Company on the lines of the old Contract and Finance Company and for the same purpose.

Through this concern, and in other ways, he built and absorbed lines in Texas and Louisiana until he had a railroad through from San Francisco to New Orleans, with connecting steamships thence to New York. Then he effected consolidations of all the roads owned and leased by the Sacramento Big Four, issued flood after flood of stocks, exchanged all the stock issued for construction into the dividend-paying securities of the amalgamated company, and finally massed the whole into the Southern Pacific Company of Kentucky, with $74,866,463 of preferred and $197,849,259 of common stock, paying 7 per cent dividends on the preferred and 6 per cent on the common, and owning besides $415,330,000 of stock in proprietary companies, to say nothing of bonds—an exhibit at which the observer may well stand aghast, and to which there is no parallel in the world.

For most of these stocks no money was ever paid. They represent no investment. Only clever and successful scheming.

On all of them we furnish year by year the profits, collected from the living expenses of the masses.

In this grand total of dividend-bearing securities is included all the stocks gathered in so many devious ways by the Contract and Finance Company, the Western Development Company, and the Pacific Improvement Company, so that not one dollar represented by these transactions is today without its direct significance to you and me, for we furnish those dividends.

How grave this significance really is, we may judge from the fact that within the last three years we have had the pleasure of paying greatly increased rates to make up increased dividends on increased stock.

Year after year increased capitalization.

Increased rates to support that capitalization.

Increased cost of living caused by increased rates.

How long can we keep this up?

CHAPTER VII.

MR. HUNTINGTON WRITES TO FRIEND COLTON.

In the White House one day:

Mr. C. P. Huntington—Mr. President, when you called on me in New York for a subscription for the campaign there did I not draw a check to you for $100,000?

The President of the United States—You did, Mr. Huntington.

Mr. Huntington—Then am I not entitled to the appointment I asked of you?

The President of the United States—You are, Mr. Huntington, and you shall have it.

Unluckily this dialogue is not a bit of imagination nor an excerpt from fiction, but part of an actual conversation. I have no doubt many other similar conversations have occurred at the White House and elsewhere. This is the only one I have been able to verify. It is verified by the man that heard it.

Suppose the appointment Mr. Huntington desired from the President to have been to a federal judgeship. Suppose the man he choose for the place to have been one of his attorneys and henchmen. Suppose an issue between the people and the railroad to come before this judge.

Toward which side would you expect the judge to incline?

And then you are to understand that although this instance of compulsive power over the government of the nation seems very startling and abnormal, it was of small moment compared with the total power to which the railroad company attained.

Beginning in 1862, when Leland Stanford was elected governor of California, the railroad monopoly steadily developed upon new lines what in the end became incomparably the greatest political machine ever known.

We shall say far too little if we merely say that this machine dominated the government of California. It was the government and all the branches thereof, not merely directing but performing.

Discerning men that wished to have a bill passed, a bill signed, an appointment made, a plan adopted, wasted no time with the puppets that nominally held office. They went directly to Mr. Stanford or Mr. Huntington and asked for what they wanted. This was the custom, even when the thing wanted had nothing to do with any railroad interest, when it might be something philanthropic or for the public good.

The real capitol of the state was moved from Sacramento into the office of the Central Pacific in San Francisco. There public policies were shaped, public questions decided, public appointments determined; not merely for the state, but often for towns and counties and occasionally, in a historic way, for the nation.

The organization that achieved these stupendous results in politics came to be an overshadowing influence in social and business affairs also. For most young men that cherished any ambition it held the future in its grasp; it could make or unmake.

If a young man wished to distinguish himself in politics or in a public career, he had no chance except by close alliance with the railroad company; if he sought any nomination, he must seek it through the company's agents.

If he was a lawyer, the railroad company could make him distinguished and successful, or it could deprive him of clients and make him a failure. If he wished to be a judge, the railroad company chose the judges; he must apply through the company.

If the young man was in business, the company could make him prosperous or it could ruin him.

If he published or edited a newspaper or a magazine, he could obtain subsidies from the railroad company; or risk bankruptcy if he had its ill-will.

The very position in society of his wife and, therefore, her comfort and peace of mind; his own standing in the community, the position and to some extent the opportunities of his children; came to depend chiefly and sometimes wholly upon his attitude toward this truly imperial power that had seized the State of California.[1]

This power controlled also most of the channels of public opinion. Some newspapers and magazines it owned outright and published in its interests; hundreds of others it controlled through subsidies, the secret pay roll, advertising, and passes. Very well known newspapers and famous editors were regularly paid for their influence; one editor was hired at $10,000 a year merely to write and to publish eulogies of Mr. Stanford.

This power went into the church also and into the schools. It secured the assistance of clergymen, educators, and historians.

Many a clergyman with an annual pass in his pocket went about speaking well of the railroad and of the four men of Sacramento. If the pass were insufficient to get him, why, there was always the liberal subscription to the church charity. Church societies were not forgotten, nor Sunday schools. One denomination organized a league with branches all about the state. Almost at once this league was controlled by men favorable to the railroad company.

---

[1] They exerted a terrorism over merchants and over communities, thus interfering with the lawful pursuits of the people. They participated in election contests. By secret cuts and rapid fluctuations they menaced business, paralyzed capital and retarded investment and development.—*Pacific Railroad Commission Report*, p. 141.

No trick escaped the vigilance that steered the machine and had no partisan preference in politics, no denomination in religion, but worked and plotted and mined without ceasing to augment and maintain colossal power.

All these and still other influences were like strings attached to many puppets, and all the strings led into the office of the railroad company. With one pull upon the strings the many puppets were set dancing.

A great part of their dancing was designed to conceal the real movements of the company, to make deviltry appear plausible, or to prevent the people at large from seeing that popular government had been abolished.

After a time a condition resulted in which the railroad company could not undertake an act so injurious that great numbers of respectable men would not applaud and support it; and the public became calloused to charges of wholesale corruption that were opposed or refuted from so many eminent sources.

After a time, too, there grew up a condition in which neither any laws nor constitutions, nor any kind of public revolt nor public protest, nor the nation, nor contracts, nor pledges, nor guaranteed rights, nor any consideration of morals, nor any other creature, seemed to avail against this Power that year after year defied every attempt to restrain it, until men lost heart and settled into sullen submission under a tyranny they could not throw off.

Periodically there had been angry revolt when the people had attempted to regain their government; anti-railroad conventions had been held, good and honest men nominated and elected to office. Every such rebellion had ended in the same abject failure.

The good men elected to office found themselves utterly unable to combat a system so vast and so marvelously buttressed. With the best of intentions and the most resolute will they were always defeated and helpless.

The state courts had stood by the company; or if these courts, too, happened to be captured temporarily by the people, then the company (which was interstate) resorted to the federal courts and thence invariably returned triumphant, so that no essential condition was changed. In a few months the people relapsed into their lethargy, and the company regained the full measure of its political ascendency.

It could do as it pleased, this company; the state had created it, and now it had displaced its creator. It could do as it pleased and levy upon the people practically unlimited tribute. It had the power to make transportation rates and through these rates it caused the people to pay for every cent expended by its political machine. Every subsidy, every "legal expense," every dollar paid for "explaining things," every charitable subscription, every hired legislative agent, every county boss, every phase of the vast organization, was charged against the people and taken from them in transportation rates, not once, but many times. The people paid for their own undoing.

They paid for it then, they pay for it now, they will continue to pay for it more and more, in cash taken out of their earnings and likewise in the increased cost of living.

This great political machine was much more efficient than Tammany's or any other machine that ever existed, because it was nonpartisan; it dominated the Democratic organization as easily as the Republican. Political manipulation it reduced coldly to the exact principles of science and business. It made politics a matter of scientific corruption and perfect organization, and by these means it secured astonishing results.

In every county in California the railroad company maintained an expert political manager whose employment was to see that the right men (for railroad company) were chosen as convention delegates, the right kind of candidates named and elected, and the right things done by men in office.

Often this manager would be the Republican boss of a Republican county, or the Democratic boss of a Democratic county. In important or doubtful counties he would be merely the railroad boss with whom the Republican boss and the Democratic boss must deal for money, votes, and success. Under him he had as many subordinates as he needed to care perfectly for the wards and rural districts, and through these assistants, he watched, reported, and forestalled any attempt to defeat or evade the system.

At the head of this vast department was always a man of peculiar gifts known formally as the railroad company's General Solicitor, but by the cynical part of the public called by a name far more expressive if less euphonious. He had a staff of well-drilled and able assistants; to each of these sub-departments was assigned. One looked after the Nevada legislature, one cared for Utah, one for Arizona, one for New Mexico, one for local politics in San Francisco. Each had his own corps of assistants and ample funds to buy such public officers as he might need.

With such an origination, so supplied with money, and so defended by respectability, the railroad company could select its own United States Senators, Members of Congress, County Supervisors, and everything between.

The money cost, of course, was great; but as the cost was saddled directly upon the people, this was not a matter of importance to the company. It was equipped with funds to buy whatever was needed, and it had very active support in ways and from men that cost little or nothing. This at first seems strange, but on reflection will be found to be true and to represent a universal condition in this country. The railroad company took and still takes advantage of the following elements that exist in every community:

1. Men that can be fooled by party loyalty.

2. Men that are eager for political careers and know there is no chance except by serving the money power.

3. Merchants that can be controlled through their banks, or terrorized,[2] or brought into line with rebates.

4. Men that believe the railroad company and all great corporations to be part of "our set" and feel a class-conscious satisfaction in allying themselves against the riffraff and the ignorant rabble "envious of us of the better orders."

5. Men that are fooled by the purchased press.

6. Men that can be had for a pass or two.

Beyond these remains the class that must be secured with money, including bosses, heelers, professional politicians, repeaters, colonizers, floaters, lodging-house keepers, the keepers of such dives and disorderly houses as cannot be controlled through the police, the saloon keepers that cannot be controlled through the breweries.

All of these were fully utilized by the political department and secured for the railroad company through the control of the state legislature.

Expenses, of course, did not end when the state officers were chosen. Many senators and representatives worked on the basis of a regular salary of $5,000 merely to kill all bills that the company wished to have killed, but with the proviso that for passing bills the company wished to have passed there must be extra compensation.

All United States senatorships were also outside of the regular price, and charged as extras. To elect a senator for the full term, the regular price was $3,000 a vote; for terms of four years or two years, discounts were made from this tariff.

Besides, there were local bosses to be paid and their rates were sometimes unreasonable. Thus Abe Ruef, the convicted boss of San Francisco, told Detective Burns

---
[2] Pacific Railroad Commission Report, p. 141.

that William F. Herrin, the present political manager for the Southern Pacific, paid him $14,000 for the control of the San Francisco county delegation to the Republican State Convention of 1906, which was rather a high price; and on special occasions the price of senatorships and other offices have been suddenly advanced in a way that would be very annoying to the railroad company if it were not able to charge the price to the public.

About all this let no one think there is surmise or inference; least of all is there any exaggeration. We are dealing with an inside view of the situation furnished chiefly by one that was long of the railroad's political department, a high executive that for years beheld and was a part of every movement in the game. This man, James W. Rea, of San Jose, personally honest in spite of his employment, has made an explicit and detailed statement concerning all of these conditions.[3] The railroad company has had ample opportunity to deny what Mr. Rea has averred on his own knowledge and from his own long experience, and the railroad company has not challenged one word of his story. So, even if it were not supported in a thousand ways by ten thousand facts and witnesses, fair-minded men would say that here must be the plain, unpleasant truth.

Yet all this time we are to bear in mind that this monstrous and corrupt machine was not deliberately designed by the four men of Sacramento nor at first desired by them, notwithstanding the unequaled power that it conferred. In truth it was at first forced upon them by conditions and then grew because of other conditions and not because of any man's depravity. Many causes combined, as in human affairs many causes always do combine, to press them irresistibly along the one course.

---

[3] San Francisco *Call*, July 4, 1908.

There were first, Stanford's natural aptitude for politics and political maneuvering, and his election as the first Republican governor of California; but there were also many other and greater influences.

From the beginning the whole enterprise was involved in politics because of the grants and subsidies that were sought from cities, counties, and the state.

Then it needed much legislation for various purposes, and it began to face many harassing lawsuits growing out of its peculiar and illegal tricks of management. The easy way to get the laws it needed, to kill laws that interfered with it, and to win the control of the courts, was through political action. As to the kind of action, there was always the example of Mr. Huntington's brilliant success with Congress. Men would hardly be flesh and blood if they were not impressed with that.

Of the original supporters of Engineer Judah's railroad project were four stockholders that had not been frightened out of the enterprise by Mr. Huntington's threat of "buy, sell or the work stops." These were Samuel Brannan, the two Lambards, of Sacramento, and John R. Robinson. After the completion of the road all men saw that its business was enormous and its profits must be great, but for some years there were either no dividends or the dividends were disproportionate to the earnings. Brannan, the Lambards, and Robinson therefore brought suits agains Stanford, Huntington, Hopkins and Crocker, for an accounting of profits alleged to have been diverted.

These suits had a very peculiar history. In all of them the allegations shown by the bills of complaint were of the most outrageous fraud. Thus the bill in the Robinson case, a digest of which I have before me, alleges that neither Stanford, Huntington, Hopkins, nor Crocker ever paid a cent for their stock,[4] that the only stock ever paid for was that held by Robinson, the Lambards, Brannan, and the counties of San Francisco, Placer and Sacramento; that these counties had bought stock as subsidies and that Stanford, Huntington, Hopkins and Crocker subsequently repurchased this stock out of the earnings of the road; that after these four men had seized control of the road they never held a stockholders' meeting, never paid for their stock, and appropriated for their own use $15,000,000 worth of real estate granted to the road for terminals by the city of San Francisco, the city of Sacramento, and the state of Nevada.

The bill recites the huge gifts received from the United States, from the state of California and the various counties, and then declares the actual cost of building[5] the road to have been as follows:

---

[4] This allegation should be compared with the finding of the minority report of the Pacific Railroad Commission, which at page 9, charges Leland Stanford with swearing, on September 18, 1871, that $54,283,190 of Central Pacific stock had been paid in, whereas the paid-in stock was only $760,000. This is designated in the report as one of the false statements under oath contained in affidavits now on file in the Interior Department at Washington.

[5] It is interesting to compare these statements with certain testimony given before the Pacific Railroad Commission. For instance, take the charge made for building from the eastern base of the Sierras across the plains. This was, as above stated, at the foothill rate, $32,000, although the act provided that on ordinary or nearly level ground the rate should be only $16,000 a mile. At page 3662 of the testimony, Mr. Charles Crocker being on the stand, I find this:

QUESTION: Is it not a fact that four-fifths of the distance between Reno and Promontory Point [525 miles] consists of easy, rolling land, where there was no special difficulty of construction?
ANSWER: Yes.

This means that for these 420 miles Messrs. Stanford, Huntington, Hopkins and Crocker charged the Government $13,440,000; whereas they should have charged but $6,720,000. The charge to the Government more than sufficed to build these 420 miles and left $3,000,000 in the hands of the Big Four, besides the land grant, their own bonds at $32,000 a mile and all the stock that they issued.

The equal of this operation has not been known in the history of railroad building.

For the first 18 miles .... $11,500 a mile
For the next 150 miles less than........... 42,000 a mile
For the remainder of the road to the six
 hundred and ninetieth mile less than.... 21,000 a mile

On this the four men of Sacramento drew from the federal government $16,000 a mile for the first seven miles, $48,000 a mile for the next 150 miles, and $32,000 a mile for the rest of the distance.

If the road had been built at actual cost, the entire charge for construction and equipment would have been $19,212,960 as against the $55,000,000 and more charged by the Contract and Finance Company—which was another name for Stanford, Huntington, Hopkins, and Crocker.

The bill also alleged that of the first mortgage bond issue of $27,500,000 these men had seized $22,000,000 for themselves, and that great sums of money that rightfully should have been available for dividends had been diverted and withheld.

In spite of the grave nature of these charges against their personal honor, the men implicated did not allow the cases to come to trial where they could prove their innocence.[6] On the contrary, they compromised each suit by buying the stock held by the complainant. For some of this stock the price paid was $400 a share, for some $500, and for some $1,700.

As the highest estimate of the real market value of the stock was at this time about 60, it will be seen that the men had luxurious taste in such things.

It appears also from certain testimony and may be noted as of interest that the attorneys that brought the suits, Alfred A. Cohen, Delos Lake, and John B. Felton, subsequently passed into the employ of the railroad company and remained there until they died.[7]

---

[6] Pacific Railroad Commission Report, p. 2779.
[7] *Ibid.*, pp. 2775, 2776, 2779, 2831, 3653.

These and many other significant incidents, the growing unrest in the state, the bitter complaints of shippers and merchants, the feeling plainly expressed that the railroad monopoly was a menace to the public, indicated the necessity of controlling public functions and building a political institution. In plain terms, if the power of the government were not seized the people were practically certain to inflict vast injuries upon, or perhaps destroy, the profits that these four saw looming ahead of them. From one point of view political control was a matter of self-preservation; later, of course, it became a matter of enormous advantage, but at first it was only a necessity.

If there had been nothing else, the relations of these four men to the federal government would have driven them inevitably into politics. The $27,500,000 of government bonds issued in their behalf were a lien on their property and they were obligated to pay the annual interest. Their purpose was to default on these interest payments for the present and eventually to evade the payment of principal and interest. Their only chance to succeed in any such scheme was to become a great political power, and first of all to own the state of California and wield it as a solid block in Congress and in the national conventions.

There was also to be considered the chance of enormous profits that lay in getting from Congress more rich grants from the public domain for their various plans of railroad extension, because in one such grant would lie a return greater than the entire cost of political control, including the expenses of "explaining" many things to many public men; and there must have been something very alluring in the idea of defraying by public grants the cost of heading off competition and maintaining the traffic monopoly of the West.

The wonderful career of Mr. Huntington in Washington showed the way by which these things could be done.

He had laid the cornerstone of the enterprise in political manipulation and the illicit control of public officers. But for his achievements with Congress there would have been no colossal fortunes for him and his associates, and without the like achievements in Sacramento and Washington no more millions could be added to these fortunes even if still greater disasters did not occur.

Governor Stanford at all times, Mr. Crocker much of the time, and Mr. Hopkins some of the time, looked out for Sacramento. I shall recite now some of the strange expenditures they made. In some cases these were charged up to "expense," in some to "legal expenses;" in all cases they were without explanation.[8] You are to understand that I am quoting from an incomplete list, covering only a few of the years:

1875.
Dec. 31. Leland Stanford $171,781.89
Dec. 31. Leland Stanford 8,877.15
No date. Leland Stanford 15,137.00
Dec. 31. Leland Stanford 15,177.33
1876.
Feb. 6. Western Development Company 26,000.00
Feb. 8. Leland Stanford 20,000.00
Feb. 17. Leland Stanford 20,000.00
July 30 to Sept. 30, 1877. Leland Stanford 83,418.09
Aug. 30. D. D. Colton 1,000.00
Sept. 22. Western Development Company 50,000.00
Sept. 22. Western Development Company 29,974.13
Nov. 2. D. D. Colton 7,500.00
1877.
Sept. 7. Leland Stanford 50,000.00
Oct. 26. Mark Hopkins 5,000.00
Nov. 1. Leland Stanford 83,418.00
Dec. 27. Leland Stanford 52,500.00
1878.
Feb. 14. Leland Stanford 10,000.00
June 7. Leland Stanford 13,000.00
June 28. Leland Stanford 111,431.25
Sept. 3. Leland Stanford 12,000.00
Sept. 4. S. T. Gage 3,000.00

[8] See Pacific Railroad Commission Report, p. 2999. Mr. Cohen, attorney for the railroad, here makes an admission about these expenditures that can be construed to mean only the worst about them.

Sept. 27.	Leland Stanford	38,156.03
Oct. 4.	D. D. Colton	3,290.00
Nov. 12.	Leland Stanford	48,816.94
Nov. 12.	Leland Stanford	18,168.71
1879.		
Mar. 25.	C. Crocker	26,452.60
Mar. 28.	C. Crocker	3,100.00
May 1.	C. Crocker	40,000.00
May 6.	C. Crocker	40,000.00
June 29.	Western Development Company	40,745.25
July 23.	Leland Stanford	500.00
Aug. 2.	Leland Stanford	789.50
Sept. 27.	Leland Stanford	38,156.03

When the Pacific Railroad Commission sought to learn something about these expenditures Mr. Stanford, under oath, could not remember about them or else took refuge in a refusal to answer, whereupon Justice Field and Justice Lorenzo Sawyer sustained his refusal.

Then the Commission tried to obtain from Charles F. Crocker, Vice-President of the railroad and son of the original contractor, some explanation of these and cognate mysteries. I will give a specimen of Mr. Crocker's explanation. He was asked:

"What was the nature of these payments?"

To which he answered lucidly: "They were general in their character."

On being pressed for a more specific definition he said that they were "expenses for various purposes." Being again pressed to be explicit, he said:

"Anything and everything that they [the officers of the company] might consider advantageous to the company and which required the expenditure of money."

Question—Do you know, directly or indirectly, of the expenditure of any money on account of the Central Pacific Railroad Company for the purpose of influencing legislation?

Mr. Cohen (attorney for company and the same Cohen that brought the Robinson suit)—I advise you not to answer that question.

Witness—By advice of counsel I decline to answer that question.[9]

As to the inevitable results of such a system, dealing on a vast scale in rottenness, I will give a few incidents much more significant than any description could possibly be. From them the discerning will see clearly enough what a bedraggled political prostitute California had become.

Mr. Rea says that when Mr. Felton was nominated for the United States Senate he was to fill an unexpired or short term. Sixty members of the legislature organized a Strikers' Union or Black Horse Brigade and demanded $180,000 in a lump sum for their votes. This, for a short term, was a strong advance over market rates.

Mr. Rea protested vigorously. The striking legislators conferred, and then informed Mr. Rea that they had determined to insist upon their terms and unless they got $180,000 they would proceed at once to elect one Johnson, an unknown farmer of the San Joaquin Valley.

This same James W. Rea, to whom we are indebted for this close inside view of the machine at work, was at one time a state railroad commissioner. In that capacity he made a ruling that, for reasons not necessary to detail here, the Southern Pacific did not like. Officers of the railroad and other interests demanded that this ruling be reversed. Rea refused to reverse it. He was then threatened with the venal press. He defied the venal press. At last he was summoned before C. P. Huntington, who happened to be then in San Francisco. Huntington ordered him to reverse his ruling. Once more Rea declined.

"Then," said Mr. Huntington, "I shall have to give the word to impeach you in the legislature and I hate very much to do it."

So within a few days the legislature began impeachment

---

[9] Pacific Railroad Commission Report, testimony of C. F. Crocker, p. 2998.

proceedings against Rea. There was pending at the time a reassessment bill that would be an advantage to the railroad and for which many legislators had been bribed to vote. When Rea was testifying before the House in the impeachment trial he ripped into this reassessment bill, exposed its true nature, and denounced the corruption that had been used in its behalf. The next day the official records were mutilated so as to take from the stenographer's report every reference he had made to the reassessment bill. The public, therefore, never knew that he had made a revelation on this subject, and the House proceeded to pass the impeachment bill.

Mr. Rea had, however, impressed certain facts upon certain senators, and one of the facts was that he knew perfectly well what were the conditions in that body, which senators were getting $5,000 a year each as "negatives"— that is to say, for merely killing bills that the railroad desired to have killed—and which of them had received more for extra services. Some of these got the idea that he intended to make a sweeping and sensational expose of the whole business of bribery. They came to him and opened negotiations that ended in the dropping of the impeachment proceedings and the concealing of disagreeable facts about eminent statesmen.[10]

People became so accustomed to such stories that conditions were regarded as a matter of course, and were talked of with a certain naive candor inexpressibly startling to visitors of a more Puritanical habit.

When in 1885, Leland Stanford was elected to the United States Senate (an event that was to have unexpected results) the state laughed and discussed the price as it would discuss the orange market. A few days after the legislature's action the late Senator James G. Fair was standing

---

[10] See Mr. Rea's full statement and examination in the San Francisco *Call,* July 4, 1908.

in front of the Palace Hotel in San Francisco, meditatively gazing into the street and chewing a toothpick.

A reporter approached and, being old friends, the two began to chat. "Senator," said the reporter, "how much do you think Stanford's election cost him?"

"Well," said Senator Fair, pausing evidently to make some mental calculations, "I can judge of that only by my own experience. From what it cost me in Nevada I should say it must have cost Stanford not less than a million."

Under the blight of years of railroad domination the public conscience was slowly seared and corruptionists grew bold while the public-service corporations worked together.

At the session of 1897 the San Francisco *Examiner* unearthed a condition of legislative corruption that would have appalled another state. To complete the evidence some telegrams were needed that had been sent via the Western Union. An investigating committee subpœnaed these telegrams. The Western Union undertook to rush them out of the state over the Central Pacific. Just before they could cross the Nevada line the *Examiner* succeeded in reaching a village constable with antique courage. He held up the train, found the box containing the telegrams, and sent it back to Sacramento under guard.

When it was opened it was found to contain evidence that the railroad company had not changed its methods since the days when Mr. Huntington "explained things."

To be seen at its best, any such incident should be studied in connection with the table of unexplained expenditures[11] offered on another page and then in connection with the Southern Pacific's rate tariff. Into these it will be found to fit quiet charmingly. Of course every excursion into the legislative vote market was charged up with the rest to "legal expenses" and (also with the rest) went into the

---

[11] Pacific Railroad Commission Report.

capitalization upon which we are privileged to pay our substance in the increased cost of living.

We shall now, if you please, return to Mr. Huntington in Washington and see how he fared in the underworld. It is really an extraordinary story, for he went there a country merchant without experience in public affairs, without acquaintance or influence, and he managed to win from Congress first one huge grab at the public resources and then another, until he appeared the very Colossus of lobbyists. In the history of Congress no man has come before it with balder propositions of private gain nor maintained them with anything like his success.

Yet about this we should be under no misapprehension. Mr. Huntington was no wonder-worker, no spellbinder, no wielder of the magic of eloquence. He was a practical man. We are not to believe that he entered Washington an unlettered trader and by force of argument swayed great statesmen to his will. He led against Congress a band of legislative experts, well supplied with money; they did the rest.

From 1862 to 1896, he spent most of his time in Washington and attended and narrowly scrutinized every session of Congress. In those thirty-four years he passed through Congress a great many bills that he wanted to have passed; he killed innumerable bills that he wanted to have killed; he utterly wrecked and ruined the almost life-long plans of his one great competitor; he exercised in all administrations and upon most departments a sinister and imperial power; and on only two occasions was he really defeated.

The history of parliamentary government shows no fellow to this career.

I am going to let Mr. Huntington tell what he will about it.

He had in his employ in 1862, and for many years thereafter, one General Franchot, quite well known in Washington; also one Beard, one Bliss, one Sherrill, and others. Before the Pacific Railroad Commission in 1887, he was asked about the nature of General Franchot's ministrations.

"He was," said Mr. Huntington, largely, "a very honorable man whom I had known since I was a boy, and he had my entire confidence."

The Commission had discovered (from other sources) that Franchot drew from Mr. Huntington $30,000 or $40,000 every year without vouchers, and Mr. Huntington was asked to throw light on this strange fact. He said:

"We had to get men to explain a thousand things. A man who has not had the experience could hardly imagine the number of people that you have to explain these matters to." [12]

Still the Commission was not quite content with this luminous answer and wanted to know more. It appeared that in 1873, for instance, General Franchot's work in Washington had cost $61,000, without any vouchers. Mr. Huntington sounded still the pipe of praise.

"He was," said he, "of the strictest integrity and as pure a man as ever lived; and when he said to us 'I want $10,000,' I knew it was proper to let him have it." [13]

Examination by Commissioner Anderson:

QUESTION.—How could Mr. Franchot personally earn $30,000 or $40,000 a year in explaining things to members of Congress?

ANSWER.—He had to get help. He had lots of attorneys to help him.

Q.—Whom did he have?

A.—I never asked him.

Q.—How do you know he had?

A.—Because he told me so. He said, "For these explanations

---

[12] Pacific Railroad Commission Report, Testimony of Huntington, p. 25.

[13] Pacific Railroad Commission Report, Testimony of Huntington, p. 34.

MR. HUNTINGTON WRITES TO FRIEND COLTON

I have to pay out a little here and a little there and that aggregates a great deal."[14]

Q.—In addition to explaining with words do you not suppose they explained with champagne and expensive dinners?

A.—Very likely. I never gave a dinner in Washington.

Q.—Was not a great deal of it spent in cigars and champagne dinners?

A.—I think so. Not so much, but perhaps some of it was to get some able man to sit down and explain in the broadest sense what we wanted to have done.[15]

It appears that up to 1887, the total expenditures of the Southern Pacific at Washington (without adequate vouchers) were $5,497,539.[16] The important point about these expenditures is that they were, for the most part, of money that really belonged to the people of the United States because it was money that should have been paid into the National Treasury as interest on the road's indebtedness. To use public funds to induce public servants to give away more public funds seems an extraordinary achievement in the history of legislation, but one of which the Southern Pacific gentlemen were easily capable.

Subsequently Mr. Huntington, examined under oath, was asked this question:

Q.—In regard to the range of discussion that was to be permitted between the members of Congress and the apostles that you sent to them, was that generally confined to Mr. Franchot and Mr. Sherrill, or did you take a hand in that?

A.—Probably it was done more or less by General Franchot, Mr. Sherrill and myself.

Q.—As a matter of fact, did they from time to time consult with you?

A.—They did.

And then for the first and only time in all these examinations Mr. Huntington was shaken out of his wary self-possession and ability to dodge and twist.

---

[14] *Ibid.*, p. 38.
[15] *Ibid.*, p. 38.
[16] Pacific Railroad Commission Report, p. 39.

Q.—But what I want to get at particularly is that no portion of these moneys was to be considered as covered by the ordinary expenditures of a railroad for purchases of property and materials. Those would be specific vouchers. So that as to all the unexplained vouchers we may assume that they were for moneys expended for imparting information to Congress, or to the departments, or for some purpose of that character?

A.—That I cannot say. Most of the money was expended, no doubt, to prevent Congress and the Departments from robbing us of our property.[17]

I put down all these things to complete the study of an intensely interesting human document. You observe no doubt, how agilely Mr. Huntington glides over the thinnest places and how honest he looks, how plausible he makes his cause look.

So, then, we should have interest in noting in the succeeding table of Mr. Huntington's unexplained vouchers, observing first that "I. E. Gates" was a confidential clerk in his employ and that here, as in the former case, the list we present is not complete.

Eleven years of expenditures for "explaining" things in behalf of the Central Pacific and Southern Pacific—being some of the unexplained vouchers charged to "expenses" upon which the officers of the company refused to throw any light—make this showing:

Year	Amount
1870	$ 63,581.03
1871	13,498.72
1872	73,361.83
1873	7,348.46
1874	52,844.94
1875	197,311.54
1876	299,301.37
1877	279,573.06
1878	471,081.06
1879	244,298.08
1880	197,809.36
Total	$1,900,009.83

[17] Pacific Railroad Commission Report, p. 37 et seq.

In the foregoing lists the most interesting exhibits are those of 1877-78 when Huntington was defeating Tom Scott, and for the years in which the legislature was in sesson at Sacramento. In running over the lists of unexplained expenditures one can usually define the legislative sessions by the crowded entries.

In 1884 the sums drawn by Charles F. Crocker without explanation total $404,710 and in the early part of 1885, $55,000. S. T. Gage, one of the railroad's legislative agents, drew out $18,150 in 1884 and $119,341 in the first part of 1885—about the time that Leland Stanford was drawing $40,066.95 for a similarly unexplained purpose.

Here is the way some of these items look in the records for part of one month:

```
1885.
Mar.  7.  S. T. Gage......$   2,500.00      Mar. 20.  S. T. Gage.....    15,000.00
Mar. 10.  Chas. F. Crocker    5,000.00      Mar. 21.  S. T. Gage.....    21,000.00
Mar. 12.  S. T. Gage.....     3,000.00      Mar. 23.  Chas. F. Crocker  15,500.00
Mar. 16.  Chas. F. Crocker   29,000.00      Mar. 23.  S. T. Gage for
Mar. 17.  S. T. Gage.....    41,000.00                H. H. Cummings.....  1,250.00
Mar. 18.  S. T. Gage.....     3,000.00      Mar. 23.  S. T. Gage....     8,500.00
Mar. 19.  S. T. Gage.....     9,000.00
                                                      Total ...........$153,750.00
```

All without explanation. The legislature was in session. It was the legislature that about this time elected Leland Stanford to the United States Senate to succeed J. T. Farley, Democrat.

Mr. Huntington was not pleased with the legislature's choice. For years he and Stanford had been growing estranged. The reason is generally understood in California; but being related to private life and scandal need not be gone into here. Huntington had thought A. A. Sargent should go back to the Senate and he took unusual ways to make known his resentment when Stanford took the place for himself.[18]

In 1888 he suddenly gave out an interview containing a statement that was construed to mean that Stanford had

---

[18] See Mr. Charles Dwight Willard's interesting book, "The Free Harbor Contest," p. 59.

paid $500,000 of the railroad company's money for his election to the Senate. This angered Stanford and an open breach was imminent. It was patched up in some way, the common report being that Stanford had threatened Huntington with counter revelations equally damaging.

Subsequently Huntington revenged himself by securing Stanford's removal as president of the Central Pacific, which place he had held continuously since the organization of the company in 1861.

Very interesting disclosures might have been made on both sides concerning other uses of the company's money. Thus it appears now that one of the most famous editors of San Francisco was on the pay roll at $10,000 a year, a famous Washington correspondent for a well-known New York newspaper received $5,000 a year, and one reading the lists is continually startled by the recurrence of names that are also the names of senators and public officers very prominent in their day.

All of these expenditures are unexplained otherwise than as "expenses" or "legal expenses."

But the final light as to Mr. Huntington's methods in Washington and what he meant by "explaining things" is contained in the following remarkable correspondence:[19]

NEW YORK, November 6, 1874.

FRIEND COLTON: As you now seem to be one of us I shall number your letters, or rather mine to you, as with those sent to my other associates in California * * * I notice what you say of Hager and Luttrell, and notwithstanding what T. says, I know he can be persuaded to do what is right in relation to the C. P. and S. P. but some political friend must see him, and not a railroad man, for if any of our men went to see him he would be sure to lie about it and say that money was offered him, but some friend must see him and give him solid reasons why he should help his friends. Yours truly, C. P. HUNTINGTON.

---

[19] Evidence in Ellen M. Colton versus Stanford, et al.

The congressional directories give the names of John S. Hager, of San Francisco, as a Senator from California in the Forty-third Congress and John K. Luttrell, of Santa Rosa, as a Representative in the Forty-fifth Congress.

NEW YORK, November 20, 1874.

FRIEND COLTON: Herewith I send you copy of bill that Tom Scott proposes to put through Congress this winter. Now I wish you would at once get as many of the associates together as you can and let me know what you then want. Scott sent me these copies fixed as he wants them and asked me to help him pass them through Congress, or if I would not do it as he has fixed them, then he asked me to fix it so that I will, or in a way that I will support it.

Now do attend to this at once and in the meantime I will fix it here and then see how near we are together when yours gets here. Scott is prepared to pay or promises to pay a large amount of money to pass his bill, but I do not think he can pass it, although I think that this coming session of Congress will be composed of the hungriest set of men that ever got together and the d—— only knows what they will do. * * *

Would it not be well for you to send some party down to Arizona to get a bill to build in the Territorial legislature granting the right to build a R. R. east from the Colorado River (leaving the river near Fort Mojave), have the franchise free from taxation on its property and so that the rates of fare and freight cannot be interfered with until the dividends of the common stock shall exceed ten per cent? I think that would be as good as a land grant. It would not do to have it known that we had any interest in it, for the reason that it would cost us much more money to get such a bill through if it was known that it was for us. And then Scott would fight it if he thought we had anything to do with it. If such a bill was passed, I think there could at least be got from Congress a wide strip for right of way, machine shops, etc. Yours truly, C. P. HUNTINGTON.

NEW YORK, December 1, 1874.

FRIEND COLTON: Your letters of November 20th, 21st and 22d are received. * * * Has any of our people endeavored to do anything with Low and Frisbie? They are both men that can be convinced. * * * I will see Luttrell when he comes over and talk with him, and maybe he and we can work together, but if we can brush him out it would have a good effect and then we could do or at least try to get some better timber to work with. * * * And in this connection it would help us very much if we could fix up California Pacific income and extensions on the basis we talked of even if we had to pay something to convince Lowe and Frisbie. Yours truly, C. P. HUNTINGTON.

NEW YORK, May 1, 1875.

FRIEND COLTON: Yours of the 17th of April, No. 17, is received and contents carefully noted. * * * I notice what you say of Luttrell; he is a wild hog; don't let him come back to Washington, but as the House is to be largely Democratic, and if he was to be defeated, likely it would be charged to us, hence I should think it would be well to beat him with a Democrat; but I would defeat him anyway and if he got the nomination, put up another Democrat and run against him, and in that way elect a Republican. Beat him. Yours truly, C. P. HUNTINGTON.

NEW YORK, September 27, 1875.

FRIEND COLTON: Yours of the 18th with inclosure as stated is received. * * * Scott is making the strongest possible effort to pass his bill the coming session of Congress. * * * If we had a franchise to build a road or two roads through Arizona (we contracting, but having it in the name of another party) then have some party in Washington to make a local fight and asking for the guarantee of their bonds by the United States, and if that could not be obtained, offering to build the road without any, and it could be used against Scott in such a way that I do not believe any politician would dare vote for it. Can you have Safford call the legislature together and grant such charters as we want at a cost of say $25,000? If we could get such a charter as I spoke of to you it would be worth much money to us. * * * Yours truly, C. P. HUNTINGTON.

Safford was Governor of Arizona.

NEW YORK, October 19, 1875.

FRIEND COLTON: I have given Gilbert C. Walker a letter to you. He is a member of the forty-fourth Congress, ex-Governor of Virginia, and a slippery fellow, and I rather think in Scott's interest, but not sure. I gave him a pass over C. P. and got one for him on U. P. So do the best you can with him but do not trust him much. Yours truly, C. P. HUNTINGTON.

The Congressional Directory gives the name of Gilbert C. Walker of Richmond, Virginia, as a member of the Forty-fourth Congress.

NEW YORK, November 10, 1875.

FRIEND COLTON: Dr. Gwin is also here. I think the doctor can do us some good if he can work under cover, but if he is to come to the surface as our man I think it would be better that he should not come, as he is very obnoxious to very many on the Republican side of the House. * * * I am, however, disposed to think that Gwin can do us some good; but not as our agent but as an anti-subsidy Democrat, and also as a Southern man with much influence. * * * But Gwin must not be known as our man. * * * Yours etc., C. P. HUNTINGTON.

William M. Gwin, of San Francisco, appears in the Congressional directories as a Senator from California in the Thirty-sixth Congress.

December 10, 1875.

FRIEND COLTON: I had a talk with Bristow, Secretary of the Treasury. He will be likely to help us fix up our matters with the government on a fair basis. Yours truly, C. P. HUNTINGTON.

Benjamin H. Bristow, of Kentucky, was Secretary of the Treasury in the second administration of Grant.

Here are extracts from other letters signed, "Yours truly, C. P. Huntington," and addressed "Friend Colton:"

NEW YORK, December 22, 1875.

* * * I think the Doctor will return to California in January. I have just returned from Washington. The doctor [Gwin] was unfortunate about the R. R. committee; that is, there was not a man put on the committee that was on his list, and I must say that I was deceived and he was often with Kerr and K was at his rooms and spent nearly one evening. The committee is not necessarily a Texas Pacific, but it is a commercial com. and I have not much fear but that they can be convinced that ours is the right bill for the country. If things could have been left as we fixed them last winter there would have been little difficulty in defeating Scott's bill; but their only argument is it is controlled by the Central. That does not amount to much beyond this: It allows members to vote

for Scott's bill for one reason, and give the other, that it was to break up a great monopoly, etc. If these damn interviewers would keep out of the way it would be much easier traveling.

Michael C. Kerr, of Indiana, was Speaker of the House.

"Yours of December 30th and the 1st inst., Nos. 120 and 121 received; also your telegram that William B. Carr has had for his services $60,000 S. P. bonds; then asking how much more I think his services are worth for the future. That is a very difficult question to answer as I do not know how many years Mr. Carr has been in our employ or how far in the future we should want him. In view of the many things we now have before Congress, and also in this sinking fund that we wish to establish, in which we propose to put all the company's lands in Utah and Nevada, it is very important that his friends in Washington should be with us, and if that could be brought about by paying Carr, say $10,000 to $20,000 per year, I think we could afford to do it, but of course not until he had controlled his friends. They could hurt us very much in this land matter, although I would not propose to put the land in at any more than it is worth, say $2.50 an acre. I would like to have you get a written proposition from Carr in which he would agree to control his friends for a fixed sum, then send it to me. * * *

William B. Carr was an influential politician in San Francisco.

NEW YORK, January 17, 1876.

* * * I have received several letters and telegrams from Washington today, all calling me there, as Scott will certainly pass his Texas Pacific bill if I do not come over and I shall go over tonight, but I think he could not pass his bill if I should help him; but of course I cannot know this for certain, and just what effort to make against him is what troubles me. It costs money to fix things so that I would know that his bill would not pass. I believe with $200,000 I can pass our bill, but I take it that it is not worth this much to us.

NEW YORK, January 29, 1876.

* * * Then on our side we have Sargent, Booth, Jones, Cole, and Gorham in the Senate to help us. * * * Scott is working mostly among the commercial men. He switched Senator Spencer of Ala-

bama, and Walker of Virginia, this week, but you know they can be switched back with proper arguments when they are wanted; but Scott is asking for so much that he can promise largely to pay when he wins, and you know I keep on high ground. All the members in the House from California are doing first rate except Piper, and he is a damned hog; anyway you can fix him. I wish you would write a letter to Luttrell saying that I say he is doing first rate, and is very able, etc., and send me a copy.

According to the congressional directories Aaron A. Sargent and Newton Booth were Senators from California. John P. Jones was a Senator from Nevada. Cornelius Cole had been a Senator from California in the Forty-third Congress. George C. Gorham was Secretary of the Senate. The name "George C. Gorham," appears in the Huntington accounts. George E. Spencer was a Senator from Alabama in the Forty-fifth Congress. Gilbert C. Walker was a Representative from Virginia. William A. Piper was a Representative from California. He was of radical views. By this time it would seem that Luttrell had been convinced.

NEW YORK, April 27, 1876.

* * * Scott has several parties here that I think do nothing else except write articles against the Central Pacific and its managers, then get them published in such papers as he can get to publish them at small cost, then sends the papers everywhere, and there is no doubt that he has done much to turn public sentiment against us. If it was known that the C. P. did not control the S. P. I think we could beat him all the time, although he has about the same advantages over us in Washington that we have over him in Sac. [Sacramento]. If he wants some committeeman away he gets some fellow (his next friend) to ask him to take a ride to New York or anywhere else, of course on a free pass, and away they go together. Then Scott has always been very liberal in such matters. Scott got a large number of that drunken, worthless dog Piper's speeches printed and sent them broadcast over the country. He has flooded Texas with them. The Sac. *Record-Union* hurts us very much by abusing our best friends. There was a no. [number] of that paper came over some little time since that abused Conkling, Stewart and some other of our friends, with Bristow's name up for president. * * * If I owned the paper I would control it or burn it. * * *

Roscoe Conkling was a Senator from New York. His name occurs in the Huntington accounts. William M. Stewart was a Senator from Nevada. Bristow was a prominent candidate for the Presidency; at the time this letter was written, he was Secretary of the Treasury. The Sacramento Record-Union was at that time a railroad organ.

NEW YORK, May 2, 1876.

Herewith I send copy of telegraphic dispatch that came over yesterday. Who is this Webster? Is it not possible to control the agent of the Associated Press in San Francisco? The matters that hurt the C. P. and S. P. most here are the dispatches that come from S. F. [San Francisco]. Scott has a wonderful power over the press, which I suppose he has got by giving them free passes for many years over his roads. * * *

NEW YORK, May 12, 1876.

* * * I sent Hopkins an article yesterday cut from the *Commercial Advertiser*;[20] today I met one of the editors, Norcutt; he told me Scott paid for having it published; that he would not have let it gone into the papers if it had been left to him, etc. * * *

NEW YORK, June 7, 1876.

* * * I hope Luttrell will be sent back to Congress. It would be a misfortune if he were not. Wigginton has not always been right, but he is a good fellow and is growing every day. Page is always right, and it would be a misfortune to California not to have him in Congress. Piper is a damned hog and should not come back. It is shame enough for a great commercial city like S. F. to send a scavenger like him to Congress once. * * *

NEW YORK, June 12, 1876.

* * * I notice what you say of Wigginton, Luttrell and Piper. The latter should be defeated at almost any cost.

Peter D. Wigginton, of Merced, and Horace F. Page, of Placerville, were Representatives from California in the Forty-fifth Congress.

---

[20] This newspaper has passed into new hands since the date of this letter.

June 24, 1876.

Parrott (Gorham) is, or was, writing a brief on fares and freight to influence, I was told, one of the judges of the Supreme Court. They are sure to do their worst but my better judgment tells me to take the scamps into camp.

New York, March 7, 1877.

* * * I notice you are looking after the state railroad commissioners. I think it is time. * * * I stayed on in Washington two days to fix up R. R. Committee in the Senate. Scott was there working for the same thing, but I beat him for once, certain, as the committee is just as we want it, which is a very important thing for us. * * *

March 14, 1877.

* * * After the Senate R. R. Committee was made up Scott went to Washington in a special train, and got one of our men off and one of his on, but they did not give him the com. Gordon of Georgia, was taken off, and Bogy of Missouri, put on.

John B. Gordon, of Atlanta, was a Senator from Georgia; Lewis V. Bogy, of St. Louis, was a Senator from Missouri in the Forty-fifth Congress.

I gave today a letter to Senator Conover of Florida. He is a good fellow enough and our friend after he is convinced we are right.

Simon P. Conover was a Senator from Florida in the Forty-fifth Congress.

New York, March 24, 1877.

* * * You write: "Our receipts are not enough to meet payrolls and imperative demands here." I have no knowledge of what the receipts have been this month, but for January and February, this year, on all our roads, they were nearly three millions of dollars, which was nearly $400,000 more than in the same months of 1876 and one-half must have been profits.

Million and a half profits in two months!

April 3, 1877.

* * * We should be very careful to get a U. S. Senator from Cal. that will be disposed to use us fairly and then have the

power to help us. Sargent, I think, will be friendly, and there is no man in the Senate that can push a measure farther than he. * * *

Aaron A. Sargent was a Senator from California in the Forty-fifth Congress.

NEW YORK, April 20, 1877.

I wrote Crocker on the 12th inst., in relation to Jones' Los Angeles road. A few days after I saw Jones I met Gould. He told me Keene had bought it [meaning the railroad at Los Angeles owned by Senator Jones of Nevada]. Of course, I said I was glad to hear it, as we did not want the road at any price; that I made Jones an offer for it because we wanted him to help us with our (C. P. and U. P.) sinking fund bill in Congress, and was very glad it [the railroad] had got out of the way, and that I saw nothing now to prevent friendly relations between Jones and ourselves, etc.

On the Sunday following A. A. Selover came to my house and said he came from Gould and Keene and that in the panic or break in Panama a few days before Jones would have broken if G. and K. had not come in to help him out, and to do it they had to take Jones' railroad, etc., and he asked me, after some beating about, if we wanted the road at $480,000. I told him that we did not want it at all but that we would take it so as to work in harmony with Jones, and that I had made him an offer as I wrote Crocker, and my impression was our people would do that now, but I was quite sure we would rather G. and K. would keep the road, if by that Jones could be made our friend, etc. What do you think of all this? I am rather disposed to think G. and K. have not bought the road but hold it as collateral.

NEW YORK, May 7, 1877.

* * * I notice what you say of Conover, the Florida Senator. He is a clever fellow but don't go any money on him. * * * The $70,000 that I let Jones have are tied up for ten years. I think we can make more than the interest on the amount paid for Jones' road out of our other roads by not running the Jones road at all; and Jones is very good-natured now and we need his help in Congress very much; and I have no doubt we shall have it. We must have friends in Congress from the West coast, as it is very important, I think, that we kill the open highway, and get a fair sinking fund bill by which we can get time beyond the maturity of the bonds that the government loaned us to pay the indebtedness;

and I think if any Republican is elected in Sargent's place, he (Sargent) is worth to us, if he comes back as our friend, as much as any six new men, and he should be returned.

NEW YORK, May 15, 1877.

Yours of the 7th inst. is received. I am glad you are paying some attention to General Taylor and Mr. Kasson. Taylor can do us much good in the south. I think, by the way, he would like to get some position with us in Cal. Mr. Kasson has always been our friend in Congress and as he is a very able man, has been able to do us much good and he has never ——— [21] us one dollar. I think I have written you before about Senator Conover. He may want to borrow some money, but we are so short this summer I do not see how we can let him have any in Cal.

I have just given Senator Ingalls, of Kansas, a letter to you. He is a good fellow and can do us much good. * * * Senator Morton is coming over; also his brother-in-law, Burbank. They are good fellows, but B. means business, not here but in W.

Scott is working everywhere for his open highway, but I think we can beat him; but it will cost money.

The Congressional Directory gives the name of Oliver P. Morton as a Senator from Indiana.

June 1, 1877.

* * * There has been quite a number of Senators and M. C. in the office here in the last few days; they all say Scott is making his greatest effort on his Texas and Pacific (open highway) and most of them think he will pass it; this man Hayes, most people say, is for it to conciliate the South; he may be, but I hardly believe he is; but I have no doubt he is for many things he should not be for. * * *

The reference is to President Hayes.

NEW YORK, September 10, 1877.

FRIEND COLTON: * * * As to Colonel Hyde writing a report about the harbor of San Diego. I would like such a report as he could

---

[21] See Pacific Railroad Commission Report, p. 3851. In the original the word left blank here is said to look like "cost." Some authorities agreed to accept it as "lost," which although it seems to make no sense had doubtless a more dulcet sound in some ears. John A. Kasson, of Des Moines, was a Representative from Iowa and later United States Minister to Austria. John J. Ingalls, of Atchison, was a Senator from Kansas.

write, and if he would write one to suit for $250 I would give it, and if he would not we shall have to go without it. * * *

(Letter of March 4, 1878, suggested that army officers be let in on the Oakland water front job.)

NEW YORK, October 5, 1877.

Yours, No. 15, is received. I notice your remarks on our matter in Cal. I have no doubt there is many things to annoy you. The dispatches about crossing the Colorado come over very well. I think Gould has had as much to do with stopping us on the bridge as Scott has, although I have had no reason for so thinking up to this morning (see clip from *Tribune*), except Jim Wilson, of Iowa, is their man, and has much influence with McCrary.

Sec. of War was in Washington when the first order went out to stop work on the bridge, and Gould came in twice, and Dillon once, to tell me that the Sec. of the Interior had his war paint on and was to attack us in his message, etc., etc. I thought at the time they were trying to cover up something, and rather supposed it was to check us on S. P. * * *

George W. McCrary, of Iowa, was Secretary of War in the administration of Hayes. Carl Schurz was Secretary of the Interior in the same administration. The bridge was at a government reservation. McCrary and Schurz stopped it. James Wilson, of Traer, was a Representative from Iowa in the Forty-fourth Congress. According to "Who's Who," the home of James Wilson, at present Secretary of Agriculture, is at Traer, Tama County, Iowa, and he was in Congress from 1873 to 1877 and from 1883 to 1885.

NEW YORK, October 20, 1877.

* * * I think Safford had better be in Washington at the commencement of the regular session, to get Congress to confirm the Acts of Arizona.

I saw Axtell, Governor of New Mexico, and he said he thought if we would send to him such a bill as we wanted to have passed into a law, he could get it passed with very little or no money; when if we sent a man there they would stick him for large amounts. * * *

MR. HUNTINGTON WRITES TO FRIEND COLTON

October 30, 1877.

* * * The committees are made up for the Forty-fifth Congress. I think the R. R. Com. is right, but the Com. on Territories I do not like. A different one was promised me. * * * I think there never was so many strikers in Washington before.

November 9, 1877.

* * * I do not think we can get any legislation this session for extension of land grants or for changing line of road unless we pay more for it than it is worth. * * * Some parties are making great effort to pass a bill through Congress that will compel the U. P. and C. P. to pay large sums into a sinking fund, and I have some fears that such a bill may pass. Jim Keene and others of Jay Gould's enemies are in it and will pay money to pass.

NEW YORK, November 15, 1877.

* * * If we are not hurt this session it will because we pay much money to prevent it, and you know how hard it is to get it to pay for such purposes. * * * I think Congress will try very hard to pass some kind of bill to make us commence paying on what we owe the government. * * * Every year the fight grows more and more expensive. * * *

NEW YORK, November 22, 1877.

* * * Matters never looked worse in Washington than they do at this time. It seems as though all the strikers in the world were there. I send with this copy of one of their letters I received yesterday, all of the some tenor. The one I send is from ex-Senator Pomeroy.

The inclosure in a letter of advice from Pomeroy to Huntington, outlining a scheme by which Congress could be controlled for the railroad, and closing with fulsome expressions. For Pomeroy, see Mark Twain's "Gilded Age;" also Mr. Huntington's accounts for 1876. Pomeroy had been a Senator from Kansas in the Forty-third Congress.

November 24, 1877.

* * * I notice what you write of the Santa Monica road. I am satisfied with that trade and when you write pay Jones no part of the $25,000, because there is an unsettled account of, say, $6,000, I think you forget his position. I have paid him the $25,000 as he told me he needed it very much. Jones can do us much good and says he will.

December 5, 1877.

* * * I have just received telegram from Washington that Matthews and Windom have been put on Senate R. R. Committee in place of Howe and Ferry. This looks as though the Texas and P. had control of the Senate as far as appointing coms. are concerned. I am not happy today.

Stanley Matthews, of Cincinnati, was a Senator from Ohio; William Windom, of Winona, was a Senator from Minnesota; Timothy O. Howe, of Green Bay, was a Senator from Wisconsin; Thomas W. Ferry, of Grand Haven, was a Senator from Michigan.

December 17, 1877.

* * * The Texas and P. Company have been fighting us for years, but have had but little money, but have used passes and promises largely; but the latter, as they say, is about played out, and some little time ago they joined teams, as I am told, with the North[ern] P[acific]. They had a little money to use as they had no mortgage on floating debt as I am told. They have made a little money on this end of their road and I think are using it. Jay Gould went to Washington about two weeks since and I know saw Mitchell, Senator from Oregon, since which time money has been used very freely in Washington and some parties have been hard at work at the T. & P.—N. P., that never work except for ready cash and Senator Mitchell is not for us as he was, although he says he is, but I know he is not. Gould has large amounts of cash and he pays it without stint to carry his points. * * *

John H. Mitchell, of Portland, was a Senator from Oregon.

January 12, 1878.

* * * Matters do not look well in Washington, but I think we shall not be much hurt, although the boys are very hungry and it will cost considerably to be saved.

January 22, 1878.

* * * The *World* again published today that the C. P. and S. P. [Central Pacific and Southern Pacific] owe fourteen millions floating debt, and it hurts us very much, and I don't see how we can carry our floating debt here unless this debt can in some way be transferred; that is the larger portion of it. The *World* is con-

trolled by Tom Scott.[22] A few months ago I could have had it in our interest, by paying its losses, or in other words, paying the bills that they [The *World*] could not pay, which would be from $2,000 to $5,000 a month. I did not think it wise to do it. * * *

February 23, 1878.

* * * The Sub. Com. of the R. R. Com. of the House have agreed to report Scott's T. and P. Bills through to San Diego and I am disposed to think the full Com. will report it to the House. It can be stopped but I doubt whether it would be worth the cost. * * * Scott no doubt will promise all the, say $40,000,000, that the act would give him. * * *

NEW YORK, May 3, 1878.

* * * The Texas and Pacific folks are working hard on their bill, and say they are sure to pass it, but I do not believe it. They offered one M. C. one thousand dollars cash down, five thousand when the bill passed, and ten thousand of the bonds when they got them, if he would vote for the bill.

NEW YORK, June 30, 1878.

I think your letter to McFarland was good. * * * I think in all the world's history never before was such a wild set of demagogues honored with the name of Congress. We have been hurt some but some of the worst bills have been defeated, but we cannot stand many such Congresses.

NEW YORK, September 30, 1878.

* * * I think you are right about Field not sitting in the Gallatin suit. * * *

Albert Gallatin had been a member of the firm of Huntington & Hopkins at Sacramento. He brought suit to prevent the Central Pacific from setting aside its sinking fund. Justice Stephen J. Field was of the Supreme Court of the United States. For many years he was actively supported in some quarters for the Democratic nomination for the presidency. The California State Democratic convention of 1884, held at Stockton, considered charges against Justice

---

[22] This newspaper had undergone changes of editorial management and ownership since the date of this letter.

Field based upon his decisions in cases wherein the Southern Pacific Railroad was interested. As a result of these charges, the convention formally read Justice Field out of the Democratic party.

I have used the past tense in describing the political degradation of this State of California, but I might as well have written much of it in the present. Forms have changed somewhat and methods; the methods of the railroad company remain the same.

Still, the huge political machine works on corrupting and corrupting, or trying to corrupt. Still, the railroad boss operates in every county, and still the head spider sits in his office and spins his evil webs. Since the political revolution of 1910 that put Governor Hiram Johnson at the head of the Republican party, the railroad, for the first time in its history, is blocked in its schemes. But its aims have not changed.

This is the influence that brought to naught the work of the reformers in the legislative session of 1909 as graphically described in Mr. Franklin Hichborne's book on that subject.[23] This is the influence that expects to determine who shall be the next governor, who shall fill every office below him, who shall be judges.

Finally, this is the influence, concealed and sinister, that stopped the graft prosecution in San Francisco; that enabled Calhoun, Schmitz and the rest to escape; that defeated Francis J. Heney at the polls; and morally this is the influence responsible for the hand that tried to assassinate him.

---

[23] "Story of the Session of the California Legislature," by Franklin Hichborne, San Francisco; 1909. It is really a most meritorious work and ought to be widely noted.

SOUTHERN PACIFIC DISBURSEMENTS AT WASHINGTON (WITHOUT ADEQUATE VOUCHERS) FOR "EXPENSES."

1872.
Jan. 13.	R. Franchot....$	33.00
Jan. 18.	R. Franchot....	13,200.00
Mch. 11.	C. P. Huntington	1,000.00
Mch. 15.	R. Franchot...	1,000.00
Mch. 23.	C. P. Huntington	500.00
Apr. 26.	C. P. Huntington	500.00
May 11.	C. P. Huntington	500.00
May 17.	C. P. Huntington	1,000.00
May 17.	R. Franchot...	5,000.00
June 5.	R. Franchot....	5,000.00
July 31.	C. P. Huntington	500.00
Aug. 24.	C. P. Huntington	500.00
Sept. 24.	R. Franchot...	19,295.50
Oct. 2.	I. E. Gates.....	5,000.00
Nov. 1.	I. E. Gates.....	500.00
Nov. 15.	C. P. Huntington	1,000.00
Nov. 21.	I. E. Gates....	500.00
Nov. 29.	I. E. Gates....	4,000.00
Dec. 28.	I. E. Gates....	200.00
Dec. 31.	"Services in 1872"	13,233.33
	Total ....$	72,461.83

1874.
Jan. 13.	R. Franchot....$	500.00
Jan. 16.	I. E. Gates....	200.00
Mch. 14.	Fisk & Hatch.	12,139.94
May 14.	C. P. Huntington	500.00
June 15.	Fisk & Hatch.	1,910.00
June 22.	C. P. Huntington	20,000.00
June 27.	R. Franchot....	3,700.00
July 9.	R. Franchot.....	150.00
July 10.	I. E. Gates....	200.00
July 11.	I. E. Gates....	200.00
Sept. 11.	C. P. Huntington	5,000.00
Oct. 16.	I. E. Gates....	281.00
Oct. 23.	I. E. Gates....	200.00
Nov.	Gen. Dwyer, U. S. Commissioner	1,000.00
Dec. 2.	"W. A. W." paid by C. P. Huntington...	4,863.48
Dec. 29.	C. P. Huntington	2,000.00
	Total ....$	52,844.42

1876.
Jan. 4.	N. T. Smith, for amount paid H. Brown.$	5,000.00
Jan. 24.	C. P. Huntington	2,500.00
Feb. 26.	C. P. Huntington	5,000.00
Mch. 9.	I. E. Gates.....	2,000.00
Mch. 12.	Jas. H. Storrs.	1,125.35
Mch. 24.	I. E. Gates....	500.00
Mch. 29.	I. E. Gates....	5,000.00
Apr. 23.	C. H. Sherrill..	15,000.00
May 9.	C. H. Sherrill..	300.00
May 24.	I. E. Gates....	5,000.00
June 2.	C. H. Sherrill...	2,000.00
June 4.	C. H. Sherrill...	1,000.00
June 30.	C. P. Huntington	5,000.00
July 2.	I. E. Gates.....	200.00
Sept. 5.	C. P. Huntington	1,000.00
Sept. 7.	"Legal expenses"	10,440.00
Sept. 15.	C. P. Huntington	1,000.00
Sept. 20.	C. P. Huntington	3,000.00
Oct. 5.	C. P. Huntington	1,500.00
Oct. 15.	C. P. Hunttington	2,000.00
Oct. 24.	C. P. Huntington	1,000.00
Oct. 26.	H. Hopkins, order	5,000.00
Nov. 1.	Leland Stanford	83,418.08
Nov. 9.	I. E. Gates.....	5,000.00
Nov. 16.	I. E. Gates.....	5,000.00
Dec. 8.	I. E. Gates.....	2,500.00
Dec. 18.	I. E. Gates.....	5,000.00
Dec. 19.	I. E. Gates.....	1,000.00
Dec. 26.	C. P. Huntington	2,000.00
Dec. 28.	Leland Stanford	52,500.00
	Total ....$	279,483.43

1878.
Jan. 11.	C. P. Huntington.$	1,150.00
Jan. 28.	I. E. Gates.....	1,600.00
Feb. 14.	L. Stanford....	1,000.00
Feb. 20.	C. P. Huntington	2,500.00
Mch. 18.	C. P. Huntington	5,500.00
Mch. 19.	C. P. Huntington	4,500.00
Apr. 12.	I. E. Gates....	1,750.00
Apr. 18.	I. E. Gates....	200.00
May 4.	James H. Storrs.	1,000.00
May 20.	I. E. Gates....	5,000.00
May 25.	I. E. Gates....	1,500.00
May 27.	I. E. Gates....	5,000.00
June 7.	L. Stanford....	13,000.00
June 22.	I. E. Gates....	2,000.00
June 25.	I. E. Gates....	500.00
June 28.	L. Stanford....	111,431.25
June 29.	Joseph H. Bell.	38,500.00
June 29.	C. P. Huntington	99,167.20

Mch. 31.	I. E. Gates....	5,000.00	Aug. 2.	A. J. Howell....	200.00
Apr. 1.	C. P. Huntington	5,000.00	Aug. 3.	James A. George	300.00
Apr. 6.	C. P. Huntington	5,000.00	Aug. 15.	C. P. Huntington	42,855.06
Apr. 19.	"Attorney" fee.	5,000.00	Aug. 15.	New York Items	1,166.66
May 4.	Anna Franchot..	25,000.00	Aug. 19.	T. M. Norwood	287.95
May 12.	I. E. Gates....	5,000.00	Aug. 29.	John Boyd.....	200.00
May 15.	I. E. Gates....	5,000.00	Sept. 3.	Leland Stanford.	12,000.00
May 19.	I. E. Gates....	1,000.00	Sept. 3.	A. J. Howell....	200.00
June 2.	S. C. Pomeroy	1,000.00	Sept. 3.	J. A. George...	150.00
June 3.	I. E. Gates....	5,000.00	Sept. 4.	T. M. Norwood.	1,000.00
June 19.	I. E. Gates....	10,000.00	Sept. 4.	S. T. Gage.....	3,000.00
June —.	New York newspapers, Tribune, Times. World and Bulletin....	3,381.45	Sept. 14.	I. E. Gates....	1,500.00
			Sept. 14.	O. M. Bradford	75.00
			Sept. 23.	D. D. Colton..	1,200.00
			Sept. 23.	J. A. George..	150.00
July 19.	C. H. Sherrill..	3,000.00	Sept. 27.	I. E. Gates....	5,000.00
July 26.	I. E. Gates....	10,000.00	Sept. 27.	J. G. Prentiss..	60.00
July 12.	S. L. H. Barlow	2,000.00	Sept. 28.	I. E. Gates....	2,000.00
Aug. 18.	R. B. Mitchell.	1,500.00	Oct. 1.	D. D. Colton....	3,460.00
Aug. 21.	S. W. Kellogg.	600.00	Oct. 1.	John Boyd......	200.00
Sept. 12.	Lyman Trumball	10,000.00	Oct. 1.	John Boyd......	204.00
Sept. —.	R. Franchot..	15,698.92	Oct. 1.	J. A. Howell....	200.00
Oct. 4.	C. P. Huntington	500.00	Oct. 1.	J. A. George...	250.00
Oct. 5.	C. P. Huntington	2,500.00	Oct. 3.	I. E. Gates.....	5,000.00
Oct. 14.	C. P. Huntington	6,300.00	Oct. 4.	D. D. Colton....	3,290.00
			Oct. 5.	I. E. Gates......	2,000.00
Oct. 17.	I. E. Gates....	5,000.00	Oct. 7.	I. E. Gates.....	1,000.00
Oct. 21.	I. E. Gates....	5,000.00	Oct. 7.	J. E. Forney....	300.00
Oct. 23.	I. E. Gates....	1,000.00	Oct. 10.	I. E. Gates.....	2,000.00
Oct. 26.	I. E. Gates....	700.00	Oct. 19.	I. E. Gates.....	6,000.00
Oct. 30.	I. E. Gates....	1,000.00	Oct. 22.	I. E. Gates.....	3,500.00
Oct. 10.	Legal expenses	2,500.00	Oct. 24.	C. P. Huntington	3,000.00
Nov. 3.	D. D. Colton...	8,000.00	Oct. 26.	I. E. Gates.....	10,000.00
Nov. 8.	D. D. Colton...	8,000.00	Oct. 28.	I. E. Gates.....	10,000.00
Nov. 13.	I. E. Gates....	1,000.00	Nov. 2.	John Boyd.....	224.00
Nov. 14.	I. E. Gates....	1,000.00	Nov. 2.	T. M. Norwood.	1,083.98
Nov. 15.	I. E. Gates....	1,000.00	Nov. 11.	I. E. Gates.....	500.00
Nov. 16.	C. P. Huntington	5,000.00	Nov. 13.	I. E. Gates.....	1,500.00
Dec. 1.	I. E. Gates.....	3,000.00	Nov. 21.	C. H. Sherrill.	1,000.00
Dec. 7.	I. E. Gates.....	1,000.00	Nov. 21.	O. M. Bradford.	75.00
			Nov. 22.	J. A. George...	100.00
Total		$178,180.37	Nov. 27.	I. E. Gates.....	500.00
1877.			Nov. 27.	T. M. Norwood	500.00
Jan. 3.	"Legal" expenses.$	10,000.00	Dec. 2.	John Boyd.....	200.00
Jan. 8.	I. E. Gates......	5,000.00	Dec. 5.	I. E. Gates.....	10,000.00
Jan. 15.	"Legal" expenses	5,000.00	Dec. 9.	I. E. Gates.....	2,800.00
Feb. 6.	Western Development Company.......	26,000.00	Dec. 17.	I. E. Gates.....	10,500.00
			Dec. 23.	John H. Flagg.	100.00
Feb. 19.	I. E. Gates....	10,000.00	Dec. 26.	I. E. Gates....	500.00
			Total		$447,630.10

CHAPTER VIII.

MRS. COLTON LEARNS ABOUT PHILANTHROPY.

On October 8, 1878, General David D. Colton was brought to his home in San Francisco suffering from a perilous wound that he had received either in some mysterious accident or from somebody's dagger.

Mrs. Colton was then in New York. She was telegraphed for and hastened homeward in special trains, but could not reach San Francisco until October 14th, five days after her husband's death.

General Colton was in several ways remarkable, but chiefly as the only man that Collis P. Huntington seemed to like or in whom he placed the least confidence. For two of his partners Huntington entertained undisguised contempt, and for the third (one may say) a kind of tolerance; but he seemed really drawn toward Colton; in his long career almost the solitary instance of human weakness and one that cost him dear.

In earlier days in California, Colton had been a rather picturesque figure. He was once the sheriff of Siskiyou County and in that capacity had bravely withstood and quelled a mob. In San Francisco he practiced law, did some work for the multifarious and usually shady enterprises of the Southern Pacific, organized the form of its plunder that was called the Rocky Mountain Coal and Iron Company, and by his superior cleverness, won Huntington's reluctant regard.

Before long he was admitted to the partnership; not, of course, to all of the good things, nor to many of them, but to choice bits that made him a millionaire. Thus when the

Western Development Company was organized, he received a one-ninth share of that precious concern; and he was president of and held much stock in the Rocky Mountain Coal and Iron, which was then selling to the Central Pacific at $8 a ton coal that was worth $4 or less.

General Colton's will left everything to Mrs. Colton, who was appointed sole executrix. She had known almost nothing about his business and she was greatly prostrated by his sudden death; but with confidence she relied upon his late associates, who had been his and her dear friends. As she wrote to Mr. Huntington in the early days of her affliction, "I know that you and Mr. Crocker will advise and take care of the wife of David D. Colton." Particularly to her near neighbor, Charles Crocker, she looked for guidance, because the families had been very intimate. When Mr. and Mrs. Crocker went to Europe, Mrs. Colton took the two oldest Crocker boys into her household as if they were her own children.[1]

When General Colton died—or was killed—Mr. Crocker was on his way home from abroad. He spent a few days in New York and conferred there with Mr. Huntington. On the night of his arrival in San Francisco, Mrs. Colton saw with great relief his carriage drive up to his door, and at once sent him a note asking him to come to see her. He excused himself for that night, but visited her the next morning and wept as he dwelt upon General Colton's splendid qualities, and his own and Mrs. Colton's great loss, by which he seemed to be greatly affected.

Meanwhile, Mr. Charles E. Green, General Colton's secretary, had prepared for Mrs. Colton an inventory of the estate. It showed possession of the following securities:[2]

---

[1] Colton versus Stanford et al., testimony, pp. 2485-90.
[2] Many of these securities can be traced by reference to the Pacific Railroad Commission Report, testimony of Doughty, p. 5256.

MRS. COLTON LEARNS ABOUT PHILANTHROPY

    408 shares Rocky Mountain Coal and Iron stock.
10,000 shares Occidental and Oriental Steamship Company stock.
20,000 shares Central Pacific Railroad Company stock.
34,900 shares Southern Pacific stock.
5,555 5/9 shares Western Development Company stock.
    749 shares Amador Branch Railroad stock.
    111 shares Berkeley Branch Railroad stock.
  2,649 shares California Pacific stock.
    556 shares Colorado Steam Navigation stock.
    650 First Mortgage Southern Pacific bonds, $1,000 each.
    100 First Mortgage Southern Pacific bonds, $500 each.
     75 First Mortgage Amador Branch bonds.
     11 First Mortgage Berkeley Branch bonds.
      3 Los Angeles County Bridge bonds.

In a few days Mr. Crocker called again, and, as Mrs. Colton said afterward, she was impressed with a great change in his manner. Apparently he has mastered his grief for his dead friend and his lips found no more words of condolence for the widow. On the contrary, he was stern and severe.[3] He said austerely that General Colton had left his affairs much confused; that he was in debt to his associates and to the companies with which he had been connected; that many of the securities in his estate had been obtained by means of a dividend of the Western Development Company;[4] that this dividend had been improperly declared by General Colton without warrant, and that all persons sharing in that dividend would be obliged to return the securities received from it.

"We are going to return our dividends," he concluded, "and as you have got to return yours, you had better do so today—before night. Will you?"[5]

---

[3] Colton versus Stanford et al., testimony, pp. 2485-90.
[4] I take this to be the dividend of September 4, 1877, described in a previous chapter. More than a year seems to have elapsed before the discovery that the securities must be returned—and by the way, they never were returned.
[5] Colton versus Stanford et al., testimony, p. 2792.

Mrs. Colton, being much taken aback, said she would seek advice and decide what to do. Mr. Crocker went on to say that General Colton, a short time before his death, had subscribed for 30,000 shares of a new issue of Southern Pacific stock. This stock, Mr. Crocker said, would be heavily assessed to build the road.[6] Of course, he said, she would not wish to pay the assessments and she had better cancel the subscription at once. She made haste to say that she certainly would, and he went his way.[7]

A few days later he returned and his manner was still more forbidding. He said (according to Mrs. Colton) that the Western Development Company was insolvent, heavily in debt, and must have the return of all the securities included in that improper dividend to which he had before referred; that General Colton owed his late associates $1,000,000, for which he had deposited as collateral 20,000 shares of Central Pacific[8] and 20,000 shares of Southern Pacific stock, but that the value of the collateral would not cover the face of the note; that the 408 shares of Rocky Mountain Coal and Iron in General Colton's effects really belonged to his four associates, being held in trust for them; and finally, that General Colton proved to be greatly in debt to all the companies. He demanded a settlement of all these claims and told her if she wished she could have them verified by her personal counsel.

---

[6] I can find no indication anywhere that this stock was ever assessed, and certainly there was not the slightest reason why it should be. As for the building of the road, that, as we have previously seen, was provided out of the earnings and sinking fund of the Central Pacific and out of the Western Development and Pacific Improvement Companies.

[7] Colton versus Stanford et al., testimony, p. 2797.

[8] In 1877 Central Pacific paid 8 per cent dividends. Neither Central Pacific nor Southern Pacific was on the market, both being closely held by Mr. Stanford and his friends. An 8 per cent stock ought to be worth at least 80, at which price General Colton's Central Pacific collateral would be worth $1,600,000 without considering the Southern Pacific stock, which is now worth 137.

MRS. COLTON LEARNS ABOUT PHILANTHROPY 201

Now, Mrs. Colton's personal counsel was, of course, her husband's personal counsel, Mr. Samuel M. Wilson, whom Mr. Crocker had highly recommended. Mr. Wilson was also one of the Central Pacific's regular and trusted attorneys and, according to subsequent testimony, in receipt of a salary of $12,000 a year from the railroad company.[9] Mrs. Colton had already sought this gentleman's advice. She obediently told Mr. Crocker she would be guided by Mr. Wilson.

Mr. Crocker's manner on this visit was so disagreeable and the widow was now so thoroughly alarmed that when he sent word of his next call, she thought it well to have some women friends about her, and thus avoided the discussion of business. Mr. Crocker did not come again, and she never spoke with him thereafter.

Mr. Wilson was now presumably investigating General Colton's affairs. After a time, he informed Mrs. Colton that the situation was far worse than Mr. Crocker had pictured it. General Colton was not only heavily in debt to the companies he represented, but his associates charged him with repeated acts of embezzlement. They had told Wilson (he said) that all the securities in the estate would not suffice to pay the General's debts; that they held enough claims to take from Mrs. Colton[10] everything she had, including her home; and they threatened, in a manner "stern and severe and determined and implacable," that unless she made a settlement and surrendered her stocks and bonds they would make public her husband's criminal acts and blacken his name and memory.

Mr. Wilson was good enough to say that he did not believe these charges, but the railroad company had all the

---
[9] Colton versus Stanford et al., testimony, p. 6626.
[10] Colton versus Stanford et al., testimony, p. 2812.

books and records and, therefore, to prove General Colton's innocence would be impossible.[11] Hence the best plan was to make terms with the associates. Mrs. Colton was greatly distressed.

Her misery was somewhat lightened when Mr. Wilson suggested that she employ a mediator, who, because of his ability and experience was likely to secure some concession. The helping hand thus in her dark hours extended to the widow proved to be the hand of Mr. Lloyd Tevis, who, Mr. Wilson said, would be just the man. Mr. Tevis is not unknown in these annals, having been the originator of the ingenious plan whereby the Big Four got possession of Wells Fargo & Co.,[12]—of which branch of the Big Four's activities he was now the president.

Mr. Tevis made what he called an investigation and reported (according to Mrs. Colton) that General Colton's debt was of great magnitude and the Western Development Company was insolvent, but Messrs. Stanford, Huntington, and Crocker had been induced to make a concession to the widow of their old friend. She must deliver to them all the securities that were in controversy, but 200 of the Southern Pacific bonds might be deposited with Wells Fargo & Co., and from these she might for ten years draw the interest.

In other words, they granted her a pension for ten years.

Of the rest of the fortune they made a thorough job. They even insisted that 50 shares of Southern Pacific that General Colton had given to his daughter as a wedding present should be returned to them[13] and that Mrs. Colton should surrender uncut interest coupons amounting to $6,000.

---

[11] *Ibid.*, pp. 2523-7.
[12] Pacific Railroad Commission Report, p. 3116.
[13] Colton versus Stanford et al., testimony, p. 2820.

MRS. COLTON LEARNS ABOUT PHILANTHROPY 203

The two men in whom she had most confidence, Wilson and Tevis, having thus assured her that no other way could be found from the sorry situation, she was almost persuaded to surrender. On the morning of August 27, 1879, she still hesitating, word was sent to her that Mr. Huntington was about to return to New York, that he would leave that afternoon at 3 o'clock,[14] and unless she signed the settlement before that time the Big Four would make no terms with her. Thus menaced, she brought herself to sign an instrument by which she accepted the terms demanded, and surrendered all her securities. The 200 Southern Pacific bonds were delivered to Wells Fargo & Co., who refused to give her any receipt for them. She also executed a release for $304,060.33 which the Western Development Company had owed to her husband.

On their part the Big Four canceled the note for $1,000,000 held by them against General Colton, and agreed to keep secret the charges of embezzlement.

Mrs. Colton knew very little about business, but she was intelligent, and she felt intuitively that there had been fraud[15] in these transactions although she knew not wherein it lay. One day, some months after she had been impoverished in this masterly fashion, she was reading a newspaper

---

[14] As a matter of fact, Mr. Huntington did not leave San Francisco that afternoon nor until September 8th, twelve days later.

[15] QUESTION: You signed this paper and yet you say you rebelled against it?
ANSWER: Because I saw no justice in it.
Q. What was the injustice?
A. Robbery.
Q. A robbery? How was it robbery?
A. It simply had arrived at the point that it was my money or my life.
Q. Isn't that a rather strong way of putting it?
A. I think not. I was in the condition of a man attacked by a highwayman upon the roadside.
Colton versus Stanford et al., cross examination of Mrs. Ellen M. Colton, to be found in the record, p. 2816.

and her eyes fell upon an inventory of the estate of Mark Hopkins, recently deceased. She noticed in the list many securities of the kind she had surrendered, and that the value of these as given in the list was very much greater than the prices at which the same securities had been estimated in her enforced settlement.

This set her to thinking and the more she reviewed her experience, the clearer grew her conviction that she had been wronged. She abandoned Mr. Wilson as her counselor and sought other advice. Her new attorney, Mr. G. Frank Smith, set on foot an investigation and obtained therefrom results that greatly astonished him.

For example, the schedule of the insolvent Western Development Company that Wilson said he obtained from the Big Four or their agents asserted an indebtedness by the company of $11,910,030.44 as follows:[16]

To Charles Crocker $2,219,541.73
To Leland Stanford 1,763,734.85
To Mark Hopkins 4,087,692.10
To C. P. Huntington 3,519,701.43
To D. D. Colton 319,360.33

This and no more. No mention was made of the fact that these five men were the sole owners of the company; that not one of them had ever paid in one cent for his stock; that they then owed the company $5,000,000, nor that the company's alleged indebtedness represented only the securities and moneys that had been advanced in their names from the Central Pacific and other funds for its devious and crooked operations, and for which they knew they would shortly be repaid about five-fold.[17]

---

[16] Colton versus Stanford et al., defendants' exhibit E.

[17] The exact nature of these operations has been sufficiently described in a foregoing chapter, but I may remind the reader here that, according to the testimony before the Pacific Railroad Commission, the Southern Pacific was built out of the diverted earnings and sinking fund of the Central Pacific. The Southern Pacific was on through business a parallel line that had the same owners

Mr. Smith was further informed that in the list of assets in this amazing schedule were most glaring omissions. Thus no mention whatever was made of these items that should have been included:[18]

$462,000.00 due from the Northern Railroad and subsequently paid in bonds.
748,000.00 due from the Northern Railroad in other items and a little later paid in bonds.
7,340.32 due from California Pacific stock.
92,640.00 due from the San Pablo & Tulare Railroad.
3,753.00 from the Pacific Improvement Company.
5,766.15 interest due on Northern Railroad bonds.
36,437.03 interest due on San Pablo & Tulare bonds.
4,986.07 interest due on San Francisco, Oakland & Alameda bonds.

The schedule also set down as a worthless asset $832,800 due from the Los Angeles & San Diego Railroad; Mr. Smith was assured that within a year this debt was paid in good bonds and stocks. Another debt of $45,640.53 carried in the schedule as a worthless asset had already been paid in gold. The Los Angeles & Independence Railroad was put down as worth $100,000 when $300,000 appeared to have been paid for it, and since its purchase it had returned $114,318 in dividends. The Colorado Steam Navi-

---

and owed the government nothing. The money that built it should have gone to pay the Central Pacific's debt to the national treasury. Curious collateral testimony about all this exists in the Colton letters of Mr. Huntington. In the letter of May 8, 1875, Mr. Huntington says: "All the material I buy here is paid for by the Central Pacific. Some of it, like the six coaches sent, I know are for the S. P. (Southern Pacific), but just whether they are to be charged to the S. P. or the Western Development Co. I do not know." In other letters he complains of the enormous floating debt of the Central Pacific that this system was piling up. "Our liabilities (Central Pacific) are getting very large here for a company with such large receipts and with no apparent outlay except interest on bonded debt and operating expenses." In his letter of March 24, 1877, he figures the profits of the Central Pacific at $750,000 a month. These were being used to pay for the building of the Southern Pacific, rendering both stock and bonds of that road "velvet" for the fortunate projectors.

[18] These and many others are to be found in the testimony, pp. 2623-31.

gation Company was entered as an asset of $150,000, whereas in the last three years previous to the making of the schedule this company had paid $110,000 in dividends. On the other hand, in the liabilities, an item of indebtedness entered at $298,208.35, should have been $269,415.73, and there were other apparent inaccuracies that might be thought very surprising in a statement emanating from a business enterprise of such magnitude and standing.

According to the information gathered by Mr. Smith, many other goodly items were missing from the assets, such as Iowa county bonds, Sioux City & Pacific bonds and the like, and no mention was made of such possessions as the contract to extend the San Pablo & Tulare road forty-six miles at $25,000 a mile in bonds and $40,000 a mile in stock (actual cost of construction less than $20,000 a mile),[19] nor of other contracts and items.

It appeared further than none of the other beneficiaries of the Western Development Company's dividend had returned any of his stocks and bonds, but on the contrary, twenty-two days after General Colton's death, these men had wound up the Western Development Company (which they controlled) and organized in its place the Pacific Improvement Company, of which they alone were owners. They then transferred to the new company all of the Western Development Company's possessions and contracts, by which device they froze out all the Colton interests. From the operations of the Pacific Improvement Company they derived by the end of 1882 $20,000,000, which they had divided among themselves, although if General Colton had lived he certainly would have had a share of it.

Furthermore, the investigation seemed to show that the

---

[19] Most of this amazing revelation of the inside history of the concern seems to have been obtained from a discharged employee. As it was never seriously controverted I am obliged to suppose it to be correct.

charge of "embezzlement" was absurd and the claim of debt quite as tenuous.

The total debt alleged against Colton was made up of $666,000, his share of the "insolvent" Western Development Company debt; $160,000 he had "embezzled"; $125,000 due to the companies he had managed; and the $1,000,000 note secured by collateral.

But it appeared that there had been paid on the $1,000,000 note the sum of $250,000, so that the debt was $750,000 instead of $1,000,000. The embezzlement charge when sifted down had no more excuse than this, that Colton had drawn from the company money without returning vouchers.[20] But it appeared that all of the partners had done this; indeed, the whole concern, when the light was thrown upon it, looked like a riot of perquisites, "melons," "benefits," and other good things of the kind. Mark Hopkins had drawn from the Southern Pacific on September 30, 1871, $151,560.59, and no accounting was made of this sum until 1880, two years after his death. Mr. Huntington when in New York drew from the Western Development apparently at his will and never returned any voucher. In three years he had drawn $400,000. Governor Stanford took out $45,638.84 without explanation. Mr. Crocker, without warrant or apparent authority, took from the treasury 500 Southern Pacific bonds to buy the Oakland water front. It seemed a fair contention that if Colton was an embezzler, these men were embezzlers, no less.[21]

As for Colton's share of the alleged indebtedness of the alleged insolvent Western Development Company, it ap-

---

[20] There was an allegation that he had deposited for the company $228,618.47 in silver and then obtained credit for his own benefit on a pretense that the deposit was in gold. This was never established, but even if it were true it was not significant, because such seemed to be the custom. The Central Pacific had done the same thing with $2,000,000 of silver. Colton versus Stanford et al., testimony, p. 2741.

[21] Colton versus Stanford et al., testimony, pp. 2638-39.

peared from the information that there was no true indebtedness and the company was not insolvent at all but fat with rich assets that never had been divided.[22] From its organization to Colton's death it had shared among its stockholders $21,000,000. At Colton's death it had on hand, as the investigation revealed, $22,810,500.43 subject to claims, real and imaginary, of $11,316,497.22.

In payment of these debts that did not exist, there seemed to have been taken from Mrs. Colton securities at much less than their real value. Her Southern Pacific bonds, for instance, were scheduled in her settlement at 60, while in March of the same year they had sold at 100, and at the time of the settlement were traded in by the Big Four at 94. The Rocky Mountain stock they appraised from her at $16.24 a share, must have been worth about par.[23] And so on.

Upon the discovery of these and many other allegations of a like nature, Mr. Smith advised Mrs. Colton to bring suit at once for the annulling of her contract and the return of her securities. Mrs. Colton still clung to a belief in the sincerity of one of the men that had professed so much affection for her husband. With the large and unctuous sentiments of Leland Stanford she was unable to reconcile the idea of despoiling the defenseless, and she wished an appeal to be made to his sense of justice.

Mr. Smith had other views. For some time he had been attentively considering the sense of justice possessed by these men and had acquired of it a very low estimate. He told Mrs. Colton that an appeal to any of them was quite useless. Nevertheless, she insisted, and on March 11, 1882,

---

[22] It may be interesting to note that as brought out in the trial the "Nob Hill" palaces of Stanford, Hopkins, and Crocker were built out of the Western Development Company. Colton versus Stanford et al., testimony, p. 8877.

[23] Pacific Railroad Commission Report, testimony of Leland Stanford, p. 2938.

he wrote to Leland Stanford outlining Mrs. Colton's story, her confidence in the goodness and justice of her old friend, and her plea that she be not utterly plundered. Mr. Smith closed with this comment:

> "Knowing how repugnant uncontested settlements are to your associates, I have acted in the premises contrary to my own belief of any possible advantage that can accrue to her from this or any other amicable overtures on her part." [24]

To this letter no answer was returned. The fact did not astonish Mr. Smith and, one may think, need not have astonished Mrs. Colton. Later she recalled an incident that, upon a more suspicious nature, might have acted to prevent the writing of such a letter. General Colton's office had been in the railroad company's building, and in a safe in that office were still kept all the securities belonging to the estate. According to her subsequent testimony,[25] Governor Stanford came into this office one day and found there Mr. Green, who had been Colton's secretary. The safe was open.

Governor Stanford remarked to Mr. Green that he was very anxious about the security of the property in that safe. He said that the art of safe-blowing had been so developed that a safe-blower could open such a safe even in a building where there were watchmen. He thought General Colton's property should be removed to a safer place, and suggested that such a place would be the vault of the railroad company. Mr. Green reported this conversation to the Widow Colton. She testified that she acted at once upon Governor Stanford's suggestion; but the safer place to which she transferred the property was not the railroad company's vault, but a box in a safety deposit company's care.

On May 21, 1882, Mrs. Colton's suit was filed in San

---

[24] Colton versus Stanford et al., testimony, pp. 2607-8.
[25] *Ibid.*, p. 2905.

Francisco. The answer of the defendants[26] was a general denial of the bill of complaint, a definite assertion of Colton's embezzlements and defalcations, an astounding reiteration of the insolvency of the Western Development Company, and a plea that the statements made to Mrs. Colton were made in good faith and on credible information.

The defendants demurred to some points in the plaintiff's bill, and Judge Hunt promptly overruled the demurrer. Whereupon counsel for Stanford *et al.* secured the removal of the case to the Sonoma County Court at Santa Rosa. It came to trial in November, 1883, before Judge Jackson Temple, a jury being waived.

Judge Temple was afterwards a member of the California Supreme Court.

After the usual manner of things disagreeable to the railroad company, the fifteen volumes of testimony taken in the case have mysteriously vanished from the court records at Santa Rosa, but I succeeded in finding copies at Sacramento and can unreservedly commend their perusal to anyone that cares to know the true manner in which the railroads of the United States have been conducted, or how far (under present conditions) men will go for the sake of money and the power that abides in money. In these respects I know of no

---

[26] They did not mention their real defense, which, though inadmissible as a plea in a court of justice, was not without merit, at least from their point of view. It was this: Messrs. Stanford, Huntington, Hopkins, and Crocker had desired to avail themselves of General Colton's superior cunning and cleverness. The securities they bestowed upon him were merely the wages for his services. When they were deprived of his services they did not purpose to continue the wages. For the most part the securities represented no investment. They were merely manufactured by the Big Four at their convenience and for their profit. All were liens upon the enterprise and carried substantial interest, and the Big Four could see no reason why property manufactured in this way should be enjoyed by General Colton's estate after they had ceased to derive anything from General Colton's wits.

The substance of this argument was frankly stated by Mr. Crocker to Mr. Wilson and will be found in the testimony, Ellen M. Colton versus Leland Stanford et al., at p. 2841.

other volumes of equally impressive instruction. Whoever reads them will face the primitive human passions made so naked and real before him that he will seem to himself to have dipped backward into the jungle.

On October 8, 1885, Judge Temple filed his opinion. It cleared General Colton's name from the absurd embezzlement charge, but held on almost all other points for the defendants, in some instances adopting the very language of their answer. The chief ground of the decision seemed to be that Mrs. Colton's contract was sound in law, made by her in full knowledge of its terms and basis, and contracts must be upheld (Miles versus McDermott, 31 Cal. 273; Woods versus Carpenter, 11 Otto 143; Le Roi versus Mulliken and Moore versus Moore, 56 Cal. 90, if I have the citations right). Also that she was not so much prostrated by her husband's death that she was unable to exercise perfectly all her mental faculties, that she had very able counsel, and by them she was fully informed as to the situation and her rights.

In the subsequently filed "Findings of Fact and Conclusions of Law," Judge Temple considered seventy-seven points, and on seventy-two of them found for the defendants.

The case was appealed December 15, 1886, and in January, 1890, the Supreme Court handed down a decision sustaining Judge Temple.

For Mrs. Colton, therefore, the net result of her suit was a heavy bill of costs that she must pay.

Mr. Huntington had won. He had defeated and crushed the widow of his old friend, and the securities that were the prizes of the long conflict rested in the coffers of the Four of Sacramento. But Mr. Huntington had his own costs to pay. For it was in this case that the Colton letters, printed in a previous chapter, were produced, and the real nature of his Washington operations proved to the world. From this time on those letters were hung about his neck.

CHAPTER IX.

SPEAKING OF WIDOWS AND ORPHANS.

For many years now this colossal institution had been the virtual ruler of the state, setting up this officer and pulling down that, filling places in the government with obedient henchmen, controlling the parties and selecting their candidates, holding avenues to distinction and even to success, choosing judges and commissioners, nominating jurors, and with equal facility influencing legislators and witnesses.[1] Men or even communities that conspicuously opposed the machine were made to suffer. As the railroad built extensions of its lines it levied tribute upon towns thus brought within its reach and sometimes inflicted very serious injury upon those that refused to make grants of land or of money.

For some such offense the city of Stockton was a long time on the company's black list and hindered in its growth. Silveyville was practically annihilated, the new town of Dixon being built, in a spirit of revenge, three and a half miles away. Bakersfield having once incurred the company's displeasure, the town of Kern, three miles off, was developed to crush Bakersfield.

It would be easy to multiply the instances that to all except Californians must seem improbable fiction. The city of Oakland, now one of the fairest and most prosperous in California, was once obliged to fight for its mere existence against the railroad company as against a public enemy. Some

---
[1] Allegations of very flagrant witness-bribing were made in San Francisco, April, 1896, in the case of Louis Schmidt, who confessed he had been bribed by agents of the railroad to testify falsely in the damage suit of Mary Quill.

very extraordinary scenes were witnessed in that contest. A visitor would have thought a civil war was raging. The company fenced off public streets by night and the citizens tore down the fences by day; the company drove piles across the water front slips and the citizens fought to remove them; the company tried to strangle the town by strangling its ferry service and the citizens underwent strange privations to maintain a semblance of their rights.

The power and supremacy of this company were not limited to state nor to municipal affairs. Merchants or shippers that supported any plan to secure relief through competition found their shipments delayed and their rivals helped with rebates. Lawyers that unduly pressed obnoxious suits found their practice vanishing. Some men were ruined for their opposition; some were made rich for their assistance. No one need wonder that to oppose the railroad came to be regarded as fraught with greater danger than the average man could afford to face.

This brings me to the incident that best illustrates the truly autocratic power that these men grasped and the wanton spirit in which they used it.

One of the triumphs of Mr. Huntington s method of "explaining" things to members of Congress (at a cost of millions of dollars added to the company's capitalization) was a bill passed in 1866 granting to the railroad company in alternate sections 12,800 acres of public land for every mile it should build from San Francisco to a point at the southeastern corner of the state; or half the land in a strip forty miles wide along its right of way. The line was laid out and the railroad's lands designated. Subsequently it somewhat changed its route and therefore the land to which it was entitled under the act.

At that time, and for years afterwards, only a small part of the line had been constructed and there grew up a question whether the railroad were really entitled to certain parts of the land it claimed in Fresno, Tulare and some other counties. The rulings[2] of four Secretaries of the Interior, an Attorney-General, and a Commissioner of the Federal Land Office, supported the view that the railroad company had no right to this property, but the company continued to claim the land and to sell it.

Meantime many settlers had come into the Fresno-Tulare region.[3] Some had secured their titles from the government before the railroad's route was changed. These now found their farms to embrace sections claimed by the company. Many others, coming after the final determination of the line, had taken railroad lands at the company's invitation and under terms set forth by the company's circulars. These speedily had troubles of another sort.

The company's circulars, signed by its officers, setting forth the attractions of the Fresno-Tulare region and offering unusual inducements to settlers, had been widely scattered over the Middle West. They dealt in an apparent spirit of frankness and truth, describing the lands as of an excellent quality but dry—a fault easily remedied by irrigation, when the soil would be found to be of surpassing fertility. Terms would be remarkably easy. Here are paragraphs from one of the circulars.

On page 6—The company invites settlers to go upon their lands before patents are issued or the road is completed, and intends in such cases to sell to them in preference to any other applicant and at a price based upon the value of the land without the improvements put upon them by the settlers.

---

[2] The dates of these decisions were as follows:
Secretary Browning, July 14, 1868.
Secretary Cox, November 2, and November 11, 1869.
Secretary Delano, May 9, 1873, and February 26, 1874.
Secretary Schurz, August 2, 1878.
Attorney-General Devens, July 16, 1878.
Commissioner Drummond, January 28, 1874.
[3] About 240 miles southeast of San Francisco.

On page 7—If the settlers desire to buy, the company gives them the first privilege of purchase at a fixed price, which in every case shall only be the value of the land without regard to improvements.

On page 9—The lands are not uniform in price but are offered at various figures from $2.50 upward per acre; usually land covered with *tall timber* is held at $5 per acre and that with *pine* at $10. Most is for sale at $2.50 to $5.

In ascertaining the value, any improvement that a *settler* or *other persons* may have on the lands will not be taken into consideration; neither will the price be increased in consequence thereof. Settlers are thus assured that in addition to being accorded the first privilege of purchase they will be protected in their improvements.[4]

In response to the liberal offers many farmers came from Missouri and Illinois and took up land. They found the country a sandy waste and worthless until, by uniting their efforts and capital, they had constructed an irrigation system, whereupon the soil became exceedingly fertile.[5]

Meanwhile, although they made repeated applications, they were unable to get their titles from the railroad company. The reason why they could not get their titles was because the company had not taken out its patents, and the reason why it had not taken out its patents was because so long as it had no patents on its lands it could not be taxed for them. This was the simple little plan it uniformly pursued and thereby deprived the counties and the State of California of millions of dollars in taxes.[6]

---

[4] These circulars were subsequently confirmed by letters from agents of the railroad company to individual settlers.

[5] They constructed two inadequate ditches before they got one that carried enough water. It was twenty miles long and was dug chiefly by the voluntary labor of the settlers, most of whom were extremely poor and lived in destitution until the water began to flow around their lands. Many of the settlers, while they worked on the ditch, lived upon corn meal ground in hand coffee mills and upon fish that they caught. None of them understood irrigation and they were obliged to learn by experience. There is extant a very pathetic letter from a woman of education and refinement, Mrs. Mary E. Chambers, a sister of one of these men, giving a vivid account of the hardships the settlers endured in these years.

[6] For explicit testimony on this point, see Pacific Railroad Commission Report, p. 146.

But in 1877 the company began to take out its patents, and soon afterwards to demand payment of the settlers.

Then the settlers learned to their amazement that the land was not to be paid for at $2.50 an acre but at from $25 to $40 an acre, and that all the improvements they had made were counted in the price. Even the irrigation ditch that they had constructed at their own expense and with their own labor became a great factor in the increase. The land was not to be offered to them first; it was to be thrown on the market for any purchaser.

When the settlers found that the company really intended thus to violate its agreement they protested, showing the circulars and the promises therein. They offered to pay the company at the stipulated prices, but all protests, offers and arguments were alike without avail; and, the company preparing to press its claims, many of the threatened farmers formed a Settlers' League to defend by united action what they believed to be their rights. Four times they had petitioned Congress (without result, of course), and now they resorted to the law. A test case was tried in the Federal Court and on December 15, 1879, Judge Lorenzo Sawyer (who afterwards held Leland Stanford to be immune from disagreeable questions) rendered a decision upholding the railroad company in all its contentions. From this decision the perplexed settlers prepared to appeal to the United States Supreme Court.

Meantime the railroad company had begun to sell the settlers' lands and four or five men moved into the region and built houses under the railroad company's warrant. In June, 1879, a band of men came by night to the place of Perry C. Phillips, a purchaser from the railroad, removed the inmates and all the contents to a place of safety, and burned the house to the ground.[7] After this the company found great difficulty in selling any of the lands.

---

[7] It is denied that the Settlers' League had any connection with this affair.

What went on in the minds of the railroad managers is only to be surmised, but from subsequent events the conclusion seems reasonable that after so many years of autocratic rule they were greatly nettled by this active and so far successful opposition. The settlers believed that, following the usual custom, both sides should now halt to await the Supreme Court's decision. As to this the railroad company had another opinion. Ignoring the pending litigation, it sharked up from the north two hardy men to whom it promised land without charge if they would succeed in breaking the settlers' position. One of these men, Walter J. Crow, was reputed to be among the best rifle and revolver shots in the state, and the settlers thought they knew the purpose for which he was employed. The antecedents of the other, M. D. Hartt, are not so well known.

Hartt and Crow went into the region, and soon after, with other men that had obtained land from the railroad, they exhibited this notice, which they said they had received:

> Tulare County, April 24, 1880.
> You are hereby ordered to leave the country.
> By Order of the League.

The Settlers' League did not send out these notices and had no knowledge of them. At the same time reports were sent abroad that bands of armed and masked men were riding up and down the district making threats and committing outrages, although the residents were not aware of such matters.

Next, the railroad company went into the Federal Court, secured writs of ejectment, placed them in the hands of A. W. Poole, United States Marshal of the district, and demanded that he serve them at once, remove the settlers, and put Hartt and Crow in possession.

The marshal, of course, was obliged to comply, and on Monday, May 10, 1880, he went to Hanford, Tulare County,[8] the trading town that had grown up near the settlers' lands.

Major T. J. McQuiddy, president and leader of the Settlers' League, upon which he had always urged moderation and patience, learned that night of the marshal's arrival and understood well enough his errand. With the secretary of the league Major McQuiddy drew up the following address:

To the United States Marshal:—

Sir: We understand that you hold writs of ejectment issued against settlers of Tulare and Fresno counties, for the purpose of putting the Southern Pacific Railroad Company in possession of our lands, upon which we entered in good faith and have by our own patient industry transformed from a desert into valuable and productive homes.

We are aware that the United States District Court has decided that our lands belong to said Railroad under patent issued by the United States Government.

We hereby notify you that we have had no chance to present our equity in the case nor shall we be able to do so as quickly as our opponents can complete their process for a so-called legal ejectment, and we have therefore determined that we will not leave our homes unless forced to do so by a superior force. In other words, it will require an army of 1,000 good soldiers against the local force that we can rally for self-defense, and we further expect the moral support of the good, law-abiding citizens of the United States sufficient to resist all force that can be brought to bear to perpetuate such an outrage.

Three cases have been appealed to the United States Supreme Court and we are determined to submit to no ejectment until said cases are decided.

We present the following facts:

First—These lands were never granted to the Southern Pacific Railroad Company.

---

[8] It is now in Kings County.

Second—We have certain equities that must be respected and shall be respected.

Third—The patents they hold to our lands were acquired by misrepresentation and fraud, and we, as American citizens, cannot and will not respect them without investigation by our government.

Fourth—The Southern Pacific Railroad Company have not complied with their contract both with our people and with our government, and therefore for these several reasons we are in duty bound to ask you to desist.

By Authority of the League.

Early the next morning before this could be delivered to him, the marshal hired a buggy and accompanied by W. H. Clark, the railroad's grader or appraiser of lands, he drove three miles northeast to the nearest of the farms covered by the writs of ejectment—the farm of W. B. Braden, a member of the League.

In another buggy close behind came Hartt and Crow, heavily armed with revolvers, rifles and shotguns, the shotguns being loaded with small bullets or slugs instead of shot.

It happened that on this day the League was having a picnic some miles away; whether this fact influenced the action of the railroad company and its traveling batteries I do not know. Braden was at the picnic; no one was in the little cottage. The marshal entered, carried out all the household goods, piled them in the road, and formally declared Hartt to be in possession of the premises.[9]

This was about nine o'clock in the morning. The marshal and Clark, closely followed by Hartt and Crow, drove to the next place, the farm of one Brewer, over the border of Fresno County, and about three and a half miles from Braden's. They encountered on the road a settler named J. H. Storer, an old friend of Marshal Poole's, and Poole

---

[9] Four loaded cartridges were left on Braden's doorstep, probably as an indication of what would be the result of any resistance on his part.

reined in for a time while the two talked. Storer said the settlers hoped for a compromise with the railroad company and he would try to arrange one.

When they drove on, Clark, the grader, reproved the marshal for talking with Storer because Storer was the partner of Brewer, whom they had come to dispossess.

About ten o'clock they arrived at Brewer's place. He was harrowing in his field. Both buggies drove into the yard, past the house, and about two hundred yards west into the field. At this moment there appeared about fifteen of the settlers in a group, some mounted, some on foot, advancing toward them. The settlers carried no visible arms; among them all were only five small pocket pistols. Marshal Poole descended from his buggy and went forward, saluting them courteously. The foremost of the settlers addressed him quietly, asking the marshal not to serve any writs until the case then pending in the Supreme Court should be decided. He also handed to the marshal the address that Major McQuiddy had drawn up.

Marshal Poole read the document and said his duty was to serve the writs then and there. The settlers replied without vehemence that they would not allow him to serve them.

They now closed about the marshal and demanded that he give up his revolver and surrender to them, whereupon he would be conducted in safety to a station whence he could leave the county. He said he would yield to force and go away but he would not give up his revolver, although he promised not to use it. Two of the settlers, Archibald McGregor and John E. Henderson, were then told off to guard the marshal and Clark to the railroad station at Kingsburg.

All this Hartt and Crow watched narrowly from the other buggy about seventy-five feet away. As the conference with the marshal ended, Hartt reached down and seized a rifle.

"Let's shoot," said he.

Without shifting his watchful gaze from the group of settlers, Crow put a hand upon his companion's arm.

"Not yet," said he, "it isn't time."

James Harris, from the group about the marshal, rode up to Hartt and Crow and cried:

"Give up your arms!"

He was within a few feet of the buggy. Crow laid his hands upon a shotgun before him. He raised it deliberately; he fired it into Harris' face.

Henderson spun around at the sound and whipped from his pocket a small caliber revolver. He caught a glimpse of the body of Harris slipping to the ground. He spurred forward, trying to fire his revolver at Crow. The hammer clicked on the cartridge but the arm was not discharged. Hartt started to descend from the buggy. As he leaned over the wheel Henderson's revolver worked at last and the bullet struck Hartt in the abdomen.[10] At the same instant Crow, from his raised gun, shot Henderson dead.

Crow leaped to the ground with a revolver in one hand and carrying other weapons. He was firing rapidly into the group of settlers. Iver Kneutson was shot dead before he could draw his revolver. Daniel Kelly fell from his horse with three bullets through his body. Archibald McGregor, who was armed with only a penknife, was shot twice through the breast. As he ran screaming toward a pool of water, Crow at one hundred and seventy paces shot him in the back. He fell over and lay still. Crow fired his shotgun and Edward Haymaker, also unarmed, fell, struck in the head.

---

[10] Hartt stated before his death that he had been sitting in the buggy with his feet on the dashboard and was in that position when he was shot. The autopsy disproved this assertion for the bullet entered at the upper boundary of the abdomen and traversed the whole abdominal cavity downward, showing that he had been shot from a pistol held above and almost parallel with his body.

All this happened, as it seemed, in an instant. A stupefaction had fallen upon the spectators; they could but stand and stare. J. M. Patterson awoke first. He bounded forward crying, "This has gone far enough! It must stop!" One or two ineffectual shots were fired. As they rang out, Major McQuiddy, who all the morning had been trying to overtake the marshal, hurried upon the scene and took charge of the disorganized settlers.

Crow still stood there, weapons in hand, menacing the crowd. McQuiddy spoke rapidly to the marshal, protesting against any further action. As the two advanced, Crow suddenly doubled forward and dodged past the corner of the barn toward a field of standing wheat.

"Don't let that man escape!" shouted McQuiddy, and as Crow disappeared into the tall grain some one—just who is not likely ever to be known—followed upon his trail.

McQuiddy now turned to the wounded and ordered them to be carried to Brewer's house while messengers rode for surgeons. The bodies of Harris, Henderson and Kneutson were placed upon the porch; they were dead. Within the house Kelly, McGregor and Hartt were moaning and twitching with agony. Two doctors were brought from the village and found that all were mortally hurt except Haymaker.[11]

This made six persons done to death that morning—on the Southern Pacific's corruptly obtained and wrongly held grant from the public domain.

Very soon there was another. Crow, dodging through the wheat, was making for the house of one Haas, his brother-in-law, and likewise an opponent of the settlers. As he ran he came to the irrigation ditch and turned off along its course; a ditch tender working below saw him running. At a mile and a half from Brewer's there was a bridge where the road crossed the ditch. Major McQuiddy had

---

[11] McGregor and Kelly died before morning and Hartt on the 12th.

sent men on horseback to try to catch Crow. These were watching for him at the bridge. Haas and his hired man drove up from the other direction in a wagon containing six guns and a supply of ammunition.

"Where's Crow?" asked Haas, seeing the roup by the bridge.

At that instant a cry arose, for Crow broke into sight along the ditch. He stopped, dodged back, and whipped up his rifle, aiming it at George Hackett. Before he could fire, a shot rang behind him. He swayed, turned a little and pitched over upon his face—dead. He had been shot through the chest.

The moment the news of that morning's work reac..ed Hanford, the railroad company announced that its telegraph office there had been closed and the operator driven away by the League, and that owing to the armed insurrection in progress all trains, passenger and freight, had been annulled. At Goshen, the other nearby station, no telegrams were received except for the railroad company.

By these means the company secured control of the news and the first reports described a bloody and unprovoked attack by desperadoes on the authority of the United States. In San Francisco five eminent railroad officers, including Charles Crocker and W. W. Stowe, at that time the Southern Pacific's political manager for California, hastened to newspaper offices and explained the innocence of the company and the depravity of the ruffians that had defied the Federal authority.

Later the effect of these communications was somewhat marred by the appearance in San Francisco of Walter Leach, the Hanford telegraph operator, and his statement that he had been removed and his office closed not by the League, but by the railroad company.

The sheriff also sent word that there was no disturbance and no reason why trains should not run. Furthermore, independent reporters, notably one for the Visalia *Delta,* got to the scene and sent out unvarnished reports. Yet it is not to be denied that a certain impression was created by the railroad company's tainted news, that this impression still persists, and that to this day the affair is far from clear in many minds to which it should be no mystery.

The funeral of the slaughtered settlers on the 12th was very impressive. All business and work were suspended in the region and in a procession of vehicles more than two miles long, a thousand farmers followed the hearses to the cemetery. McGregor and Kelly were single, but Harris and Henderson had each a wife and a child, and Kneutson left a wife and nine children. All of these were presently evicted from their homes.

There was no further disturbance. The farmers were disheartened by the deaths of their comrades and by the obviously resistless power of the railroad, against which no rights, no law, no protest, and no appeal could prevail. On May 26th five of them went to San Francisco to make what terms they could with this supreme power. As soon as they alighted in the city they were arrested and thrown into jail, charged with conspiracy and resisting a Federal officer. Not one of them had been anywhere near the massacre.

Subsequently they were released, but other arrests were made, many indictments found, and John J. Doyle, W. H. Patterson, Purcell Prior, William B. Braden and Courtney Talbot were tried before Judge Lorenzo Sawyer, who practically ordered the jury to convict. The jury refused to convict of conspiracy but found the prisoners guilty of resisting the marshal. They were sentenced to five months' imprisonment each and were sent to jail.

As for the land, the railroad company won that handsomely, for after the terrible work of that May day the appeals of the three test cases were abandoned by the discouraged and penniless settlers and Judge Sawyer's decision stood. Years afterward the same issue was raised again in another county of the state, and, being carried to the Supreme Court, the court ruled against the railroad and upheld the principle for which the settlers had contended,[12] so that their position must have been as legally sound as it was morally just.

But the land for which they had contended was none the less lost to them and became a part of that total on which you and I have the pleasure of paying interest charges, for it was all swept into the capitalization. Other additions thereto occasioned by this episode were not great: something for legal expenses, something for newspaper articles, something for political dirty-work men, something for Hartt and Crow, and a few other similar items. That was all, because the funerals of the farmers killed were paid for by friends and neighbors and cost the company literally nothing. No doubt these necessary expenses would have been borne by the orphaned and dispossessed families of the deceased if the railroad company had left them anything to pay with.

This is the battle of Mussel Slough, to which you may have heard some reference. It is all over now; the Southern Pacific is triumphant. But for years the settlers of Tulare County held memorial services on each anniversary of that bloody day at Brewer's Farm. They remembered, though the rest of the world and the railroad company speedily forgot.[13]

---

[12] Southern Pacific Company versus Groeck, 74 Fed. 385, 183 U. S. 690. In the case of Boyd versus Brinckin, decided by the California Supreme Court a few months after the massacre the same principle was involved and was upheld by the unanimous decision of the Court, Chief Justice Sharpstein writing the opinion.

[13] The authorities for this chapter are the statements of survivors of the massacre; the statements of eyewitnesses published at the time; the accounts printed by the San Francisco *Chronicle, Alta California, Bulletin, Call,* and *Examiner,* and particularly the detailed reports in the Visalia *Delta;* the rare pamphlet entitled "The Struggle of the Mussel Slough Settlers;" testimony given at the trials; and the account printed in the Atlas of Kings County.

CHAPTER X.

WHAT THE LAW DOES FOR US.

In the grip of the great power of the Southern Pacific Railroad, the people of California learned that they had small advantage from those wonderful gifts of nature wherewith their state ran over. One resource after another was discovered and developed, gave forth its promise of prosperity, and was incorporated into the money-making machine of the railroad monopoly, or asphyxiated by its high rates.

The richness of the land was for the railroad company and not for the producers.

Orange growers found that while they could raise the best and cheapest of all oranges and in unequaled abundance, the freight charges absorbed the profits of their toil.

California wines attained a just celebrity; but if they were to be shipped by rail, the freight rates barred them from general use and defeated the wine growers.

Wonderful crops of deciduous fruits, peaches, plums, apples, cherries and pears, sometimes rotted on the trees; no man could afford to ship them to market.

This rich adobe soil, surpassingly fertile, was found to produce such wheat as never before had been seen; stalks six feet high, with large, firm berries, a prodigious yield; but when vast areas had been sown in wheat, the farmers discovered that at the freight rates exacted by the railroad monopoly no profit lay in wheat growing. All the world was eager for California wheat; vessels came from Liverpool around Cape Horn to get it, and for the carriage of a few miles from the farms to the seaport the railroad charged so much that nothing remained to the farmer.

Here lay the world's vineyard, orchard and granary; what Swinburne calls God's three chief gifts to man, his "bread and oil and wine," showered upon it in overmeasure, and the railroad monopoly took the tilth of all for its own coffers. This great state, seven hundred and seventy miles long and about two hundred and fifty miles wide, timbered, watered—with so much gold that even now over eighteen million dollars' worth is taken yearly from its soil; with silver, platinum, petroleum, and other mineral wealth; with fertile soil; with the advantage of a singularly delectable climate; with so much variety of products—seems to have been endowed with every good thing that nature knows, and beyond any other region of earth. One might think that all the natural forces had intelligently combined to see how much they could do here for man and his life; and, to crown their work, had attracted a population of the best fiber the American race had produced.

And yet the population of this splendid state in 1900, thirty-one years after the completing of the transcontinental railroad, was only 1,485,053. This is the showing of its growth by the United States census:

```
1850 .............................................    92,597
1860 .............................................   379,994
1870 .............................................   560,247
1880 .............................................   864,694
1890 ............................................. 1,208,130
1900 ............................................. 1,485,053
```

From 1890 to 1900 only 277,000 increase. Is not that significant?

COMPARATIVE AREAS AND POPULATIONS.

	Area in Square Miles	Population
California	158,360	1,485,053
France	207,054	38,961,945
Germany	208,830	63,886,000
Japan	147,655	49,732,952
Italy	110,550	32,475,253
Belgium	11,373	7,074,910
Massachusetts	8,315	2,805,346
New Jersey	7,815	1,883,669
Illinois	56,650	4,821,550

The true garden spot of the world, and after forty years of railroad domination it had in 1910, 2,377,549 inhabitants in an area greater than Ohio, Illinois, Indiana, Massachusetts and New Jersey together; more than forty per cent larger than Italy with about one-fifteenth of Italy's population! So that to this day, after the traveler has apprehended something of the unmatched resources of the country, the greatest of all its wonders is its sparsely populated areas.

The same lawless power that perverted the government and seized the courts has throttled California's development and deprived its people of the products of their industry. Men have sown, and this power, cunningly adjusting its rates for that purpose, has year after year taken the harvest.

You say: For this abnormal condition there must have been a remedy. This nation of ours is ruled by law and majorities. It must have been possible to subdue or to regulate this railroad. The fault must have been with the people.

No—no fault with the people. The people were all right. The fault lay in the system. The choice offered to the people was between nominal rule by the Republican party and nominal rule by the Democratic party. When they wearied of railroad tyranny under the name of a Republican administration, they revolted and introduced railroad tyranny under the name of a Democratic administration. The monopoly controlled the Democratic administration as easily as it had controlled the Republican. It was a power too great to be withstood and made great by the money of the community that it now oppressed.

But how about the law? How about the blessed thing called regulation? How about the government supervision of corporations?

That is the very thing I want most to tell you about. Come, now, you that think you can deal with this problem by regulation. Come and have a good look at this exhibit. It will not give you cheer but it ought to furnish unlimited instruction.

Law? There was nothing but law; and constitutions; and provisions; and orders; and amendments; and fresh statutes; and then more law; all aimed and shaped to regulate, restrict and control this monster, and the monster never gave a hoot for all of them. Every step of its progress had been marked by the violation of some law or some article of the holy constitution, and it strode calmly and cheerfully over all, never minding in the least.

For instance: There was an article in the Constitution of the State of California that expressly forbade a certain kind of lease between railroad companies. So the monopoly made something like a dozen leases of that variety. There was a section of the penal code that forbade an interchange of stock between railroad companies. So the monopoly proceeded to interchange the stock of its subsidiary railroad companies. There was an article in the state constitution providing that the state railroad commissioners should have the power to fix passenger and freight rates. And when on one famous occasion these commissioners undertook to exercise this power, the monopoly brushed the commissioners out of its way and continued to make its own rates in its old fashion on its old basis.

And what was that basis? All the traffic would bear. Some of these incidents should be told in detail.

1. Thus Section 20 of Article XII of the Constitution of California contains this provision:

> And whenever a railroad corporation shall for the purpose of competing with any other common carrier lower its rates for transportation of passengers or freight from one point to another, such railroad rate shall not be again raised or increased from such standard without the consent of the governmental authority in which shall be vested the power to regulate fares and freights.

For many years the oppressed and defrauded merchants of San Francisco held to the belief that the one sure remedy for their troubles was in competition. If they could only get another railroad, competition would compel the Southern-Central-Pacific oligarchy to reduce rates and practice decency. Many times their hopes of competition had been raised from many sources, but always to be disappointed. The new line was seized, controlled or absorbed by the oligarchy, or headed off if it was approaching from the East. At last the merchants formed their own company and built their own line from San Francisco Bay down to rich San Joaquin Valley, 200 miles and more.

At once the new line made rates much lower than the Southern Pacific's tariff, and the Southern Pacific was obliged to meet the reductions. Beautiful proof of the virtue of competition as a cure-all! But the Atchison, Topeka & Santa Fe—which had acquired the old Atlantic & Pacific (a land grant railroad across Colorado and New Mexico)—now extended its line westward, secured an entrance to California and appeared on the scene to offer the grandest promise of a perfect competition. If the Santa Fe could be brought to San Francisco there would be a competing outlet to the Atlantic. So the merchants sold their San Joaquin Valley line to the Santa Fe and amidst great rejoicing the Santa Fe entered San Francisco early in 1900.

Immediately, the Santa Fe and the Southern Pacific restored the rates in the San Joaquin Valley generally to the basis that had prevailed before the merchants' road was built, and the people of San Francisco discovered too late that the addition of a new line to their facilities made no difference in their situation, for the simple reason that the Southern Pacific owned $17,000,000 of stock in the Santa Fe and the two roads had a close traffic and trackage arrangement. Two roads with but a single thought; two tariffs that gouged as one.

Among the passenger rates that had been reduced by the merchants' road competition was the passenger rate from San Francisco to Fresno. This had been $5.90; it was cut to $3.75. When the merchants' road was sold, the old rate of $5.90 to Fresno was restored. This was in March, 1900. Mr. E. B. Edson brought suit to test under the constitution the legality of the restored rate, and the State Board of Railroad Commissioners joined him. In the Superior Court Judge George H. Bahrs gave judgment for Edson and the commissioners. The Southern Pacific appealed, and on May 23, 1901, the Supreme Court reversed Judge Bahrs and remanded the case for a new trial.[1]

On the retrial in the lower court in July, 1904, Judge Frank H. Kerrigan decided in favor of the railroad company, holding that the rate had never been reduced.

The ground for this decision is worth noting. It seems that when the Southern Pacific reduced the rate to Fresno to $3.75, it issued a new form of ticket good only for the day of issue. The old style of ticket, price $5.90, and good for six months, it still kept on sale. Nobody ever wanted or bought the old style of ticket at $5.90, but it could be bought if desired. Hence, in Judge Kerrigan's opinion, there had been no reduction of rates.

---

[1] Edson et al. versus Southern Pacific Company, 133 Cal., 25.

Edson and the commissioners now appealed. Chief Justice Beatty wrote the decision of the Supreme Court, which entirely upheld the railroad company, and affirmed the validity of the $5.90 charge—not because the rate had not been lowered, but because it "had not been lowered for the purpose of competition within the proper construction of the constitution." Judge McFarland, an associate judge of the Supreme Court and previously a Southern Pacific attorney, concurred with Chief Justice Beatty, but added an even stronger opinion of his own, in which he fiercely attacked Section 20 of Article XII of the constitution, speaking of it as containing "a drastic and ruinous penalty."

One might think that on such grounds any law anywhere could be upset at any time.

Incidentally, it may be interesting to note that Judge Bahrs was retired to private life at the end of his term and Judge Kerrigan was elevated to the Appellate Court.

2. Among the choice presents the four gentlemen of Sacramento gathered from the United States was a land grant for building a railroad from Roseville, eighteen miles north of Sacramento, to Portland, Oregon. This grant was of every alternate twenty square miles (ten on each side of the track) conditioned upon the building of the road the entire distance. The Congenial Four built only as far as Redding, 152 miles, but they took possession of the land grant for the entire projected line of the road.

It was immensely valuable land, comprising some of the best timber on the continent. In 1882 the time limit for completing the road had long expired so that, except for the line from Sacramento to Redding, the grant was forfeited. To reclaim it an act of Congress was necessary. Every attempt to pass such an act and to return to the public the land justly belonging thereto was defeated. The four gentlemen had no more right to the land than they had to the Washington monument, but they held it nevertheless, and reaped millions from it.

In the election of 1882, Mr. Barclay Henley, a young attorney of Santa Rosa, who had studied the land grant question, was nominated for Congress on a platform demanding that the forfeited land grants should be returned to the public domain. On this issue he was elected and promptly introduced bills [2] for the reclamation of the forfeited grants of the Roseville-Portland line, for the reclamation of the forfeited land grants of the Northern Pacific—colossal grabs that have somehow escaped the attention they deserve— and some other bills having similar objects. The Congenial Four bitterly fought the bill that sought to make them disgorge, bringing down Judge Dillon and General Roger A. Pryor from New York to argue in their behalf before the Public Lands Committee of the House, and filling the lobbies with their hired men.

But Mr. Henley had absorbed the whole subject and he made of it so clean and masterly an expression that he carried the House with him. After a time, the only active opposition he encountered was from the late Thomas B. Reed, of Maine, sometime Speaker of the House. When the vote came all the bills were passed by large majorities. They went next to the Senate. There they were promptly buried, nor could any argument or appeal ever resurrect them. The four congenial gentlemen remained in possession of the land to which they were not entitled, and it is today reflected in the capitalization of the Southern Pacific railroad that the public pays exorbitant freight and passenger rates to support.

This must be a cheerful thought to all of us. First we are cheated of millions upon millions of acres of our lands, rich in those natural resources we are now so anxious to con-

---

[2] For the particularly interesting debate on the first of these bills, see *Congressional Record,* Forty-eighth Congress, First Session, pp. 4814-22. The pleas made in behalf of the railroad are a revelation to anyone that will dig them out.

serve; next we pay freight rates on the value of the land that has been stolen from us; then as the value of this land increases with the increase of population, it becomes additional capital on which to base additional rates to lay additional burdens upon the ultimate consumers, 85 per cent of whom are poor or very poor. The finite mind seems incapable of a grander concept.

3. But the land grab story has still a sequel not less delectable. It shows how even the best of movements for the public benefit may easily be twisted into further advantages for the fortunate and further burdens for the people at the bottom.

About fifteen years ago the need of conservation began to be forced, very tardily, upon our attention by the obvious fact that we should shortly be without timber as without public lands. Congress, therefore, set apart regions as inalienable forest reserves for the nation. An honest man in the Senate, looking over the project, saw that while its main features were admirable, it contained one defect, easily remedied. It did not provide for the cases of men that had settled upon the land now sequestered for public purposes. That is to say, in the middle of a reserve a settler might be tilling a farm, and by the establishing of a forest reserve about him might find himself utterly cut off from communication with the rest of the world, whereby his farm would be made valueless.

This senator, therefore, introduced a measure providing that any dwellers on the land taken for forest reserves should have the right to exchange their farms for an equal amount of public land elsewhere. This just and reasonable amendment fell into the hands of an eminent friend of the Interests in the Senate and another in the house. They changed the words "dwellers on" to "holders of" and, at the last minute before the end of the session, it was rushed through the Senate, giving no chance for amendment.

WHAT THE LAW DOES FOR US 235

The railroad companies immediately took advantage of this provision. They gave up fifty millions of acres of worthless barrens in Nevada and Arizona where nothing ever grew, or ever would grow, but cactus and sagebrush, and received in exchange choice timber lands in Oregon, Northern California and Washington, nor could any protest or outcry avail to check this monstrous fraud.

Only by a narrow margin did they fail of getting those invaluable coal deposits in Alaska that are now the subject of national controversy. They had planned to grab all such lands, but found they were stopped by the fact that the homestead law did not extend to Alaska. Their newspapers in all parts of the country then began to demand amendment of the law so that Alaska should be thrown open to homestead entry. When the agitation had proceeded long enough, a bill to this effect was introduced in Congress and slated for immediate passage. One man, Judge Joseph H. Call, of Los Angeles, well known as an opponent of corporation knavery, discovered what was afoot and hastily warned a group of honest Congressmen. By these the bill was so amended as to exclude the railroads from the benefit of the extension.

Meantime, those choicest timber lands in California, Oregon and Washington, before referred to, had been obligingly withheld from entry. When the schemers found that they were beaten off from Alaska, the timber tract was as opportunely restored to entry and the railroad companies filed for and grabbed it all—about fifty million acres. I suggest that the next Conservation Conference in this country devote itself to this little fact.

4. But to return to the experiences of California. And here I come upon the main story I desire to tell because it illustrates so sweetly just how much effect rate regulation, supervision, restriction, Hepburn bills, commerce courts, strenuous gentlemen, and the like agencies, can have upon

railroad companies when the railroad companies do not care to observe such trifles.

Also something else. It illustrates and shows us precisely how and to what extent you and I and all of us pay for these fortunes; pay for them once when they are made and then the interest on that, and the interest on that, many times over, until the dollar we paid forty years ago for Mr. Huntington's "explanations" to Congressmen has become two dollars that we pay year after year; until all the wealth that was stolen, filched, and conveyed from any one of these enterprises in the palmy days of its looting, is the basis of a bill annually presented to us and for which we must dig up the money.

If the looting were done when it was done and we were rid of it thereafter, the case could not be so bad. But every dollar of loot in any railroad enterprise, all the bribe money and "legal expenses," the jobs in the construction accounts and the swindles in the interlacing leases, become, all of them, just so many additions to the capital account on which interest must be paid through the rates that come home to us all.

With this little preface, necessary to make clear the true meaning of the characters and incidents we shall introduce, we are now ready for our story.

About thirty years ago this idea of curing evils by regulating them laid strong hold upon the people of California, and in the brave new constitution of 1879, to which we have before referred, they determined to deal once and for all with the railroad monopoly question. So in Section 20 of Article XII, they gave to the Board of Railroad Commissioners every conceivable power "to establish rates of charge for the transportation of passengers and freight by railroad and other transportation companies," to supervise and control such companies, and to enforce its will upon them. For failure to obey the commissioners' rulings, severe penalties were provided, the companies to pay heavy fines and their officers to be punished with fine and imprisonment. The section concludes with this explicit statement:

In all controversies, civil and criminal, the rates of fares and freight established by said commission shall be deemed conclusively just and reasonable.

The force of regulation could no farther go. Even the most fervid regulationist has never suggested anything approaching this achievement.

Some years afterwards, the state legislature, finding that for some reason blessed regulation did not produce the expected good things, tried to strengthen the commission's hands with the majesty of statutes, enacting that whenever the commission determined upon a rate it should file the new tariff schedule with the railroad company affected, and that twenty days after the new rate should go into effect and become the law of the land.

Although it possessed these unequalled and ample powers, the commission never did a blessed thing but make reports and draw its several salaries; it was armed with thunder bolts and used only goose quills. Mr. Huntington wrote once to General Colton: "I notice you are looking after the state railroad commisisoners. I think it is time."[3] Whether this "looking after" had any relation to the prevailing inertia, the reader can surmise as well as I.

But it appears that in 1894 there was one of the periodical revolts against the Southern Pacific, which had so long been the constituted authority and government of the state, and this treasonable and unruly spirit, seizing upon the Democratic party, found expression in the following resolution that the Democratic State Convention of that year embodied in its party platform:

Resolved, That the charges for the transportation of freight in

---
[3] Letter of March 7, 1877. See foregoing chapter.

California by the Southern Pacific Company of Kentucky[4] and its leased lines, should be subjected to an average reduction of not less than twenty-five per cent, and we pledge our nominees for Railroad Commissioner to make this reduction.

You must recall the marvelous and perfect political organization of the Central Pacific before you can comprehend the force of the revolt that produced this resolution. The truth is the grain growers were threatened with ruin. Some of them were supporting the burden of heavy mortgages while from their abundant crops the railroad was filching most of the profits. They were, therefore, in the mood of men not to be trifled with.

No doubt the passage of that resolution was a treasonable act that the railroad's political department could easily have prevented. A few years before, it would have done so, but it had learned that regulative laws and constitutional provisions were really ineffective; and besides, there was the memory of that bloody May day at Brewer's Farm. The country had made so much fuss about the killing of a few farmers; "The Massacre at Mussel Slough" it was universally called, and the Southern Pacific the murderer of those men. It was not nice for professed philanthropists and art connoisseurs. Even the subsidized editors always gagged a little about Mussel Slough.

Evidently there was a point of endurance beyond which men could not be driven with entire safety to the drivers. Wisdom and experience indicated that no harm could come from such a resolution nor from a campaign conducted on these lines; it was only a useful and desirable vent for public clamor that otherwise might have worse results.

So the convention nominated its candidates on this platform, and the party went into the campaign with at last the similitude of an issue to fight for. The state that year was

---

[4] The various consolidations of the Central Pacific, Southern Pacific, and a score of other lines had been merged into a company bearing this name incorporated in Kentucky, March 17, 1884.

in one of its moods for a change from the machine that had a Republican name to the machine that had a Democratic name, and two of the three Democratic candidates for railroad commissioner were elected, constituting a majority of the Board.

In August, 1895, seven months after taking office, the commissioners reached (one would think with sufficient deliberation) the important matter of freight rates, and on September 12th and 13th adopted two resolutions, the first declaring a reduction in grain rates of not twenty-five but eight per cent, and the other expressing an opinion that all rates should be reduced, and at some time the commissioners would get to work and reduce them—perhaps when the robins should nest again.

To this lame and impotent conclusion came the revolt of the grain growers and the valorous resolve of the Democratic State Convention.

But you should wait a little; the best is yet to come. This is a very famous case and tested to the utmost the whole power of the regulative theory. If there ever were in the United States railroad rates that ought to be reduced, they were the grain rates in California; and if there ever could be anywhere a force able by law and constitution to reduce such rates, it was the California Board of Railroad Commissioners.

Whatever rates that Board might decide upon (said the constitution of the state) should be valid and "in all controversies, civil or criminal, the rates of fares and freights established by said commission" should "be deemed conclusively just and reasonable."

Note what happened.

The railroad company went straightway before Judge Joseph McKenna, then of the United States Circuit Court, now of the United States Supreme Court, and on October 14th obtained a temporary injunction restraining the commission from carrying out or enforcing the reduction it had declared.[6]

Of course. The United States Circuit Court takes precedence over authorities constituted by the state.

Soon after, the case came up again on a motion to continue the injunction and the issue was joined. There was a grand array of counsel—W. F. Herrin, successor of "Bill" Stowe as chief solicitor and political manager for the Southern Pacific, former Judge John Garber, E. A. Pillsbury, and others for the distressed railroad company; Attorney-General Fitzgerald, former Judge R. Y. Hayne, and others for the commissioners. The case lasted for more than a year.

The plea of the company was that it was too poor to afford any reduction of rates and that the action of the commissioners, unless prevented by the court, would so injure the company and decrease its revenues that it would amount to the confiscation of property expressly prohibited by the Constitution of the United States of America.

Please note this. You see now we are coming down to fundamentals. Rates could not be reduced because under existing conditions the Constitution of the United States practically forbade them to be reduced.

To show the extreme poverty of the company were adduced many figures.

First, there was the capitalization of the company and of its constituent companies, with their bonded debt. Then there was a computation showing that for the last eighteen months the whole company (which included lines in Oregon, Arizona, New Mexico, and elsewhere) had been operated at a loss—on this capitalization. Then there was a list of certain constituent lines of the Southern Pacific, to-wit: the Oregon & California, the Central Pacific, the California Pacific, the Northern Railway, the Northern California

---

[6] The title is the Southern Pacific Company versus The Board of Railroad Commissioners of the State of California. Number of the case, 12, 127.

Railway, the South Pacific Coast Railway, and the Southern Pacific of California; after which the bill of the company avers as follows:

Fifth, That none of said corporations, other than the said California Pacific Railroad Company and the said Northern Railway Company, have for more than one year last past received or been entitled to receive any profit or net income whatsoever above their actual expenses or any compensation for the use of their equipment out of the funds payable to them by your orator under the terms of said leases or otherwise, nor have any of said corporations paid, or been able to pay, any dividends to their stockholders.

This is dull legal verbiage, but I want to put it all in because it is necessary if we are to determine about the legal control of these corporations.

"Under the terms of said leases," says Mr. Word Spinner of the company's plea.

What leases?

Why the leases of the constituent companies one to another. Each of these constituent companies was made up of many other smaller companies, each leased in turn to a larger company, until there was a grand collection of leases.

Thus the California Pacific mentioned in this plea was a constituent company leased to the Southern Pacific, and the California Pacific was itself an aggregation of smaller roads covered with leases. First, there was the old Marysville & Benicia, organized under the act of 1851, which was leased to the San Francisco & Marysville of 1857, which was leased to the Sacramento & San Francisco, which was leased to the Old California Pacific, which was leased to some other road, which was leased to the present California Pacific.

The commissioners agreed that most of these leases were clearly illegal and invalid, and that the whole Southern Pacific conglomerate was an outlaw and pirate.

Section 20, Article XII, of the Constitution of California, declares that no railroad company, nor other carrier, shall combine nor make any contract with any other company "by which combination or contract the earnings of the one doing the carrying are to be shared by the other not doing the carrying."

Which was, of course, precisely the situation created by most of these leases.

Law? Well, as I said before, there is no end of law. Law on all sides of us steadily violated by this corporation. Nothing but law. As, for instance, Section 560 of the penal code of California, reads as follows:

"Every director of any stock corporation who concurs in any vote or act of the directors of such corporation, or any of them, by which it is intended either"—(And then follows a list of prohibited acts, ending with this):

Fifth—To receive from any other stock corporation, in exchange for the shares, notes, bonds, or other evidences of debt of their own corporation, shares of the capital stock of such corporation or notes, bonds or other evidence of debt issued by such corporation, is guilty of misdemeanor.

And before a committee of Congress in 1894, testifying, Mr. Huntington, President of the Southern Pacific, explicitly admitted that the Southern Pacific Railway of California, of which he was also President, had done this identical thing thus forbidden by the statute, although the law that he thus calmly admitted he had violated had never been enforced upon him.[6]

Why do we have laws if they can thus be set aside at one man's will?

But about these leases of the subordinate roads. The Southern Pacific argued that it could not afford to reduce the grain rate because all its roads, except only two, the California Pacific and the Northern, it was operating at a loss, and that the small profits on these were needed for repairs and betterments.

---

[6] The Southern Pacific Company versus The Board of Railroad Commissioners. Argument of former Judge Hayne, p. 214.

Then please observe.

A. All of these roads were owned by the same persons, who were also the owners of the Southern Pacific, so that when they made one of these leases, they leased their own property to themselves.

B. The rental so paid by one road to another became a part of the operating expense of the larger road.

C. These rentals were repeated several times and were usually at excessive rates.

D. The final road that embodied all the small roads had to make enough to pay all the rentals (to its own owners, of course) and a profit besides, and when this profit was two and a half per cent, the point was raised that it was a profit to small to justify any reduction in rates.[7]

The process may be illustrated thus. Let us suppose one of these roads to be composed of four subordinate roads successively leased. The first is one hundred miles long. It is leased for one hundred thousand dollars a year to the second company, which builds fifty miles and leases itself and the first road to a third company for two hundred thousand dollars a year. The third company adds fifty miles and leases itself and its constituents to a fourth company for four hundred thousand dollars a year. All these leases are, in reality, held by the same persons. It is evident that, in the end, they have two hundred miles of track on which the leases they hold are an exorbitant charge upon the operation of the road—to be paid to themselves.[8]

---

[7] "They own the California Pacific; they lease it to themselves at $600,000 a year; then they add the $600,000 to operating expenses and show a deficit of $54,000 a year." Judge Hayne's argument, p. 577.

[8] The California Pacific, with a total value of $1,404,935, was leased for $600,000 a year. The annual rentals of some of the other lines was almost as much as the whole value of the property leased and there was a fiction accepted by many persons that should have known better, that above these monstrous rentals there must still be profit else the road was operated at a oss.

In other words, the lease is simply a subterfuge to conceal profits that the public must furnish.

As to the railroad's poverty again, it averred in its bill of complaint, sworn to October 11, 1895, that for the year ending December 31, 1894, the income account of all its lines in California was as follows:

Gross earnings	$20,783,157.04
Interest	183,759.12
Rentals	26,572.23
Total receipts	$20,993,488.39

From which was to be deducted:

Operating expenses, renewals, improvements, et cetera.	$13,320,417.52
Taxes	659,002.10
Rentals, et cetera	792,471.21
Interest on bonds	5,472,190.24
Sinking fund payments	135,000.00
Payments to the United States for Central Pacific	179,910.27
Surplus on lines in California	$ 434,497.05

This small sum, it was declared, was required for improvements so that the lines were really operated without a profit.

Reports made by these companies to the State Railroad Commission have a somewhat different look. The form of statement required by the State Commission sets forth the total income from all sources, and the total deductions of all kinds, and the remainder is called the net income. According to these statements, the business of the Southern Pacific lines for the year ending June 30, 1894, showed the following results:

Lines in California	Net Incomes
Southern Pacific	$2,289,832.65
California Pacific	250,549.50
Northern Railway	400,058.19
South Pacific Coast. Leased	No operations
Northern California. Leased	No operations
Total	$2,940,440.34
Central Pacific in and out of the state	$1,377,720.80
Total Net Income	$4,318,161.14

WHAT THE LAW DOES FOR US

How this coheres with the railroad company's statement in its bill I can not undertake to say. As to the matter of dividends, of which the company averred there had been none, the commissioners swore that on the Central Pacific dividends had been paid in 1894 and 1895 and had been kept secret.[9]

To prove its poverty, the company filed a schedule of the total indebtedness and the interest thereon; also of the capital stock of each company; and alleged that the actual value of the roads exceeded the amount of the stocks and bonds.

Some extremely interesting developments resulted. The law of California requires assessments to be made on the full cash value of property. On June 6, 1895, four months before the beginning of this suit, Mr. A. N. Towne, General Manager of all the Southern Pacific lines, filed with the State Board of Equalization (the highest taxing body), sworn statements in which he declared the full cash value of all the franchises, railways, roadbeds, rails, and rolling stock of each of the Southern Pacific lines in California. This covered all of the company's property except such as was assessed by the various county assessors. By adding the amounts sworn to by Mr. Towne, and the amounts in the statements to the county assessors, the actual cash value of all the property of all the companies (on their own statements), including their state franchises and all else, was easily ascertained. This, put by the side of the company's statements in the bill, made a startling showing. I think we had better exhibit it all together as thus:

---

[9] These were the dividends promised to Sir Rivers Wilson after he had investigated the Central Pacific in behalf of the unfortunate English stockholders, as related in a previous chapter.

Railroad Line	Total Debt (Company's Showing)	Annual Interest Thereon	Capital Stock (Company's Showing)	Total Capitalization (Company's Showing)	Actual Cash Value Shown from the Sworn Statement	Amount of water by this showing
Southern Pacific of California	$43,652,400	$2,454,984	$68,402,000	$112,054,400	$16,119,232	$95,935,168
South Pacific Coast Railway.	5,500,000	220,000	6,000,000	11,500,000	1,079,592	10,420,408
Northern California	1,074,000	53,700	28,000	2,354,000	175,000	2,179,000
Northern Railway	9,907,000	546,910	12,896,000	22,803,000	3,445,542	19,357,458
California Pacific	6,825,500	322,125	12,000,000	18,825,000	1,404,935	17,420,565
Central Pacific	35,428,000	1,908,054	67,275,500	102,703,500	14,219,569	88,483,931

WHAT THE LAW DOES FOR US

On all this huge volume of water, the public was required to pay the rates that furnished the interest, and the company could not afford to make a reduction of eight per cent in the grain rates that were throttling the farmer.

How much of actual annual reduction in income would be produced by this reduction? How much would the company lose if it allowed the new schedule to go into effect? At the most—$100,000 a year.

Let's look into that.

One hundred thousand dollars a year. At five per cent, the annual interest on the water on the capitalization of only one line, the South Pacific Coast, would be more than five times this amount. The annual interest on the water in the capitalization of the California Pacific alone would pay the grain rate reduction more than six times. It was to support this fictitious capitalization that the grain rates must be kept up and the farmers must pay and the bread eaters must pay and all the world must pay for this gross and swollen capitalization, $10,000,000 in one line, and $80,000,000 in another, and $19,000,000 in another, all demanding interest on the bonds and dividends on the stocks.

And these bonds and stocks created for the profit of the owners of the road, neatly concealed by the leases and other devices, represented in the main nothing but the greed of the owners and the fraud of their methods. This was why the freight rates were high, the farmers were poor, and the cost of living increased.

In that chain of cause and effect, there was not a flaw.

Five per cent on the $19,357,458 of fictitious capitalization in the Northern Railway is $967,872.90; five per cent on the actual value of the Northern Railway is $172,277.10. Under the existing conditions, the Northern Railway must earn $968,000 a year; if it were capitalized for its real value, it need earn only $173,000, and it could reduce its grain rates and all other rates much more than eight per cent and still make its dividends. What the people of California and the people elsewhere were paying for was not a reasonable profit on an investment, but an unreasonable profit on a scheme of fraud; and as a matter of fact the only confiscation involved in the proposed reduction was the confiscation of a piece of the apparatus of a gigantic shell game.

Take some of this capitalization on which the railroad company demanded "a reasonable profit," and see its substance.

Into that capitalization was charged, for instance, the $2,840,000[10] that the Central Pacific paid to the Union Pacific for the overlapping lines when the two roads were engaged in their insane race for mileage. Twenty-five years had passed since that strange exhibition of frenzied competition. On this $2,840,000 at six per cent for twenty-five years, the interest would be $4,260,000, making with the principal, $7,100,000.[11] On this again the annual interest is $426,000, and the commission asked for only $100,000 a year reduction in freight rates.

In those early days of the Central Pacific, there was spent at Washington and Sacramento $6,532,329 for corruption disguised as "legal expenses," and this went into the capitalization on which the farmers must pay and the bread eaters must pay and all the world must pay. At six per cent interest for twenty-five years this would amount to $9,798,493.50. If that sum were applied to reducing the debt of the company, the annual saving in interest would be $587,-

---

[10] Pacific Railroad Commission Report, p. 3039.
[11] Mr. W. F. Herrin, chief counsel for the railroad, said in his argument, at p. 112: "The money expended by these people legitimately and honestly for the speedy construction of this road cannot be ignored. There is no equity on the part of the State of California to insist on striking out and eliminating a single dollar that was actually expended in the construction of the road. It was a legitimate investment."

WHAT THE LAW DOES FOR US

909.61—and the commission asked for only $100,000 from the railroad.[12]

Again: Before the Pacific Railroad Commission,[13] E. H. Miller, Jr., secretary of the company, gave a tabulation showing that from 1873 to 1884 (when the road was sold to the unfortunate English investors and the profits were suppressed) the dividends paid on Central Pacific stock amounted to $34,308,055. The net earnings of the road from its completion to December 31, 1886, amounted to $59,276,387.54. In the first seven years ending with 1876 the owners had received $18,000,000 in dividends besides the enormous outside profits in bonds, land grants, construction graft, other graft, expense accounts, and leases.

If from 1870 to 1876 they had been content to take one-third of the net income for their emoluments, each of them would have received $222,000 a year for each of those years; and if they had applied the remaining two-thirds of the net earnings to the reducing of the company's debt, they would have canceled $12,000,000 of that debt.

On $12,000,000 for twenty years the interest at six per cent is $14,400,000, which would be the saving effected by 1896. The annual saving in interest charge would be $720,000 if for the first seven years of its existence the owners of the road had been content with $222,000 a year each from the net profits of its operations. A careful man can always sustain life on $222,000 a year. And then—$720,000 a year of saved interest charges! All the farmers asked was that $100,000 a year should be dropped from the incalculable loot.

Instead of being content with $222,000 a year for seven years, *the Congenial Four of Sacramento grabbed off in that*

---

[12] Mr. Herrin in his argument (p. 139) declared that the operation of the roads would be discontinued if the reduction were enforced.

[13] See report, p. 2547.

time and divided $18,000,000 of profits (from the road's operation alone), and then made of their monstrous profits and of the debt they would not pay a basis for charging extortionate rates, and next, in court, a basis for defending those rates.

It seems hard to go in imagination beyond this triumph of impudence.

Or to take another illustration: If down to 1884 the owners had been content to divide among themselves yearly one-third of the net profits and to apply the rest to pay the road's just debts, they would by that time have shared $11,436,018 from the road's operations alone and would have saved for the road to 1884, $22,877,037. By the time the grain rate suit was brought this would be $39,339,901, on which the annual interest would have been $2,360,394. And all the farmers asked was that $100,000 a year should be taken from the load that they bore.

And again: From the testimony taken before the Pacific Railroad Commission it appeared that the $62,000,000 of issued capital stock of the Central Pacific Railroad Company was divided among the four gentlemen as a free gift, and the four gentlemen paid not a cent of it, and that this $62,000,000 was part of the capitalization on which interest must be paid by means of charges levied upon the public.[14]

And it appeared that all the bonds fraudulently taken from the government at the mountain rate, $48,000 a mile when the actual construction was on level ground, all these were in the account and must be paid for by charges levied upon the public.

And it appeared that all the bonds fraudulently taken from the government at the foothill rate, $32,000[15] a mile, when the actual construction was on level ground, all these

---

[14] See pages 2646, 2670, and 2377, testimony of Leland Stanford and Edward H. Miller, Jr.
[15] Pacific Railroad Commission Report, p. 3662.

WHAT THE LAW DOES FOR US

were in the account and must be paid for by charges levied upon the public.

And it appeared that all the money fraudulently taken by the Contract and Finance Company (owned by the same owners) on excessive and extravagant charges for construction and repairs—all that was in the capitalization and must be paid for year after year by charges levied upon the public.

And it appeared that the manipulation by which at the end of the construction period[16] the Central Pacific owed the Contract and Finance $3,500,000 and took for that debt the Central Pacific's notes for $5,700,000 and subsequently received in payment for these notes $7,000,000 of land grant bonds, that all this graft also was in the capitalization and must be paid for by the charges levied upon the public.[17]

And it appeared that the grafting contract[18] by which the Contract and Finance undertook to make repairs on the Central Pacific, and furnish its supplies and thereby raked off $2,000,000 a year extra profits—that all this was in the capitalization and must be paid for year after year by charges levied upon the public.

And it appeared that all the graft secured under the aliases of the Western Development Company and the Pacific Improvement Company, all the excessive bond issues, fraudulent construction charges, and magnified costs, all these were included in the capitalization and must be paid for year after year by charges levied upon the public.

And it appeared that when the Western Development Company and the Pacific Improvement Company raided the sinking fund of the Central Pacific Company,[19] that here

---

[16] *Ibid.*, p. 2682, testimony of W. E. Brown.
[17] Judge Hayne's argument, p. 509.
[18] Pacific Railroad Commission Report, p. 3227, testimony of Lewis M. Clements.
[19] *Ibid.*, testimony of C. P. Huntington, p. 32; testimony of Leland Stanford, p. 2665. In the present case, Judge Hayne's argument at p. 512.

were items of cost that went into the capitalization and must be paid for year after year through charges levied upon the public.

And it appeared that when suits were brought that threatened in a painful way the reputations of the gentlemen involved in these operations and they bought back at 400 and 500 and 1,700 the stock they quoted at 80, these expenditures also went into the capitalization. And when the directors of the company hired writers, newspapers, and magazines to praise them and their work, or to favor legislation in behalf of the Central Pacific, these expenditures also went into the capitalization.

And it appeared that the real purpose of the Contract and Finance Company and the Western Development Company, and the Pacific Improvement Company, and all the other aliases and disguises of these gentlemen was to effect exactly this result, to transform the expenditure into a fixed charge upon the public that should endure for the profit of the four gentlemen; and that all these charges could be paid only in transportation rates; and that because of all these accumulated charges and piled-up accretions of fraud, the grain rates must be exacted and the farmers must pay and the bread eaters must pay and all the world must pay.

And it appeared that there was no end to these charges. That whenever the great power that gripped and held in its fist the State of California extended in any way its operations or acquired additional lines or bought a steamship or built a branch or spent money for legislation or made an improvement or paid a rebate or made an illegal lease or straightened its corkscrew track, it piled up more capitalization, which meant more interest and dividends to be met, which meant more charges to be paid by the public.

And it appeared that when the Central Pacific defrauded the nation by building a crooked road, the public paid charges on the crookedness; and when these crooked places were made straight the public paid charges for making them straight. Whatever the railroad company did produced more capitalization, and all the capitalization produced interest and dividends to be met, and all the interest and dividends meant charges levied upon the public. And at the other end of this infallible mill stood the owners issuing the excessive securities, and adding the proceeds to their huge hoards.

Many of these matters were set forth with great force and skill by the attorneys for the railroad commission. The railroad company, by its learned counsel, excepted to certain features of the commissioners' answer, and by order of the court they were stricken out. One of the excised sections contained some of the extraordinary revelations of the tax statement before referred to. In another place, Paragraph IX of the commissioners' answer, occurs this significant passage:

That it is notoriously true that for many years last past the complainant has expended large sums of money in the employment of politicians and others to improperly influence various branches of the Federal and State Government and to obtain for themselves [itself] advantages to which it was not entitled; and to induce action on the part of various branches of the public service for the sake of its own private advancement and for that of its officers, and that a large part of the sums claimed by it as operating expenses are for such unlawful expenditures.

From this the court ordered to be stricken out the words that "it is notoriously true."

Judge McKenna's decision was filed November 30, 1896. In his accompanying opinion he confined himself chiefly to the constitutional aspects of the case and to precedent and previous decisions. He found that for the year 1894 the Pacific System of the Southern Pacific had been operated at a loss of $276,262.70, that the company could not afford to make the reduction of rates ordered by the commissioners, and that the reduction would be such confiscation of property as was prohibited by the Constitution of the United States. The clause of the California Constitution upholding rates to be promulgated by the commissioners he declared to be null and void[20] for similar reasons, and he therefore continued the injunction and knocked out the proposed reduction.

In this view Judge McKenna was in accord with the decisions of the Supreme and other courts, for the fact seems to be that under the Constitution and the system of business that we have adopted, no other decision is possible. Capital is capital; capital is entitled to just and reasonable profits; courts cannot inquire minutely as to the methods by which capitalization is piled up; and once having saddled ourselves with this burden, we must continue to bear it so long as the securities exist.

It only remains to say that in 1898 a new Board of Railroad Commissioners was elected; that on April 24, 1899, this new board rescinded the grain reduction resolution enjoined by Judge McKenna; and on May 19th the railroad company graciously consented that the case be dismissed. Which ended the last attempt of the grain growers to utilize Regulation's artful aid in their behalf. They submitted to their fate, and after a time most of the wheat fields were put to other purposes.

But if we really desire to learn just why the cost of living has increased so heavily upon us, and just why it threatens to become, before long, an insupportable condition, our investigation need go no further than this.

The history of the Southern Pacific is not very different from the history of other railroads in the United States.

Who pays the vast interest charges on the nine billion dollars of fictitious capitalization that these railroads have piled up?

---

[20] The Southern Pacific Company versus The Board of Railroad Commissioners. Judge McKenna's decision, p. 2.

CHAPTER XI.

THE STORY OF THE HARBOR FIGHT.

"The railroads of today ought not to be judged by the past."

So say the railroad attorneys, presidents, and champions, sitting pleasantly at meat. So dutifully echoes that part of the periodical press owned or controlled by the railroad interests.

I doubt not all of us would be glad to accept and to follow the injunction if only we could; but to separate the railroad of today from its past is like separating the living tree from its root.

The railroad company of today is an accretion of railroad companies of the past; the railroad management of today is an inheritance from the railroad management of the past; the railroad capitalization of today has been built upon years of devious policy; the railroad rates of today reflect forty years of scheming and looting.

If the railroad companies would cease to operate their political departments in the manner of 1878 and 1884; if they would cease to build fictitious capital on the fictitious capital of previous years; if they could avoid as a basis of rates the necessity of getting interest and dividends on this fictitious capital, we could possibly afford to forget the past and its records.

We must look back to the past because we are paying for the past. Three times a day the past comes to our tables and collects its toll.

The manner of this collection we shall now, if you please, proceed to see, and also to see how utterly futile and absurd are, and must be, all attempts to deal with the American railroad problem by doctoring symptoms with legal remedies, even when these are most justly grounded and ably enforced.

You remember, no doubt, the $27,500,000 of subsidy bonds that the United States government issued and bestowed upon Messrs. Stanford, Huntington, Hopkins, and Crocker, to facilitate the building of the Central Pacific.

These bonds were to fall due thirty years after the completion of the road.

The road was completed in 1869-70. The bonds became due in 1900.

Originally, the government stipulated that the railroad company should pay the semi-annual interest on these bonds, and the principal when due.

The company refused to pay the semi-annual interest and got from the Supreme Court a decision that it need not pay this interest until it paid the principal. This obliged the United States to advance the semi-annual interest from the treasury, which amount was charged against the company.

In 1887 the Pacific Railroad Commission was appointed to investigate the condition of the company and discover what use it had made of its resources and income, a reasonable inquiry in view of its repeated statements that it was too poor to pay the interest it owed, and would be too poor to pay the principal.

After listening to much astounding testimony of a nature extremely damaging to the company, the commission made two reports. The majority dealt lightly with the offenses that had been revealed. Governor Pattison, the minority member, returned a stinging indictment of Messrs. Stanford, Huntington, Hopkins, and Crocker, and urged the government to forfeit the company's charter for fraud and dishonesty.

Nothing was done on either report.

In 1896, the time for payment being close at hand, the debt to the government was apparently more than $60,000,000, and the company's attorneys and representatives made no secret of its intention to default on this debt.

Public sentiment demanded that some arrangement should be made. Mr. Huntington was still hovering about Congress with his agents and lobbyists.[1] He prepared a bill that provided for the refunding of the debt into bonds bearing two per cent interest and payable at a period estimated at eighty years from date.

This bill was slated for passage by the Republican machine to which Mr. Huntington had always contributed liberally.

Everybody knew that the bill was to be jammed through and Mr. Huntington was greatly pleased with the prospect.

He had reason to be pleased. The bill settled all differences with the government, and put off the day of payment so far that it probably would never come.

Mr. Huntington's pleasure was of short life. It was presently upset by two men.

At the request of Mr. William Randolph Hearst, Mr. Ambrose Bierce went to Washington, and every day for one year he wrote an article exposing the rotten features of Mr. Huntington's bill.

These articles were extraordinary examples of invective and bitter sarcasm. They were addressed to the dishonest nature of the bill and to the real reasons why the machine had slated it for passage. When Mr. Bierce began his campaign, few persons imagined that the bill could be stopped.

---

[1] The Washington correspondence of the *Chicago Evening Post*, April 22, 1896, contains this passage: "The most pitiable and at the same time the most disgusting spectacle that now offends the national capital is the Huntington lobby. The list of paid lobbyists and attorneys now numbers twenty-eight, and their brazen attempts to influence Congress to pass the Pacific Railroad Refunding Bill have become the disgrace of the session."

After a time the skill and steady persistence of the attack began to draw wide attention. With six months of incessant firing, Mr. Bierce had the railroad forces frightened and wavering; and before the end of the year, he had them whipped. The bill was withdrawn and killed, and in 1898 Congress adopted an amendment to the general deficiency bill, providing for the collection of the Pacific Railroad subsidy debts, principal and interest.

This may be held to be as wonderful a victory as was ever achieved by one man's pen, and, also, one of the most remarkable tributes to the power of persistent publicity. What it meant for California may be judged from the fact that when news was received of the death of Mr. Huntington's bill the governor proclaimed a public holiday, and in the name of the state sent a telegram of thanks to Mr. Hearst.

But it was a victory destined to have far more memorable results than these. At once the railroad company abandoned all hope of cheating the government, and resorted to a vast and difficult feat of financiering that it might provide for the payment of the accumulated debt. For months the eyes of the financial world were fixed wonderingly upon this slack wire adventure, which was regarded in some quarters as fraught with peril, in others as "a clever and ingenious contrivance," and on all sides as a new chapter in high finance.

The substance of it was this:

The amount due to the government, less deductions, was $58,800,000. For this the company gave twenty notes of equal amounts, payable semi-annually over a period of ten years, bearing interest at three per cent and secured by an equal amount of bonds.

This meant, of course, an increase of capital. The accrued interest, $30,700,000, had been due to the government. Instead of paying it to the government, the Big Four had wrongfully paid the money to themselves in dividends. They now funded the accumulated debt for us to pay.

There was next prepared a new issue of Southern Pacific stock and a new issue of four per cent collateral bonds. Next an assessment of $2 a share was ordered on the old Central Pacific common.

But to offset this assessment, the new collateral bonds were presented free to the stockholders to the amount of $16,819,000.

Then the stockholders received, share for share, $67,275,500 of the new Southern Pacific stock on which six per cent dividends were to be paid—a fine, dividend-paying stock exchange for a stock that for years had been inert and unprofitable.

Next a new Central Pacific Railway Company was organized in Utah to succeed the old, and the original part of the Millionaire Mill passed from public view forever.

The $16,819,000 of collateral bonds and the $67,275,500 of new stock made $84,094,500 of securities which must be provided for from the earnings. Nominally, the total increase in the capitalization was $47,579,000, being the capitalized interest on the government debt, and the collateral bonds; but the total paper capitalization was now $114,794,500, and all of it became interest or dividend bearing, whereas much of it had previously been of small value.

A total of $114,794,500, on which interest must be paid.

We are paying it.

Thus:

Annual dividends on the stock, 6 per cent.................$4,036,530
Collateral bonds, $16,819,000, at 4 per cent.............. 672,760
Capitalized interest on government subsidy.............. 1,200,000

    Total annual charge on us.......................$5,909,290

We have been paying this for thirteen years. So far, we have paid upon this account $76,820,770.

Then this is the way our account stands to date:

Debt of the railroad to the government.................$58,800,000
We have paid because of the refunding of that debt.... 76,820,770

We are out so far...............................$18,020,770

In thirty years we shall have paid close upon $180,000,000, which is three times the amount of the debt, and shall then be losers to the amount of $120,000,000.

It would have been enormously cheaper to give Mr. Huntington a cancellation of the debt.

Cheaper in freight rates; cheaper, therefore, in the daily living expenses of the people.

But since this debt and the annual charges that we must pay on it are directly and solely the results of the operations (before described) of Messrs. Stanford, Huntington, Hopkins, and Crocker, and of nothing else, kindly observe the impudence of the men that urge us to forget railroad history.

We might very well answer that we will forget railroad history when the railroads cease to make us pay for that history.

But the floating of the gigantic refunding scheme had another result besides the levying of additional tribute upon us. Mr. Stanford was dead, Mr. Hopkins was dead, Mr. Crocker was dead. Mr. Huntington, who had been steering and directing the new operations died (before they were completed) in August, 1900.

Some confusion followed in the public mind, with many stories of sales, purchases, and reorganizations. When this mist cleared away, men saw that the Great Millionaire Mill had passed into a new ownership.

For years the many properties of the original Big Four of Sacramento had been undergoing consolidation. For all the millions upon millions of fictitious stock issued and gathered to themselves as they had gone along, for all the fictitious capitalization in all the long list of subsidiary lines and branches, being company within company until the human mind wearied and failed to follow the ramifications —for all this there had been issued stock in the Southern Pacific Company, of Kentucky, the final consolidated concern.

Great blocks of this were now acquired from the heirs of the Big Four and through the exigencies of the refunding operations, and when the situation finally cleared there appeared as the real owners of the old Central Pacific, the Southern Pacific, the unknowable convolutions thereof, the Pacific Mail, the Morgan steamships, the Union Pacific, the whole bewildering aggregation with all its load of fictitious capital, buttressed with lordly gifts from the public domain, rich with spoils, incomparably the grandest source of riches ever known in human history—of the whole, incalculable thing, the real owners appeared as the colossal Standard Oil interests, with the late E. H. Harriman as their representative.

In the end it was the Standard Oil group that had financed the "clever and ingenious" refunding deal and had thereby seized the control of the Mill, and it is to the Standard Oil group that we pay our $5,900,000 of annual tribute to that deal, and all the other tribute on all the other deals back to the days of the Contract and Finance Company, John Miller, and the books at the bottom of the river Seine.

Is not that sweet?

Yes, we should love to forget the past if the past would only let us. But when, on $200,000,000 of fictitious stock created by the Contract and Finance Company and its successors, we furnish such dividends that the price of that stock goes up to 137, the manner in which we are to win forgetfulness of the past ought to be very carefully explained to us.

So much for the business side of forgetting. Suppose we turn now to the political side and see how that looks.

We found that, in the old days, this company was wont to maintain a great and elaborate political machine covering every corner of the state and working with perfect precision to fill all offices with persons chosen by the company. We found that this machine cost much money and the cost thereof was and is assessed upon us, who continue year after year to pay.

Always to pay.

We found that the company divided the state into districts, each with its boss; and the districts into counties, each with its boss; and that the county bosses reported to the district bosses, who reported to the chief boss, who was the company's chief counsel and attorney in San Francisco.

Then come down to these days of ours, if you will. Who is Mr. Walter F. Parker? He is the Southern Pacific leader for the southern district of California. And who report to him? The county bosses in that district. And to whom does Mr. Parker report? To William F. Herrin, chief counsel of the Southern Pacific at San Francisco.

Same old frame work, evidently.

How does the thing work today?

Like this:

In California the governor's term of office is four years.

A new governor was to be elected in 1906. Mr. James N. Gillett was then a member of Congress for California. Five months before the election, Mr. E. H. Harriman gave a dinner in Washington to men influential in politics and business. At that dinner Mr. Gillett was chosen to be the next governor of California, Mr. Harriman announcing in a few, well-chosen words Gillett's selection by the railroad company.

To ratify this choice, the State Republican Convention was called at Santa Cruz. All the railroad bosses from great to small had received the necessary word about Mr. Harriman's action, and proceeded at once to secure Gillett delegations from the counties. In Los Angeles County, which sent a large delegation, Mr. Walter Parker himself directed operations. He sat on an upper floor of the building in which the county convention was held, and a staff of messengers ran continually between his desk and his leaders on the floor. Not a move was made without his word; the delegates were marionettes; he sat above them and pulled the strings.

Likewise in San Francisco, which had a large delegation, Mr. Herrin took personal charge and operated with no less success, although upon a basis more primitive. According to a confession of Mr. Abe Ruef, the convicted boodler of San Francisco, Mr. Herrin paid him $14,000 for the control of the delegation.

Simple, neat, effective.

Of late years California has been growing more and more restless under the iron sway of the Southern Pacific. Even with the active co-operation of Mr. Ruef, former Mayor Schmitz, and their gang, Mr. Harriman did not find it perfectly easy to nominate the man he had chosen. Many persons, including some long inured to conditions, resented that Washington banquet performance. They felt that it marked the limit of railroad arrogance on one side, and of the state's subjugation on the other, and they did not like it.

Hence the Southern Pacific managers at Santa Cruz were put to rather unusual methods to fulfill Mr. Harriman's wishes.

That is to say, they auctioned the other offices for Gillett support.

In this way. If a man had ambition to be a judge, and they knew he was all right and sound on the railroad's supremacy, they said to him:

"How many votes for Gillett can you swing?"

Perhaps the ambitious one replied that he could swing fifteen. They reported this to his rival, started a competitive bidding, and the man that undertook to deliver the greatest number of Gillett votes got the place on the ticket.

Thus do we vindicate the purity of our institutions and the grandeur of representative government.

Mr. Gillett was nominated. I have on my desk as I write[2] a little picture of a happy family group, being in fact a little dinner party at Santa Cruz just after the nomination. The gentlemen in the photograph have been dining, and with pleasure I note that they seem to have been dining well. Gentlemen of a happy aspect, well dressed, contented, and congenial, no doubt; a pleasant occasion.

That handsome gentleman in the center with his hand affectionately on the shoulder of the gentleman seated before him, is Mr. Gillett, afterward Governor of California, and nominated to that high place by Mr. Harriman, as aforesaid. The gentleman in front of him upon whom he leans so trustingly, is Mr. Abe Ruef, sometime boss and boodler of San Francisco, now convicted of the dirtiest of political crimes and serving his sentence. Yes, that is Mr. Ruef; Mr. Gillett's hand is on Mr. Ruef's shoulder.

At Mr. Gillett's left stands Mr. Walter F. Parker, to whom several times, and, we must fear, rather unpleasantly, we have alluded in these chronicles. Mr. Parker is a gentleman of the most distinguished consideration. When Mr. Frank Flint, lately United States Senator from California, was publicly congratulated upon his election, he said, with touching simplicity: "I owe it all to Walter Parker."

Still farther to Mr. Gillett's left stands Judge F. H. Kerrigan, quite at ease, with his hands in his pockets. When Judge Kerrigan was a judge of the Superior Court,

---

[2] See page 369.

he decided the crucial Fresno rate case in the way related in a foregoing chapter. He is now a judge of the Appellate Court, having found promotion. Judge Bahrs, who decided the case the other way, found no promotion, but was retired to private life.

Just back of Judge Kerrigan's left shoulder is Congressman Knowland.

Next to Mr. Ruef and Mr. Gillett at their right is Mr. George Hatton, a friend of Mr. Parker and of the Southern Pacific. Next to him is Judge McKinley, and at the end is Judge Henshaw, of the Supreme Court.

Thus we may see the judiciary, statesmanship, commerce, transportation, blackmail and boodle, all pleasantly commingled and meeting on equal terms under the genial auspices of the Southern Pacific Railroad. Nothing is lacking to the picture except in the background the figure of Collis Potter Huntington in an attitude of benediction.

Mr. Gillett's name was, in the cant phrase, "submitted to the voters" of California, who nominally elected him governor. As a matter of fact, there was not much choice. The railroad company played the usual tricks, stimulated the partisan frenzy, befogged the issue, subsidized editors, flooded the state with its hired newspapers, made unthinking people believe that somehow the security of the country depended upon Gillett's election, created the impression that by voting for Gillett a man was "supporting the President," did some other things not necessary to specify here—and won.

Not by much margin, incidentally. The number of people it can fool with this kind of rot is steadily diminishing.

From this chapter of history we may learn how foolish a noise we make when we talk about any new basis of judgment for one railroad, at least. This railroad is doing in politics exactly the things that it did forty-eight years ago and forty years ago and twenty years ago and ten years ago and all times between.

Observant persons in California do not need to be told this any more than they need to be told their own names. They know it.

But elsewhere has grown up among us a strange kind of sentimental softness in regard to railroad rascality, and a willingness to accept the gold bricks of repentance and reform whenever they are offered by a railroad president with a smug face and an indurated conscience. These little incidents may show how much credence belongs to such protestations when you hear them urged in behalf of the Southern Pacific.

In California every fight to purify conditions, to reform a municipality, to stop graft, to proceed in honesty and decency, is a fight against the Southern Pacific, and that is as true of the heroic struggles of Mr. Heney, in San Francisco as of the fight for better conditions in other communities.

In Los Angeles the fight centered at first around the control of the harbor, and was fought in the open, without disguise, the citizens on one side and the Southern Pacific on the other.

Los Angeles lies a little back from the coast. Its natural harbor is San Pedro, familiar to all readers of Dana's immortal "Two Years." San Pedro is south of the city. The Southern Pacific owned the harbor of Santa Monica, fifteen miles north of San Pedro and from the city lying about west.

Neither harbor was (as it lay) in any condition to accommodate a large deep-sea traffic; both needed breakwaters and other improvements. Readers of Dana will recall his vivid descriptions of the perils of his San Pedro, the roadstead open to the terrible southeasters, the sudden rising of the gale, and the swift flight of the vessel to sea until

THE STORY OF THE HARBOR FIGHT 267

the storm should pass. This had not much changed in 1871 when Congress appropriated money to improve the harbor. The work went on for several years, and as the improvements were made the commerce of the port increased. Then Los Angeles entered upon its period of rapid growth, and the need of a commodious and safe harbor was apparent.

The people of Los Angeles wished this to be at San Pedro. At first the railroad company seemed not to care. Then its officers bought real estate at Santa Monica[3] and, in 1890, Mr. Huntington declared that Los Angeles must have its harbor at Santa Monica, or not at all.

There began now a contest that lasted eight years. Los Angeles appeared regularly before Congress asking for an appropriation for San Pedro; Mr. Huntington, through his lobbyists and Congressmen, as regularly defeated the project. All that was needed at San Pedro now was a breakwater, which could be built at no great expense. Mr. Huntington invariably knocked out the breakwater.

Meantime, army engineers had examined both harbors and reported convincingly in favor of San Pedro and against Santa Monica. Mr. Huntington was stronger than the engineers. In the face of their report, he had a bill introduced and favorably considered to appropriate $3,000,-000 for his Santa Monica scheme. He could not quite get this passed, but he could always defeat San Pedro.

In 1894 he came to Los Angeles, strode into the rooms of the Chamber of Commerce, and requested a conference. Members were summoned by telephone. When they arrived he told them they were making "a big mistake" to support San Pedro, that it was not to his advantage to have San Pedro selected, and, anyway, they could never get Congress to give money for their scheme. The announcements seemed to make little impression on his hearers. Mr. Huntington said:

---

[3] "The Free Harbor Contest," by Charles Dwight Willard, p. 80.

"Well, I don't know for sure that I can get this money for Santa Monica; I think I can. But—," bringing down his first with an explosive slam, "I know damned well that you shall never get a cent for that other place."[4]

The voice of ultimate government, you see. He knew. Not less interesting than the decree of this ruler is the fact that his listeners, the smug business men and reformers of Los Angeles, agreed not to let it be known to the populace. It might "increase the growing bitterness." When you are fighting for your life against a power like this there must be no bitterness on your side.

The issue came soon after before the Senate Commerce Committee. Mr. Huntington was there, demanding $4,000,000 for his Santa Monica. The Los Angeles people asked for a small sum for San Pedro.

The St. Louis *Globe-Democrat's* Washington correspondence of those days contains this paragraph:

The harbor contest at Los Angeles waxes warmer. C. P. Huntington was seen going the rounds of the hotels to-day and, although it was Sunday, he made no halt in buttonholing senators. Four days ago there was a decided majority in the Commerce Committee in favor of following the wishes of the two senators from California,[5] but since the arrival of Mr. Huntington at the capital it is now a matter of great doubt where the majority will be found. There is serious speculation in the minds of many people as to the means Mr. Huntington may have used to bring about this change.

Possibly the speculation would have gained additional zest from a perusal of Mr. Huntington's letters to "Friend Colton."[6]

Mr. John P. Jones was a member of the Senate Commerce Committee and an ardent champion of Santa Mon-

---

[4] "The Free Harbor Contest," p. 107.
[5] One of these, Stephen M. White, a Democrat, was a Los Angeles man and a champion of San Pedro.
[6] See the letters of Huntington to Colton, foregoing.

ica. I believe we have previously encountered the name of John P. Jones.[7]

The committee voted to postpone a decision about the two bills until it could go to Los Angeles and inspect both harbors. This put the matter over for two years, or until 1896.

Meanwhile, the people of Los Angeles had formed a Free Harbor League to fight for San Pedro. The long delay wore out the enthusiasm. In 1896 somebody suggested that probably Mr. Huntington was no less tired of fighting. A friend undertook to sound him and returned with the statement that Mr. Huntington willingly agreed to a cessation of hostilities for the rest of that session of Congress, neither side to make a move.

The next thing the people of Los Angeles knew Mr. Binger Hermann, then a Representative from Oregon and a member of the House Commerce Committee, and since with other claims to fame, had put into the River and Harbor bill two items, one of $392,000 for work on the inner harbor of San Pedro, and one of $3,098,000 to complete Santa Monica.

At this the people of Los Angeles arose in wrath, and in the clamor of their protest the committee knocked out both items.

By "the people of Los Angeles" I mean, and have meant, the majority. As soon as the railroad company announced its choice of Santa Monica, there had sprung up at once two factions in the city, the same factions that ever since have continued to struggle for its possession. On one side were the railroad's attorneys friends, and admirers and,

---

[7] About this time the New York *World* took the trouble to find out who owned Santa Monica. It discovered that the property adjoining the exclusive water front owned by the Southern Pacific was divided in eight holdings. Of this, John P. Jones and A. B. de Baker held three. All the rest of the land was in the name of Frank H. Davis, representing C. P. Huntington.

of course, the wealthy and respectable element, all lined up with Mr. Huntington for Santa Monica. On the other, the masses of the people, the labor unions, merchants without social aspirations, and others of that order, fought for San Pedro.

Santa Monica had the advantage in the influence of its supporters; San Pedro had the numbers.

Mass meetings were held by each side and resolutions passed, the San Pedro people meeting out of doors and the Santa Monicans in Illinois Hall. Both parties circulated petitions to Congress. Presently, the cause of Mr. Huntington, his friends, lackeys, and social peers, was deeply hurt by the discovery that the names on their petition were largely fraudulant. Thereafter, San Pedro had all the advantage.

The issue came April 16, 1896, before the Senate Committee on Commerce, when delegations representing both sides were heard.[8] Mr. Huntington had a majority of the Committee. Nine[9] voted to restore to the River and Harbor bill the $3,098,000 appropriation for Santa Monica; six opposed it.

When the bill reached the Senate floor, Senator White forced through an amendment that a board of five engineers should determine whether the $3,098,000 should be expended at Santa Monica or at San Pedro. In conference Mr. Binger Hermann bitterly fought this provision, which was hung up for many days, but Congressman James G. Maguire, of San Francisco, threatened that unless the item were allowed to stand, he would expose on the floor of the

---

[8] Among the champions of Santa Monica on this occasion was former Senator Cornelius Cole, whose name we encountered in the Colton letters.

[9] Frye, of Maine; Gorman, of Maryland; Elkins, of West Virginia; Jones, of Nevada; Quay, of Pennsylvania; Murphy, of New York; McMillan, of Michigan; McBride, of Oregon; Squire, of Washington.

House the whole Huntington game, and the thing went through.

Great rejoicing in Los Angeles.

The board of five engineers decided in favor of San Pedro.

More rejoicing in Los Angeles.

But here came strange developments.

The matter now rested in the hands of General Russell A. Alger, Secretary of War.

General Alger was an old friend and business associate of Mr. Huntington, who had given heavily to the Republican campaign fund.

General Alger's first achievement was to hold up the appropriation nine months, so that the Board of Engineers could not begin its work.

The Board's report was made in March, 1897, and work should have been begun four months later. Month after month went by, but the War Department did nothing about San Pedro. Los Angeles people bitterly complained. They repeatedly called General Alger's attention to the delay, and had in return bland, empty promises of immediate action. They began to understand that the real intention was to stop the work until the matter could be thrown back into Congress, and Santa Monica be substituted.

Former Congressman McLachlan, of Los Angeles, protested once more to Alger, and received the startling information that the Board's report was defective and must be carefully studied before action could be taken.

Another month went by with no sign of action. Mr. McLachlan again called General Alger's attention to the delay. This time General Alger lost his temper, declined to answer any questions, and declared that he would advertise for bids when he got ready.

Senator White now introduced a resolution, calling upon the Secretary of War for information about the delayed work at San Pedro. General Alger furnished in reply several reasons, all denounced as flimsy or baseless, and the Senate responded in a curt resolution directing the Secretary of War to begin work at once.

This resolution the Secretary of War calmly ignored.

Los Angeles people, after a time, called his attention to it.

He remarked blithely that it meant nothing to him because it has not been passed by the House.

Then some kind friends took him aside and told him that if he persisted in that view, the Senate, when it reassembled, would attend to his case in a way that would surprise him. General Alger intimated that he did not care.

By this time people in Los Angeles were deeply stirred. They united in a petition to President McKinley, reciting the facts. He referred it to Attorney General McKenna. Mr. McKenna rendered an opinion that there was no legal reason why work should not begin at once at San Pedro. General Alger let the opinion lie a month on his desk without deigning to notice it.

The Free Harbor League and the people of all Southern California seeing how Mr. Huntington had outwitted them, and that he had every prospect of defeating them at last, began a desperate campaign against Alger, trying chiefly to induce the President to force his Secretary of War to act or to force him out of office.

After three months of this, Alger was driven to the point of saying that he could not begin the work because there was no direct appropriation, and he must wait until Congress should vote again.

The people pointed out that even if this were true he could advertise for bids and make a start.

General Alger said he had no money to advertise with.

All the Los Angeles and San Francisco papers telegraphed offers to print the advertisements for nothing, and the Los Angeles Chamber of Commerce guaranteed that it would pay all advertising bills.

General Alger said this would not be dignified and got up some question that he said must be referred to the Judge-Advocate General.

The Judge-Advocate General promptly decided that the question was without substance, and that anyway, there was $50,000 available for advertising.

Meantime, Mr. McKenna had ceased to be Attorney-General, being succeeded by Mr. Griggs. General Alger now referred to Mr. Griggs the identical question that previously had been referred to and decided by Mr. McKenna.

At this the whole State of California broke into fierce and bitter complaint. It was directed at President McKinley, and at last it evoked from him a positive order that the Secretary of War should begin work.

He had wasted two years and one month.

The contract was now let, the breakwater constructed, and the harbor completed.

Its value to Los Angeles is not yet obtainable, because the Southern Pacific barricades it with some of the most extortionate rates known on this or any other continent. But the inevitable result of the railroad company's policy will be a municipal railroad to the harbor and the beginning of Los Angeles as a great seaport.

Such are the latter day operations of the Southern Pacific in national affairs. And here is a sample of its record in regard to municipalities.

By 1905 most of the valuable franchises in Los Angeles had been seized by the allied Interests, of which the Southern Pacific was the chief and commander. One was left, being the chance to build a railroad along the river bank in the city limits.

On March 26, 1906, the mayor was out of town, and one Summerland, president of the City Council, was acting mayor. The Council was in regular weekly session. At 4:30 P. M., when all routine business had been disposed of and most of the spectators had departed, an ordinance was introduced, granting to one E. W. Gilmore, "and his assigns," a franchise for a railroad on the west bank of the river from the south city limits to Alesio Street, a distance of about three miles.

This was put on passage at once. Mr. Charles D. Willard, representing the Municipal League, perceived what was on foot and vehemently protested. He went upon the floor of the Council and appealed to an honest alderman to vote against the grab. A representative of the city attorney's office joined him in strenuous objection. Nevertheless, the ordinance was jammed through.

Outside waited a carriage to take a messenger with the ordinance to Summerland's house, where he was prepared to sign it. But first the signature of the City Clerk was necessary. An underling dashed downstairs to the City Clerk's office, put the ordinance under City Clerk Lelande's nose, and asked him to sign it, giving the impression that it was merely routine legislation.

Lelande demurred, looked over the document, and refused to sign. Without his signature, Summerland could do nothing, and the ordinance was hung up.

The next day the discovery was made that because of a technical irregularity in the passing of the ordinance, it must needs be passed again, and a special meeting of the Council was called for the next day, Wednesday, March 28th, when the iniquity went through by a vote of 6 to 1.

What happened next will be found related in the following affidavit, which covers the whole story:

STATE OF CALIFORNIA, } ss.
COUNTY OF LOS ANGELES.

H. J. LeLande, being duly sworn, deposes and says:
The facts in relation to the attempted passage of what has

THE STORY OF THE HARBOR FIGHT

become generally known as the Gilmore river bed franchise are as follows:

Late in the afternoon, about 6:30 P. M., of the date when this franchise was first presented to the Council, Mr. Wilde, my chief deputy, came into my private office and placed this franchise on my desk before me, stating that "the boys upstairs were in a hurry for this," and asked me to sign it. This franchise consisted of several typewritten pages. Mr. Wilde turned it over to the last page, which contained the space for the signature of the mayor and myself, and asked me to sign it, as "the boys were upstairs waiting for it," and I asked what it was. Mr. Wilde replied, "A franchise for a spur track." I told Mr. Wilde that I would sign it in a few minutes as I was busily engaged writing a letter.

Mr. Wilde left my private office, and shortly after his departure W. R. Hervey came into my private office and asked if I had signed the ordinance that Mr. Wilde brought in, and I stated that I had not; and he said that Mr. Gilmore was going away that evening and would like to have me sign it at once, as they wished to have it published in the morning. After Mr. Hervey had made this statement I looked at the document for the first time, and then informed Mr. Hervey that I would wait and allow this to go through in the usual manner as I did not see any necessity for haste, or words to that effect. Mr. Hervey urged me as a personal favor to him and to Mr. Gilmore to sign it at once, and I again informed him that I saw no necessity to hurry this matter, and he stated that he would see that I signed it and left the office, apparently angry.

Very shortly after Mr. Hervey left the office, Mr. Gilmore came in and said that he was going to leave town that night and wanted to get this fixed up and published in the morning, and pleaded with me to sign it at once. I made the same reply to Mr. Gilmore that I made to Mr. Hervey, that "I would allow the ordinance to take its usual course." After I had made this statement, Mr. Gilmore continued to plead with me to sign the ordinance, which I refused to do.

Just before I started for home I was called up on the telephone and informed that Mr. Summerland was waiting upstairs for me to bring that ordinance. I answered "All right," but had no intention of bringing it up. I took my hat and left for home. And shortly after I had finished my dinner, Mr. Gilmore called at my residence and again pleaded with me to sign the ordinance that night, and again said that this was a matter of great importance to him and he was desirous of having the matter completed before he left the city, and offered me his political influence if I would sign it. He made the statement that I would never regret signing it.

Then, shortly after the departure of Mr. Gilmore from my residence, I came back to the office and Mr. W. F. Parker called me up by 'phone that night and wanted to know if I was going to be at my office for a few minutes. I stated that I was, and he said he was coming over. Shortly after receiving the message, Mr. Parker came to my office and asked to see the ordinance, which I allowed him to do, and he made the statement that he didn't know whom it was for, and that he was glad I hadn't signed it, and asked me not to sign it until he had found out more about it. I told him that I had not intended to sign it until the following day anyway.

The minute clerk had prepared his minutes, showing that the council had adopted the ordinance by a vote of six to one, Summerland being acting mayor in McAleer's absence, and Mr. Smith being absent. My attention was called to the fact that Councilman Houghton first voted "No" and finally changed his vote to "Yes," other business having been transacted in the interim, and at the time that Councilman Houghton changed his vote to "Yes" the chairman then announced that the ordinance had been adopted; so when the members of the Council found that we had, on Tuesday, recorded the ordinance as having been lost they met again on the next day, Wednesday, and passed the ordinance by a vote of six to one. I will furnish an exact copy of the minutes showing the above statement to be correct.

About three o'clock on Wednesday, the day the ordinance was passed, Mr. Parker called me up by 'phone and asked me if I would step down to his office. I informed him that I was quite busy and would prefer having him come to my office in the city clerk's office. He said he thought it was best for him not to come there, but would meet me at the Hotel Alexandria buffet. I replied that I would meet him there after five o'clock. I left the office about five o'clock and went to the Alexandria buffet and there met Mr. Parker in one of the little cushion places there. He opened the conversation and said, "I suppose you know what I want to see you about?" I answered that "I believe I do," or words to that effect.

One of the first questions asked me by Parker was "How MUCH WILL YOU TAKE TO SIGN THAT ORDINANCE RIGHT AWAY?" or words to that effect. I remember this distinctly because I was surprised that he would make such a statement. After which he said, "I CAN GET YOU A THOUSAND DOLLARS IF YOU SIGN THAT ORDINANCE TO-DAY AND TAKE IT TO SUMMERLAND."

My answer was that "I did not want any of that kind of money."

He also made the statement that MONEY WAS BEING SPENT AND I MIGHT AS WELL GET SOME OF IT. He said that my power was not executive, that my duty was simply ministerial, and that I might as well get the money and sign it and get it out of my hands as quickly as possible. I said that I was going to hold it until Mayor McAleer came back. He said that it didn't make any difference to him, that I was overlooking a chance to get some of the money, or words to that effect; whereupon I returned to the office.

At the time Parker and I had the conversation in the Alexandria buffet he told me that he had found out that this was for Mr. Huntington. He made this last statement as to his having found out that it was for the Huntington interests in connection with his statement that money was being used. Various other people called me up, some before this conversation with Mr. Parker, and some after, but no officials, and urged me to sign it and get it out of my hands quick, or words to that effect.

I went back to my office and stayed there until about 6:30 o'clock. In the mean time I had several calls, and I went home and stayed at home until about 8:15 o'clock, when I left home to keep from being further disturbed. Wednesday, about four o'clock, Charley McKeag was the man that sent a telegram at my request to McAleer, who was then out of the city, to return as quickly as possible. I kept the ordinance in my safe until Mayor McAleer returned.

After McAleer's return, then, to get it to the mayor, I, of course, certified it, so that he might sign it or veto it. No previous legal notice of any kind was given to the public of the intention to pass this ordinance, and no competitive bids were asked for.

(Seal) (Signed) H. J. LELANDE.

Subscribed and sworn to before me this 22d day of November, 1909.

(Signed) GEO. S. WELCH.

Notary Public in and for the County of Los Angeles, State of California.

On his return, Mayor McAleer vetoed the ordinance in

a message so virulent that one of the aldermen moved that the "insult be returned with the rest of it, unread."

The intention was to pass the ordinance over his veto, but the people of Los Angeles, whose wrath had been rising from the first news of the steal, were now in a state of dangerous excitement. Among the most orderly and law-abiding of people, they had been wrought out of their usual self-command by the audacity of the franchise grabbers, and if the councilmen had persisted in defying public opinion some remarkable scenes might have followed. But the aldermen took fright and abandoned the ordinance.

Such is the modern method of the Southern Pacific in politics.

And here is its modern method in business:

The great steamers Mongolia and Manchuria, of the Pacific Mail, in every way magnificent specimens of marine architecture, were built at Newport News for the Atlantic Transport Line, under the belief that Congress would pass the ship subsidy.

When this hope failed, the two steamers were sold to the Oregon Short Line, a possession of the Southern Pacific Railroad system.

That is to say, they were bought with the money of the Oregon Short Line. In point of fact (according to the sworn testimony of a high officer of the company), their purchase stood in the name of Mr. E. H. Harriman, by whom they were leased to the Pacific Mail, and who collected from the Pacific Mail their rental, which was $30,000 a month for each steamer.

In other words, Mr. Harriman, representing the Standard Oil interests, controlled the Oregon Short Line and also controlled the Pacific Mail. He used his control of the Oregon Short Line to buy the steamers with the Oregon Short Line's money (in his name), and then used his control of the Pacific Mail to lease the property thus secured for his own benefit.[10]

That is the way the thing is done now.

For all of it at all times we must pay.

To what extent we have already paid may be gathered from a table with which we may well conclude our reflections on this edifying subject. It does not show the total production of the Great Millionaire Mill; probably no human mind could trace, formulate, and accurately state what that production has been. It shows only a part of the wealth that, without return of any kind, we have freely bestowed upon this unparalleled institution.

CENTRAL PACIFIC—
Government land grant, minimum	$ 30,000,000
Unearned dividends on stock	34,000,000
Capitalized interest on subsidy bonds	30,700,000
Common stock (representing no investment)	67,275,500
Bonus on bonds	16,819,000
	$178,794,500

SOUTHERN PACIFIC—
Government land grant, minimum	$ 40,000,000
Donations by California councils	1,002,000
Mission Bay, donated by the state, estimated value at the time	9,500,000
Capital stock (representing no investment)	160,000,000
Dividends thereon	30,400,000
	$240,902,000

SOUTHERN PACIFIC COMPANY OF KENTUCKY—
Government land grant acquired with Morgan purchase	$ 13,000,000
Surplus capitalized (see report 1903)	100,081,022
Stock acquired under early leases	76,000,000
	$189,081,022
Grand Total	$608,777,522

---

[10] See "In the Matter of the Consolidation and Combination of Carriers. Relations between Such Carriers and Community of Interest therein," etc. Before the Interstate Commerce Commission, at San Francisco, January 29, 30 and 31, 1907. This whole edifying story of the Harriman performance is described in the testimony of R. P. Schwerin at pp. 113, 115, 156, 158, etc. At the New York hearing there were introduced the minutes of the meeting of the Oregon Short Line's Executive Committee of March 26, 1903, at which this deal was ratified.

Of this colossal sum only an inconsiderable fraction can be held to represent any kind of investment, and the greater part is to this day drawing interest and dividends from the consuming public.

Reflected in the cost of living.

CHAPTER XII.

THE STORY OF THE LEMON RATE.

And now for us, the people, who pay for all this gigantic fortune building, for fraudulent contract and political machine, watered stock and dishonest lease; who paid for all yesterday and pay for it today and will pay for it tomorrow, many times over.

Where do we come in?

In 1887, Governor Pattison, at the close of the long, patient, judicial inquiry by the Pacific Railroad Commission, of which he was chairman, delivered his opinion that the inflated part of the Central Pacific's capital amounted to a tax of $3,000,000 a year[1] upon the shippers of the country.

We have seen the means by which the inflation was achieved, the multifold tricks, swindles, and fraudulent devices. This is what such things cost us in 1887—above any fair compensation for any service performed.

In the eighteen years from the completing of the Central Pacific to the Commission's report in 1887, the four men of Sacramento had taken from the shippers of the country on this account alone $54,000,000—through the forms of illegitimate toll referred to by Governor Pattison, and above any fair compensation for any service performed.

In this total the work of the Contract and Fiance Company as producer of fictitious capital has some place. But we are to remember that, aside from this and from all other sources of sudden wealth in Governor Pattison's cal-

---
[1] Pacific Railroad Commission, Minority Report, p. 146.

culations, there was ever the staggering accretion of a thousand other operations and a thousand extravagances and excesses of power. To the one item of interest-bearing capital that Governor Pattison had in mind we must add many industrious efforts under the names of the Western Development Company, the Pacific Improvement Company, the coal and iron companies, the bridge companies, street railroad companies and countless other aliases and masks behind which these men rode the highways. All these left behind their proportionate share of burden on the public.

So did the interwoven leases, the money paid to prevent disclosure, the money spent to defeat Mrs. Colton, the money spent in shooting at the settlers of Mussel Slough, the money spent to bribe legislatures and subsidize editors, the money spent to maintain the vast political machine in California, and the money spent to defend the illegal land grants.

All this stupendous sum was piled up, aside from Governor Pattison's total. Every year the interest on it was being paid by the shippers, and Governor Pattison estimated that the small part of this tribute due to the brigandage of the old Central Pacific and the Contract and Finance Company was $3,000,000 a year—paid by the shippers.

The shippers, of course, merely passed it along, with interest, to the consumers. You and me.

So there is where we came in twenty-five years ago; to the tune of $3,000,000 a year cast into only a part of the Millionaire Mill.

Even then, and even for that small part, the tribute was beyond any justification and wholly arbitrary.

If the railroad had been built with a fair degree of honesty and had been so managed, or if it had represented only legitimate investment, it could have paid from the beginning 6 per cent interest, discharged all its obligations to the government, and saved in eighteen years $54,000,000 to shippers over the Central Pacific alone.

At the same time, the Four of Sacramento would have owned 2,495 miles of railroad absolutely free from debt and every cent of their investment would have been repaid to them.

This is not a surmise but a simple mathematical demonstration. If the enterprise had been fairly honest, the stockholders would have realized by 1887 for every dollar of their stock $1.07 in dividends, $1.11 from the land sales, and would have had $4 worth of interest in the property; so that in eighteen years each dollar would have yielded $6.18—by the methods of approximate honesty.

To the householders of America there would have been saved $54,000,000 of dishonest tolls plus interest and profits thereon.

Those $54,000,000 were the exact measure of the difference to us between honest and dishonest methods. The profit of dishonest methods for eighteen years was $54,000,000, on the Central Pacific alone.

Twenty-five years have passed since Governor Pattison reached this conclusion.

If the traffic had remained as it was in 1887, and there had been no other tribute exactions, we should have paid so far $129,000,000 in excessive charges because of crooked accounts and fraudulent contracts; on the Central Pacific alone.

The traffic has greatly increased; the operations have been repeated, extended, improved, and multiplied; more watered stocks and baseless bonds have been prodigally heaped upon the property, with more corruption, more bills for purchased legislation, more expenses of the California political machine, more payments to Abe Ruef and his kind, more expenses incurred by the W. F. Herrins and their staffs of politicians, more deals, more dishonest leases, more hired editors, more crooked bosses.

For all these we are paying year after year, just as we

pay for the original Contract and Finance Company crookedness.

So that if Governor Pattison could come back now and repeat his inquiry, he would find the annual charge that in 1887 was $3,000,000 for the Central Pacific alone *is now become for the Southern Pacific system a charge many times that sum.*

If the American householder, puzzling over the 60 per cent increase of his living expenses in fifteen years, wants a solution of his problem, let him for a time contemplate these facts. Let him also remember that they are merely typical of the general railroad condition and need only to be multiplied into the number of "systems" to furnish much of the stupendous sum represented in the augmented cost of living. For in ten years the railroad capitalization of this country, now eighteen and one-half billion dollars, has increased seven billion dollars—being in effect a National debt, the interest of which is levied upon us as tribute.

How do we pay this tribute?

Let us see. On January 1, 1909, the transcontinental railroad lines increased the freight rates 18 per cent on east-bound traffic and a little more on west-bound traffic.

Conservative authorities in California estimated that this increase of rates meant an increase of $10,000,000 a year in the living expenses of the people of California.

California has probably 400,000 families. This means an average increase of $25 a family.

Accomplished by merely one increase of rates.

By reason of this same increase of rates the market value of Southern Pacific securities rose nearly $100,000,000. By reason of this increase of market values the estate of the late E. H. Harriman, at first appraised at $149,000,000, was found on examination to be worth $220,000,000.

Twenty-five dollars taken yearly from each family in California; $71,000,000 piled upon the private fortune at the other end. From the householder to the vault of the railroad magnate a million pumps pumping dollars.

What do you get for this tax laid three times a day upon the living of your household? It is your money, the railroad company takes it from you and adds it to the great fortunes. What do you get?

Let us look into that next.

Whoever will consider carefully and impartially the subject of freight rates in America will be drawn to the conclusion that the so-called science or system of making these rates consists merely of discerning how much can be extracted from any community without inciting it to resistance, and from any branch of traffic without destroying it. Simply this and nothing more.

Now you will not believe this until I prove it to you, because you have long been accustomed to hear foolish chatter about the enormous difficulties of rate making and because, naturally, you have assumed that in making rates there is considered the cost of the service, the amount of investment and the interest thereon, with taxes, insurance, and other expenses, and what would constitute a just and reasonable profit.

I think it would be difficult to instance any railroad rate in America made on any such basis.

In America railroad rates are made under the pressure of an inexorable necessity created by fictitious capitalization and fraudulent expenditures. The necessity is to wring from every transaction the last obtainable cent. Justice has and can have no place in the consideration. What the traffic will bear is the one standard and that means, plainly translated, what the shipper can be forced to pay.

At first thought this sounds unfair and partisan. It is neither. It is only a cold statement of facts. It seems unfair because we like to think there is reason in all things. About other things I do not pretend to say, but about rate making I know there is no reason other than the reason I have mentioned. The next time you read any profound observations by one railroad lackey or another on the intricate and wonderful science of rate making and the awe with which we should regard it, you might recall some plain facts I shall now give you. They may help to a just estimate of the railroad lackey and also cheer your expense account with some delicious humor—of a certain kind.

Here we go, then, taking at random and merely as samples.

On a carload of coffee, San Francisco to New York, 3,240 miles the freight rate is $180. From San Francisco to Phoenix, Arizona, a distance of 900 miles and over the same line, the freight rate for the same car is $240.

From Pacific Coast points (San Francisco, Los Angeles, et cetera) to Phoenix, Arizona, the freight rate on sugar is $1 a hundred pounds in carload lots. From the same points to Memphis, Tennessee, about 1,200 miles farther, the freight rate on sugar is 60 cents a hundred pounds. From San Francisco to Cheyenne, Wyoming, 1,270 miles, the rate is 55 cents.

California produces most excellent raisins, but the people of the eastern states cannot generally avail themselves of this abundant product because the freight rate to the Atlantic Coast is $1.10 a hundred pounds. Yet, asphaltum is hauled from the Pacific to the Atlantic Coast for only 55 cents a hundred pounds. The raisin traffic will bear $1.10 and the asphaltum traffic will bear only one-half of that.

Cotton goes from Dallas, Texas, to China, 7,500 miles, by way of Seattle for $1.35 a hundred pounds. Of the 7,500 miles in this haul 2,500 are by rail. For hauling the same cotton from Dallas to New Orleans, 567 miles, the rate is 60 cents a hundred pounds—or nearly one-half the cost of the 7,500 mile haul to China, 2,500 miles of which are by rail.

Not long ago an American captain was in Hankow, China, loading pig iron for Los Angeles. The Chinese merchant with whom he dealt, being both intelligent and curious, desired to know what was the cost of carrying iron so far. The captain said the freight rate was $6 a ton.

"How much of that does the steamer get?" asked the merchant.

"Four dollars a ton."

"Then the iron must travel a long distance by railroad," said the merchant.

"No," said the captain, "a very short distance—only twenty-two miles from San Pedro harbor to Los Angeles."

"Show it to me on your map," said the merchant, exuding incredulity.

The map was produced and the merchant studied it carefully, following with his finger the steamer's route from Hankow down the river 700 miles to the ocean, then across 5,000 miles of ocean to San Pedro. With this he compared the almost imperceptible distance from San Pedro to Los Angeles. His conclusion was that the captain was lying; the thing was manifestly impossible. Waybills and receipts made no impression upon him. Either the captain was a monstrous and malicious liar, or the American people were crazy. Politeness and probability forbade him to accuse an entire nation of lunacy; hence the fault lay with the captain.

But the captain was not lying; he was telling the truth. The traffic between Los Angeles and San Pedro, the harbor of Los Angeles, is indispensable; therefore it can bear a great deal. You can ship some kinds of freight from an American port to a European port and back for the cost of moving the same freight from a ship in San Pedro harbor to Los Angeles, twenty-two miles. The freight rate on iron from San Pedro to Los Angeles is $2 a ton; on other commodities it ranges from $2.20 to $3 a ton. In addition, there is a wharfage charge of 50 cents a ton. Well—I told you.

You see, the traffic will bear these charges; hence they are levied. There is no other reason for them nor for any other charges that the Southern Pacific makes anywhere. It gouges and grabs what it can because it needs every obtainable cent to pay the interest and dividends on the securities piled up by the Contract and Finance Company and all the other historic devices the nature of which I have explained in the foregoing chapters. The Los Angeles merchants must have their freight from San Pedro. There is no other way to obtain it. Hence the traffic will bear these charges, which are promptly passed to the people.

How long the people will bear them I have no skill to predict.

San Pedro is the harbor of Los Angeles and within the city limits. San Diego is 126 miles from Los Angeles. The rates from Los Angeles to San Diego are about the same as the rates from one end of Los Angeles to the other. The San Diego traffic will not bear quite so much as the Los Angeles traffic.

On some kinds of freight, and including wharfage, the rate is $3.50 a ton from a ship in San Pedro harbor twenty-two miles across Los Angeles, and it is $7.50 a ton from Antwerp to San Pedro—16,000 miles or thereabouts.

The present railroad freight rates from Sacramento, California, to Reno, Nevada, are higher than the freight rates in the old days of mining, before the railroad was built, when all freight must be dragged over the mountains by mule and ox teams.[2] This, I suppose, is one of the "benefits" conferred by the Big Four upon the country.

You can ship certain kinds of freight from Liverpool to San Francisco by way of New Orleans for no more than

---

[2] Before the Interstate Commerce Commission. Traffic Bureau of the Merchants Exchange versus Southern Pacific Company et al. Docket No. 2839. Brief for complaint, pp. 100-18.

you must pay on the same freight if your shipment originates at New Orleans instead of Liverpool.[3]

Does not all this seem strange?

Yet, the Southern Pacific, it must be confessed, has no monopoly of such monstrosities.

At the mines in West Virginia soft coal is worth $1 a ton. When it has been transported to the city of Washington, 400 miles, it sells for $3.50 a ton. At Scranton, Pennsylvania, a car is loaded with anthracite coal worth less than $2 a ton. The next morning it is in New York and worth $6 a ton. Apparently, the cost of transporting coal 100 miles is greater than the cost of mining it.

In California coal is now so dear that for the poor it must seem like a luxury; and yet there are in the mountains in Colorado, New Mexico, and Utah, and in the North Pacific states, great coal deposits that might afford a cheap supply if reasonable freight rates could be had. As they cannot, coal is regularly brought to San Francisco from Australia.

Every person that consumes anything contributes to the freight rates, and everywhere these rates are made in this arbitrary and extortionate manner. The natural course of trade is continually being distorted, blockaded, and bedeviled to give more profits to the railroads, to provide them with longer hauls, or a chance for bigger rates. Communities are not allowed to trade where they can find the best terms, but only where they will yield the best pickings for the railroads. A town forty miles from St. Paul and 400 miles from Chicago was compelled to go to Chicago for its supplies because the railroads made the rates from Chicago to that town, 400 miles, equal to or less than the rates from St. Paul to that town, forty miles.

There is an impression adroitly spread by railroad press

---

[3] See 162 U. S., 197.

agents and railroad newspapers that all these conditions have passed away and the railroads have reformed their practices. As a matter of fact, there has been no essential change.

The unjust rates continue year in and year out to collect our tolls.

Some of the least defensible of these extortions are practiced in California and help materially to gather the means for the dividends and interest on the securities we have been considering.

For example, I call attention to extracts from the Southern Pacific's freight tariffs showing rates from San Francisco and from Los Angeles. If you are unfamiliar with railroad rates, I may be allowed to explain that the practice is to charge less for freight in carload lots than for freight in smaller quantities. This occasions the division into rates for carload and rates for less than carload. Bearing this in mind, study the table on the next page.

I will now recite for your entertainment a little chapter of history showing that these abuses are not only flagrant and intolerable but firmly rooted.

C. P. Huntington died in 1900.

At that time one of the American railroad executives most talked about for sagacity, energy, skill, knowledge, and results was Mr. Charles M. Hays.

Mr. Hays was selected to take the place of Mr. Huntington as head of the great Southern Pacific system. He remained less than a year when, to the amazement of the railroad world, he suddenly resigned.

Everybody knew there must have been some trouble and all railroad men knew that the trouble was not with Mr. Hays. Almost at once he was snapped up by the Grand Trunk, of which vast and extending system he is now the chief commander.

THE STORY OF THE LEMON RATE

From	To	Miles	1st Class Rate per 100 lbs.	2d Class Rate per 100 lbs.	3d Class Rate per 100 lbs.	4th Class Rate per 100 lbs.	5th Class Rate per Ton	Class A Rate per Ton	Class B Rate per Ton	Class C Rate per Ton
Los Angeles	Goshen	241	$0.79	$0.76	$0.71	$0.67	$10.80	$11.60	$7.90	$6.90
San Francisco	"	241	.63	.58	.54	.51	8.30	7.65	5.20	4.55
Los Angeles	Exeter	241	.80	.77	.73	.69	11.20	11.60	7.90	6.60
San Francisco	"	247	.67	.62	.58	.55	8.90	8.25	5.65	4.80
Los Angeles	Tulare	231	.76	.71	.67	.64	10.20	11.60	7.85	6.60
San Francisco	"	240	.69	.64	.59	.55	9.10	8.40	5.70	5.00
Los Angeles	Porterville	224	.76	.72	.68	.65	10.40	11.60	7.75	6.60
San Francisco	"	264	.73	.68	.64	.61	9.90	9.25	6.00	5.20
Los Angeles	Oil City	179	.80	.76	.71	.67	10.60	10.80	6.95	6.30
San Francisco	"	315	.90	.84	.78	.73	11.80	10.95	7.75	6.70
Los Angeles	Bakersfield	168	.71	.68	.64	.61	9.60	10.00	6.15	5.50
San Francisco	"	303	.83	.77	.72	.68	11.00	10.15	6.75	5.90
Los Angeles	Olig	218	.83	.79	.75	.72	11.40	13.30	7.55	6.90
San Francisco	"	353	.86	.79	.74	.70	11.40	10.55	7.00	6.05
Los Angeles	McKittrick	216	.76	.70	.66	.63	10.00	13.30	6.75	6.10
San Francisco	"	351	.85	.78	.73	.69	11.20	10.35	7.00	6.05
Los Angeles	Fresno	276	.80	.77	.73	.69	11.20	11.60	8.00	7.00
San Francisco	"	195	.55	.51	.47	.44	7.20	6.70	4.60	4.05
Los Angeles	Visalia	249	.79	.76	.71	.67	10.80	11.60	7.90	6.60
San Francisco	"	248	.66	.61	.57	.54	8.70	8.05	5.45	4.80
Los Angeles	Coalinga	290	.86	.78	.74	.71	11.40	14.80	8.00	7.00
San Francisco	"	269	.80	.73	.69	.66	10.70	10.05	6.20	5.45
Los Angeles	Hanford	248	.79	.76	.71	.67	10.80	11.60	7.90	6.90
San Francisco	"	233	.63	.58	.54	.51	8.30	7.65	5.20	4.55

SOME OF THE CURIOSITIES OF THE CALIFORNIA FREIGHT RATES—THE HIGHEST IN THE COUNTRY.

Mr. Hays never publicly explained his dissatisfaction, but according to close friends of his he began, soon after he took the Southern Pacific, to examine the freight tariffs by which this company gathers the interest on all these securities. Mr. Hays is known to be a just man. It seemed clear to him that the rates were indefensible and ought to be adjusted. He undertook to adjust them. The power behind the railroad that, being greater than all law and all government, had for many years thriven upon these extortions, objected to the changes Mr. Hays desired. Mr. Hays insisted; the Power insisted. Finding that the Power was supreme and that he could not do justice, Mr. Hays resigned.

How do you like this little story?

I need not inquire of certain newspaper valets and hired men of the Southern Pacific. I know they will not like it at all because at once they will see that it is true and extremely distasteful to their employers. Their natural impulse will be to deny it, a course to which they are cordially invited.

For all these things the railroad company has usually its excuse—not always, but usually.

From Oakland to Lompoc, about 314 miles, the Southern Pacific within the last three years gave to one lumber company a rate of $4 a thousand and to another a rate of $7.50. When one of the railroad's officers was on the witness stand before the Interstate Commerce Commission, he was asked why the $4 rate was made. He replied, airily, that it was to meet "water competition." This is a favorite excuse with the railroad companies. With wonderful effrontery they offer it for rates to points a thousand miles from any water route. So in this case the young man said "water competition" as if the words were a finality.

Then the commission suddenly exhibited the rate of $7.50 to the other lumber company and for once a railroad com-

THE STORY OF THE LEMON RATE

pany was silenced. Apparently, it could think of no way to twist, duck, or dodge out of the dilemma, nor even to insult, bulldoze, or browbeat the commission; a situation rare in the commission's experience.

When Manager H. A. Jones, of the Southern Pacific, came to the stand in Los Angeles, January, 1909, he was much more frank. At San Francisco and Los Angeles, and, I believe, at other junction points, the Southern Pacific exacts a switching charge (so-called) of $2.50 a car. There is no sense in this charge. It represents no service performed nor anything else except an arbitrary exaction. Mr. Jones was asked why his company levied this charge. He answered promptly and truthfully that it levied the charge "because it could get the money."

When the "water competition" bogey will not serve, the company can usually allege something about the peculiarity of the haul or of the business. One of these allegations can stand for all and is, moreover, a lovely example on its own account. Thus:

Some of the glaring inequalities set forth in the table on another page are defended (by the railroad's champions) on the ground that there is a long ascent north of Los Angeles; therefore, the rate from Los Angeles to Goshen should be higher than the rate from San Francisco to Goshen, although the distance is the same. This is as good as any other defense for the railroad; and how good this is you may learn from the fact *that 75 per cent of the goods shipped from San Francisco to Goshen have already been hauled up that hill north of Los Angeles without the least increase in rates therefor.* That is because they have been shipped from the eastern states over that route. And yet, the charge for the 241 miles from San Francisco to Goshen is about 18 per cent less than the charge for the 241 miles from Los Angeles to Goshen—*because of that hill!*

The hill is a great matter when you ship goods from Los

Angeles to Goshen. It is nothing when you ship goods from New Orleans to Goshen by way of Los Angeles.

Is it really necessary to be perfectly absurd that we may defend our sacred corporations?

Of course, the shippers, as a rule, do not care very much. Why should they? It is none of their affair; the charge merely becomes a part of the price to the consumer, and so long as that price is not great enough to interfere with trade the shipper need not bother about it. Changes in rates may cause actual losses to merchants, but high rates bear only upon the consumer. And the consumer? *Oh, well, he never knows. The charge is concealed in the prices of his beefsteak and potatoes, and while these mount steadily upon him he blames the farmer or the packer. Therefore, on with the game! It can be played without limit!*

First, the stock issued gratuitously to the fortunate insiders; then the freight rate made to secure dividends on this stock; then more stock; then more rates. All passed along to the consumer and he never objects, bless his heart, but pays his bills like a little man.

The California producer has not been so well tamed. He has been protesting forty years because the railroad company, applying its favorite formula in a way we must now consider, has steadily absorbed all his profits.

Take oranges and lemons. In the celebrated orange rate case which dragged along six years, Mr. Joseph H. Call, of Los Angeles, showed that under the prevailing freight rate the average profit left to orange growers was 13 cents a box, without any allowance for decay or damage,[4] while the railroad company took 90 cents a box for freight. That was what the orange traffic would bear.

At the end of the six years' fight through the Interstate Commerce Commission and the courts there was secured a

---

[4] Senate Committee on Interstate Commerce, Proceedings of May 17, 1905.

final judgment reducing the charge from $1.25 to $1.15 a hundred weight. This meant a saving to the orange growers of $1,000,000 a year in freight rates. The ground of the decision was that $1.15 was a fair rate. This seems to raise the questions:

(1) How about the years in which the company was collecting an unfair rate?

(2) Who is to recompense us for that imposition?

As to what lemons would bear, the railroad company slightly erred. Some years before it had conceived the idea that the lemon traffic would bear an increase of 15 cents a box in the freight rate and had accordingly, and for no other reason, announced the increase. The lemon growers protested vehemently and, of course, in vain; such protests are usually in vain. All the profit of lemon growing was swept away in that 15 cents of rate increase; the producers were now growing lemons at an actual loss. When this fact had been demonstrated, the growers began to cut down their trees and to turn the land to other crops.

This practical proof that their calculations had been wrong and the lemon traffic would not, after all, bear the additional tribute they sought to extort was all the railroad managers needed. They wanted the profits of lemon growing but they could understand that if there were no lemons there would be no such profits, so they rescinded the increase, went back to the old rate, and induced the growers to replant their orchards.

So Akbar remitted the tribute levied upon a conquered province when he found that the people had been stripped to their skins.

From this time until November 15, 1909, the lemon rate was $1 a box, California to eastern points.

Aside from freight rates, the only serious trouble about the lemon business in California is the limit of the demand. California lemons are of unusual excellence; but, after all, the lemon in its pristine state and undiluted remains more a fruit of utility than of desire; few persons, we may believe, devour lemons for delight therein. So far as the California lemon could be delivered at all in America it superseded, on merit, all others; but because of the freight rates it seldom had a chance east of the Alleghenies. The center of its distribution was Des Moines, Iowa, and the Atlantic states continued to get their lemons from the Mediterranean.

Of the annual American consumption of 12,000 carloads of lemons, California furnished only about 4,800 carloads, although quite able to furnish all.

The Californians long agitated for an increase in the import duty on lemons, that the handicap of their freight rates might be equalized and the California lemon have a chance on the Atlantic seaboard. At last their desires were gratified. The new tariff of August 5, 1909, raised the duty on lemons 50 per cent.

The lemon growers rejoiced and were exceedingly glad. Their joy lasted two months. In October, the Southern Pacific announced that on November 15th it would raise the lemon rate 15 cents a box, or from $1 to $1.15.[5]

This, you will understand, is a minimum. On some hauls the rate was raised to $1.25, $1.35, and $1.40.

Faithful to its good, old and only principle in rate making, the Southern Pacific had grabbed the additional profit for itself. The lemon traffic would now bear the 15 cents it would not bear before, and the railroad needed that 15 cents to pay dividends on fictitious stock.

This time the lemon growers combined against the extortion and brought into the case the Mr. Joseph H. Call of whom I have before spoken. I am bound to think him a

---

[5] Before the Interstate Commerce Commission. Arlington Heights Fruit Exchange et al. versus Southern Pacific Company et al. Petition, p. 17.

remarkable man, although my inclining toward such distinctions is small. Much of his life has been spent in fighting railroad corporations, apparently on conviction and principle and not for the harlotry of the professional advocate. He fought the Southern Pacific to a standstill in that settler's case (Southern Pacific versus Otto Groeck) referred to in a previous chapter and it was he that showed that in the Mussel Slough massacre the railroad company had no more legal than moral right. As special counsel for the government he recovered more than four million acres of grabbed land from the Southern Pacific.[6]

Mr. Call took up the case of the lemon growers and got in the United States Circuit Court an injunction restraining the railroad from collecting the increased rate. When it became evident that he would secure injunctions all along the line, the railroad company desisted for the time being and agreed to hold the new rate in abeyance until the issue should be determined by the higher courts.

Apparently, the counsel for the lemon growers was just in time. Since he got his injunction, the Supreme Court has decided in a similar case that railroads must be sued in the states where they are incorporated. If that ruling had applied here, the injunctions would have been dissolved and the suits began anew[7] in Kentucky, where (with great foresight) the Southern Pacific is incorporated and where it has no trackage and does no business.

Meantime, Mr. Call brought the case before the Interstate Commerce Commission. That sounds easy; in reality, it was a stupendous task. Every company that handles any part of any lemon shipment must be served with a summons. The original petition in the case contained six pages of the names of companies necessarily sued as co-defendants, about 400 in all, many of them railroads long since

---
[6] See 146 U. S., 570-619, and 168 U. S., 1-66, and 189 U. S., 447.
[7] See 215 U. S., 501.

absorbed in the great combinations.[8] An amended petition filed a few weeks later contained the names of sixty-three additional and microscopic concerns that previously had been overlooked.

Every one of these it was necessary to serve, for to sue railroad companies in this country is no holiday performance, be assured. You can sue men in five minutes, but to sue a railroad company may take five years. When at last all had been served, the Interstate Commerce Commission took up the case and on June 11, 1910, decided that the lemon rate should be $1. The railroads were expected to appeal from this decision, whereupon the contest would have been transferred to the courts—to last there for years and years. Instead of appealing, the railroads, possibly because of the very unusual public interest in the case, allowed the rate to remain at $1.

This was something of a novelty in the experience of the sorely tried American shipper. Ordinarily, the case would have been heard by the commission, which would have entered an order against the railroads commanding them to "cease and desist" from charging the $1.15 rate, so that if the railroads were to reduce the rate to $1.14½ they would be complying with the commission's order.

But the railroads would not give even so much heed to the order. They would take the matter into the Federal Courts and about four years later the complaining lemon growers would learn whether they were to keep their profits or continue to hand them to the railroad company.

You think this is pessimistic, unfair, or prejudiced, but it merely states the prevailing conditions. Most of the Interstate Commerce cases take longer. "Cincinnati and Texas Railroad versus Interstate Commerce Commission"

---

[8] Before the Interstate Commerce Commission, Arlighton Heights Fruit Exchange et al. versus Southern Pacific Company et al. Petition, pp. 3-9.

THE STORY OF THE LEMON RATE 299

took six years; "Texas Railway versus same," seven years; "Interstate Commerce Commission versus Alabama Railway," five years; "Interstate Commerce Commission versus Chicago Railway," eight years; "Missouri Pacific versus United States," ten years,[9] by which time everybody connected with the original suit had died or forgotten all about it and the court threw it out on that ground.

We are not yet through with the famous Lemon Rate, however. About the time the railroads gave up the idea of appealing to a Federal judge the Commerce Court was instituted. The railroads in due time took the lemon case thither and a year later got a decision reversing the Interstate Commerce Commission. And thus the matter stands today.

Much wondering attention was called to the lemon tariff grab, as if it were something quite new. As a matter of fact, the only strange thing about it is that anybody should think it strange. It is in line with accepted railroad policy everywhere.

The real beneficiaries of the great American protective tariff are not so much the manufacturers or producers as the railroad companies.

The railroad companies adjust their rates to just below the point where the foreign article (plus the tariff) can be laid down in any given territory.

They do not wish to see the American producer crushed, but all the money he makes they purpose to take for dividends and interest on securities a la Contract and Finance Company.

I submit the following convincing illustrations made up from Mr. Call's figures. The basis is the transcontinental railroad rates between Pacific and Atlantic or lake ports compared with freight rates from abroad.

---

[9] Before the Senate Committee on Interstate Commerce. Hearing on the Regulation of Railway Rates, pp. 1-2.

Commodity.	Average of Approximate Tariff Duty.	Freight Rate from Abroad.	Total Import Cost.	Railroad Terminal Rates.[10]
	Ton	Ton	Ton	Ton
Bituminous Coal	$0.67	$6.00	$6.67	$6.30[11]
Portland Cement	1.60	6.00	7.60	7.00[12]
Steel Ingots	8.00	6.00	14.00	12.00
Pig Iron	4.00	6.00	10.00	10.00
Structural Iron	10.00	6.00	16.00	16.00[13]
Oranges	20.00	3.00	23.00	23.00
Cotton Goods	40.00	6.00	46.00	40.00
Low Grade Dry Goods	40.00	6.00	46.00	60.00

Evidently here the railroad rate is so made that it is a shade under the tariff duty plus the freight rate from abroad. By this adjustment, the importation of the foreign article is not encouraged, but the railroad company gets the greater part of the difference in price between the foreign and domestic article. In other words, it gets the real benefit of the tariff on these commodities.[14]

We tax all else to feed the manufacturer, and fatten the manufacturer to feed the railroad company.

But to return to our lemons. The growers of that ungracious fruit have still another grievance.

To understand it well one must know about the peculiar functions of the American refrigerator car and I am not sure that I can explain that in a few hundred words, but I will try.

The transporting of perishable commodities in refrigeratory cars is now a great industry and very important to all

---

[10] "Terminal rates" are rates from one point with water transit to another, as from Chicago to Seattle.
[11] From Colorado and Utah to Los Angeles and San Francisco.
[12] From the factories in Kansas to Pacific Coast points.
[13] In car load lots.
[14] Remarkable though unintentional confirmation of this fact may be found in Before the Interstate Commerce Commission; Enterprise Manufacturing Company et al. versus Georgia Railroad Company et al. and China and Japan Trading Company versus Georgia Railroad Company. No. 981 and 994. See p. 73, letter of J. O. Stubbs to Howard Ayres.

of us because these cars bring us a large part of our daily food. Most of these cars are owned by the Beef Trust, but are used for fruit and vegetables as well as for meat. The Beef Trust compels the railroads to pay for hauling its cars (a mere disguise for a rebate) and, in addition, gouges the consumer through an onerous charge for ice.

Before 1906 the Beef Trust had contracts with the Southern Pacific by which the Southern Pacific, after it had well plucked the fruit grower, turned him over to the Beef Trust, which in a workmanlike manner finished the trimming. When these contracts expired, gentlemen that controlled the Southern Pacific could see no reason why the Beef Trust should have this good thing when they needed the money themselves, so they chased the Trust out of the game, organized a refrigerator car line of their own, collected the goodly icing charges and turned them into the treasury, whence they presently emerged as additional dividends on more watered stock.

Now it was once thought necessary that lemons, oranges, and the like fruits moving east from California must be iced all the way. Which was good for the refrigerator car lines. Eventually the growers found that by a system of precooling the fruit it would go through without icing and arrive in perfect condition. So on such shipments they placarded the cars with this notice:

"Do not Re-ice in Transit."

That was where the additional grievance came in. The notice never made the least difference to the railroad company. It did not re-ice the car, but it charged for re-icing just the same—$30 a car.[15] On something like 40,000 cars of citrus fruit a year. Good graft.

---

[15] Before the Interstate Commerce Commission. Arlington Heights Fruit Exchange et al. versus Southern Pacific Company et al. Petition of complaints, pp. 15-16. The graft involved here is not much greater than that involved in all these icing charges, which are everywhere unjust.

Others besides fruit growers had grievances. In 1896, the Southern Pacific charges on wool had become so exorbitant that wool growers were threatened with ruin and were driven back to primitive conditions. Some of them abandoned railroad transportation and hauled their wool in wagons 200 miles to a market, finding that extraordinary reversion to mediæval methods cheaper than to pay the railroad rates. To these and to the lemon growers that cut down their orchards the blessings of the railroad and its "benefits conferred" must have seemed grimly farcical.

Meantime, the cities, like San Francisco and Los Angeles, groaned, and so far as they dared, they protested.

Every approach by land was held by the Southern Pacific. Many times the people of San Francisco encouraged new lines of railroad that promised competition, and the city and county granted subsidies to such enterprises, only to see the new projects fall, one after another, into the hands of the monopoly.

But there was always the open road of the sea. Monopolies can seize the land; no one can compass the sea. Whenever years of effort to establish competition or get relief by land had ended in failure, the San Franciscans would turn to the sea.

They found no more relie_ there than they had found in competitive routes by land.

Two conditions stood in their way. Their business was with the eastern states. Therefore, it was domestic commerce. The Federal law restricted domestic commerce to American ships. There were few American ships.

The normal, easy, and cheap transit for their goods was from New York down the Atlantic coast to the Isthmus of Panama, across the Isthmus by the Panama Railroad, and then up the Pacific to San Francisco.

From New York to the Isthmus they could ship easily.

From the Isthmus to San Francisco the only steamships were those of the Pacific Mail, and the Pacific Mail was owned by the Southern Pacific.

To prevent the use of the water route and to compel shipments by rail, the Pacific Mail made a prohibitive rate between the Isthmus and San Francisco.[16]

The merchants of San Francisco endured this condition for years. To end it, some of them organized an independent line of vessels to the Isthmus. Competition.

The Southern Pacific made an arrangement with the Panama Railroad whereby for a payment of $75,000 a month[17] the railroad agreed to let the merchants' freight lie on the wharves instead of carrying it across the Isthmus. In a short time the wharves were piled high with goods the railroad made no effort to move.

The merchants surrendered before this impossible condition, the independent line was abandoned, and the situation drifted back to the undisputed control of the Southern Pacific. Its subsidy to the Panama railroad for helping to throttle California was alone sufficient to pay a fair dividend on the Panama's capital.[18]

Recently there has been another attempt (of an uncertain destiny) to revive competition. But in the main, this is the situation today.

But, you say, this is very strange. The Panama Railroad and the connecting steamship line on the Atlantic are now owned and operated by the United States government. Surely the government will not enter into an open alliance for plunder with the Southern Pacific.

No, but there is something else at work.

---

[16] The chief business of the Pacific Mail to the south was between San Francisco and the west coast ports of South America.

[17] Report of J. L. Bristow, Special Panama Railroad Commissioner, to the Senate Committee on Interoceanic Canals, 1908, p. 13.

[18] Commissioner Bristow's Report, p. 13.

The Southern Pacific continues to operate the Pacific Mail, and continues to make prohibitive rates. Today the total freight rate from San Francisco to New York *via* Panama is $8 a ton. Of this, the United States government, for the railroad haul across the Isthmus and the water haul to New York, receives $2.40; the Southern Pacific, for the shorter water haul, San Francisco to the Isthmus, receives $5.60.

To meet this condition the obvious remedy is for the government to operate steamships on the Pacific as it does on the Atlantic. Now see:

In San Francisco, Isidor Jacobs, a civic reformer noted for his courage, has been for nineteen years fighting railroad extortion. He organized the old Traffic Association of California, which brought forth the San Joaquin Valley Railroad (gobbled by the Santa Fe) and the ill-fated independent line to the Isthmus. For some years he has been laboring for a government line on the Pacific. Largely at his instigation the government sent J. L. Bristow as a special commissioner to investigate conditions pertaining to such a line.

At San Francisco, a public meeting was held under the auspices of the Chamber of Commerce, which, with the two other mercantile associations of the city, is dominated by the Southern Pacific. Some hundreds of merchants were present. Only Mr. Jacobs spoke for the government line. Other speakers praised with fulsome expressions the Pacific Mail service and management, and opposed a government enterprise.

Mr. Jacobs suggested that Mr. Bristow should invite the merchants to come to him privately at his hotel and express their opinions. Mr. Bristow adopted this suggestion, and in the next two days, about two-score of San Francisco's free and independent American citizens crept like criminals into Mr. Bristow's apartments and after exacting a pledge of

THE STORY OF THE LEMON RATE 305

secrecy told him that the Pacific Mail service was abominable and extortionate and a government line would be a boon. Many of these were gentlemen that at the meeting had expressed exactly the opposite views.[19]

"I inquired privately as to the reasons for the inconsistent attitude of these gentlemen," says Mr. Bristow. He seems to have found out. "It was further added that the tremendous power in transportation matters which this combination of steamship and railway management held over the fortunes of San Francisco shippers would tend to make them timid in expressing in public any views that would be displeasing to either company."[20]

"Tend to make them timid!" Between the tyranny of a corporation in the twentieth century and the tyranny of a satrap in the first will some one kindly point out the difference? Some one of the Glorious Spirit of Optimism preferred, but anyone will do.

San Francisco never got its government line and the Pacific Mail continues to blockade the Isthmus route. The Southern Pacific influence stopped this as it has stopped every other relief for forty years. It is a pathetic spectacle. With the open-handed Californian generosity San Francisco has given money, lands, and terminals. In return she has had chiefly kicks and scientific and multiplied extortion. I think you can hardly find in the world the fellow to that story.[21]

To epitomize it, one should look first at the magnificent Mission Bay property freely bestowed upon the railroad, and then turn to contemplate the fact that at the great Portola celebration in San Francisco, October, 1909, the Southern Pacific was the only institution that made money

---
[19] Mr. Bristow's Report, p. 4.
[20] Ibid, pp. 4-5.
[21] As to the conditions today, see report of the Senate Committee on Federal Relations, California Legislature, to be found in the Senate Journal for March 23, 1909, p. 27.

from the crowds and the only institution that refused to contribute a dollar to the expenses of the celebration.

Observe next how much your laws avail to restrain this corporation.

The Hepburn railroad rate regulation act was passed by Congress in 1906. It was the nation's third and most strenuous attempt to end railroad abuses.

Four months after it became a law all men in San Francisco that follow these matters knew the Southern Pacific was paying no more heed to the new than it had paid to the old law and was daily granting the forbidden rebate.

Complaint was made to the Interstate Commerce Commission and one year later, in October, 1907, Commissioner Lane came to San Francisco and began a hearing.

At once it was evident that the government's secret service agents and inspectors had caught the railroad red-handed. Amazing details were laid bare. It appeared that rebates abounded for favored shippers in almost every line of commerce. To record these illegal transactions the Southern Pacific maintained a set of secret books, twenty in number, called the "A" books,[22] kept in a separate room by a Mrs. Cummins and a Miss Lena Amundsen. To these books no one had access except the head manipulator of rebates, and in them were set down thousands of instances of these forbidden advantages to shippers—disguised mostly, please mark, as alleged claims for damaged goods or overcharges —under the sanction of the General Freight Agent of the Southern Pacific.[23]

Documentary evidence of these rebates was submitted and by the curious may now be found in the appendix to the testimony.

---

[22] Before the Interstate Commerce Commission. In the Matter of Rates, Practices, Accounts and Revenues of Carriers, at San Francisco, October 2, 3, 4, 1907. Testimony of J. M. Brewer, pp. 6, 7, and elsewhere.

[23] *Ibid.*, p. 7.

When the scandal had been laid bare the Southern Pacific, quite unabashed, played its trump card and retired serenely.

It offered Mr. G. W. Luce, General Freight Agent, as a witness, with the statement that he could explain these rebates if he were sworn.

Commissioner Lane was not to be so trapped. He recognized that the swearing of Luce as a witness would be an "immunity bath" for him and all his transactions. Therefore, the commissioner declined to let Mr. Luce be sworn, but said he might make any statement he cared to make. The Southern Pacific attorney would not let Mr. Luce say anything except under oath.[24] And thus the matter ended. The Southern Pacific management said, with much pretense of righteous indignation, that it could explain everything if it were only allowed, but it was not allowed—which is an excellent line of talk for gabies—and the commission, of course, was deprived of the advantage of questioning Mr. Luce.

This was in 1907. Some optimists may think that these lawless practices having been thus indubitably revealed, the Southern Pacific (in the beautiful phrase of regulation) "ceased and desisted" from them and joined the other railroads in protestations of reform. To any such persons I commend a reading of the decision of the California Board of Railroad Commissioners, filed January 12, 1909, from which it appears that one year after the revelations before Commissioner Lane the same company was dealing in the same line of rebates at the old stand.[25]

---

[24] Before the Interstate Commerce Commission. In the Matter of Rates, Practices, Accounts and Revenues of Carriers, at San Francisco, October 2, 3, 4, 1907, pp. 116, 117.

[25] Before the Board of Railroad Commissioners of the State of California, No. 102. In the Matter of Alleged Discriminations by the Southern Pacific. Pages 17 and 18 will be found particularly interesting.

This incident, so characteristic, so perfectly typical of the whole enterprise from its inception, may well close our little history.

With the concentrated bitterness that the people of California feel for the Southern Pacific, we have had nothing to do here. Purposely, I have refrained from mentioning the terms in which most Californians usually refer to the railroad, and have likewise omitted great store of material and incidents of which the import was malignant or personal or tending to place upon individuals responsibility for a general condition for which no man should be blamed.

But I do believe it to be a fair conclusion that the whole system upon which this company has been operated from its first stock subscription to this day is largely fraudulent, utterly wrong, and gravely injurious to the people of California and to the rest of the country.

I do believe it to be clear that every dollar taken unfairly or dishonestly or by clever scheming out of this property has been repaid many times from the living expenses of the people.

I do believe it certain that all this represents a situation not much longer to be endured if the nation is to survive and be free.

The highways are the people's. Let us return them to the people from whom they have been taken chiefly by chicanery, bribery, and fraud.

For all these and all the other intolerable and growing evils of our transportation system, for the increased cost of living demonstrably produced by the overissue of railroad securities, for the menace in the rapid increase of these overissues, and for the corruption that these influences always work in our public affairs, there is no other remedy.

Let us begin to apply it now.

CHAPTER XIII

THE STORY OF THE NEW HAVEN

"Great Scott!" said Mr. E. H. Harriman one day, "is there anything like that still left out of doors?"

He was speaking of a certain piece of railroad that by some chance had not been loaded to the guards with the common stock, preferred stock, debentures, first, second, and consolidated mortgages, notes and refunding certificates that now adorn the greater part of our admired railroad structure.

His astonishment was natural. Of the typical American railroad it may be observed with truth and without prejudice that its chief business has largely ceased to be the transporting of passengers and freight and become the issuing of securities for the public to pay.

Wonderful invention, the printing press! Its relations to civilization and enlightenment have been widely recognized, but no one has adequately celebrated its functions in the mysterious processes of High Finance. Yet herein its work is in one way the most important of all, for in this way it comes every day to every household and collects toll in a manner that we little suspect but can never evade.

Would you like to remove the lid from these mysteries and see for once the great fortunes in the making? Would you also like to see by an object lesson exactly why the cost of living mounts upon us? Here is your chance, then. For once the whole process is visible to the plain, ordinary citizen, and his rare and happy privilege it is to watch the dimes taken from his earnings and follow them through the dizzy evolutions of Wall Street to their final resting place beyond his reach.

Prior to 1903 the New York, New Haven & Hartford Railroad, although a great and growing octopus monopolizing the railroad traffic of a large region, was what is known as financially sound. It operated 2,037 miles of road with a main line from New York City to Boston and many branch lines through Connecticut, Rhode Island, and Massachusetts. Its capital stock was $70,897,300, its funded debt was $14,549,300, its total capitalization was $85,446,600.

Six years later its capital stock had increased 72 per cent., its funded debt had increased 1501 per cent., its total capitalization had grown to $356,737,975.

It had meantime entered upon a deliberate plan to secure an absolute monopoly of the entire transportation business of New England.

By 1903 the process of combining and unifying the steam railroads had reached the stage where there were three main New England systems—the Boston & Maine, the Boston & Albany, and the New York, New Haven & Hartford. The Boston & Maine controlled everything east and north of Boston, and the Boston & Albany and New Haven companies everything west and southwest thereof.

Between the coast points a very extensive freight and passenger business was carried on by water. Through the interior trolley lines were beginning to be of great importance and to threaten the steam lines with a steadily growing competition.

To-day *this entire vast business, steam rail, electric rail, and maritime is practically in the mailed fist of the New Haven* except what is controlled by the Boston & Albany.

But the Boston & Albany is largely controlled by the same powers that own the New Haven, and the two roads have a close traffic arrangement for their mutual advantage.

The curious spectacle is now presented of six populous and busy states whose transportation of every considerable kind is gripped by one small group of capitalists and operated by them for their sole benefit.

In that entire region, bustling with traffic, they can lay upon the inhabitants what tribute they please.

This unique and wonderful power, that makes historic conquerors like Akbar and Yenghis Khan look like pigmies, has been secured partly through the handy printing press and its issue of watered securities, partly by ignoring laws and courts, and partly by the most strange and alarming assistance of government.

First, as to water transportation.

About sixteen years ago many lines of steamboats threaded Long Island Sound between New York and points from which Boston was easily reached.

One after another the New Haven reached out and gathered them into its fold. The Fall River Line, the Providence Line, Norwich Line, Stonington Line, New Bedford Line, New Haven Line, Bridgeport Line, Hartford Line, Block Island Line, Maine Steamship Company—all taken in.

Independent lines were formed to combat this monopoly and keep down rates by means of blessed competition.

Also, the New Haven gathered these in, usually in secret and without changing their apparently independent nature. Whenever necessary, it started on its own account what pretended to be an independent line. With this it crushed a hopeful rival and brought the remains into the fold.

To-day it owns or controls practically every means of steam transportation by water routes between New York and New England.

Next, the trolley lines.

As early as 1893 the threat of this competition had become formidable. Electricity had taken the place of horse power on all the street railroads within the towns and cities; the electric railroads were now being extended so as to connect the towns. In July, 1901, the New Haven directors, designing to suppress this increasing competition, appointed a committee of unusual powers, composed of President Charles S. Mellen, Mr. Robert W. Taft and Mr. George J. Brush, to formulate and carry out plans to gain control of the trolley lines.

The committee formed a separate corporation known as the Worcester & Connecticut Eastern Railroad Company, with a capital stock of $500,000. To this company the New Haven advanced certain sums of money. With this money the new company secured two or three small electric lines. Next it brought out the handy printing press, and issued upon the property thus secured a fine line of stocks and bonds. With the proceeds of these stocks and bonds it repaid to the New Haven road all of the money advanced except $15,000.

This sum of $15,000 represented the New Haven's entire investment. The rest of the money required was supplied by the obliging public through the printing press.

In other words, here was repeated the exact process by which so many steam railroads have been acquired, by which Mr. Yerkes got possession of the street railroads of Chicago, and the Ryan-Whitney combination got possession of the street railroads of New York. It is the magic wand of high finance.

The Worcester & Connecticut Eastern now delivered to the New Haven a majority of its voting stock, consisting of 2,501 shares.

It was then ready for the next step usual in these operations. On May 18, 1904, it underwent what is called in the language of high finance "reorganization." Its capital stock was increased to $10,000,000, its name changed to the Consolidated Railway Company. The New Haven invested no more money in it, but the New Haven still held a majority of the voting stock and still supplied the control from its own officers.

The machine was now perfectly equipped and smoothly working. The Consolidated proceeded to acquire one trolley road after another, paying for them with its own debentures which it issued from the press as fast as they were required. By May 1, 1907, it had taken over in this way 500 of the 600 miles of electric railroad then operated in Connecticut and had crushed the competition of the trolley.

Meantime, our old friend, Senator Aldrich, and others in Rhode Island had been doing a little printing on their own account. On June 24, 1903, they organized a thing called the Rhode Island Company, the benevolent purpose of which was to acquire all the gas, electric light and street railroad properties of Providence and then to control the principal trolley lines of Rhode Island. To facilitate this good work, the Rhode Island Securities Company was organized under the laws of New Jersey as a holding concern. Rhode Island courts cannot touch a New Jersey company.

The New Haven road, having completed its conquest of the entire trolley field of Connecticut, now turned its attention to Rhode Island and observed with approval the Aldrich activities there.

In Providence the New Haven had a concern called the New England Loan & Trust Company, for it had long recognized the tremendous advantage of controlling money supplies. The New England Loan & Trust Company had a capital of $50,000 (all owned by the New Haven Railroad) and a charter from the obedient state of Connecticut that apparently authorized it to do anything except to hold prayer meetings. It now went to the superior court at Hartford and had its name changed to the Providence Securities Company. Next, the Providence Securities Company issued $20,000,000 of 4 per cent bonds. With these bonds it acquired the Rhode Island Securities Company, and therewith the control of the gas, electric light, and street railroad properties of Providence and the chief trolley lines of Rhode Island

It next dissolved the Rhode Island Securities, and the New Haven reigned alone in Rhode Island.

The trolley services of two states were now in its grasp.

Its Consolidated Railway Company next acquired the New York & Stamford Railroad, a trolley line from Portchester to New Rochelle, in New York, and its monopoly became perfect from New York City to the eastern boundary of Rhode Island.

So far all was well. The astute gentlemen that controlled the New Haven had for years looked longingly upon the great Boston & Maine system. It controlled an enormous traffic, it was prosperous, it was a good dividend earner, and, best of all, it was lightly capitalized, for this is the identical piece of railroad property whose discovery had excited the wonder of Mr. Harriman. To say that its capitalization had never been juggled were, of course, to say too much. But its capitalization had never been juggled to its injury, and there remained vast possibilities for juggling that had never been explored.

The New Haven, on the contrary, had been steadily juggling all these years. Its successive and enormous issues of securities were loading upon it dividend payments and fixed charges that were becoming a menacing problem. Therefore, it was in a position very familiar in these juggling operations. It must acquire some good dividend earner to swell its receipts and support its own securities, and here was the fat old Boston & Maine, a melon just ripe enough to cut. So the New Haven determined to acquire the Boston & Maine.

Throughout the Boston & Maine's territory, but chiefly in western Massachusetts, the trolley lines were threatening it with great and increasing competition. The New Haven, partly to injure the Boston & Maine, partly to extend and complete its own system, and partly, of course, to have excuse for the printing press, began now, through its Consolidated Railway and its issued securities, to acquire control of the Massachusetts trolley lines.

Here is where it struck its first snag. For many years it had dominated the politics of Connecticut and Rhode Island with a power equally supreme, no matter what party might be in nominal control of the government. In those states, therefore, it had proceeded with a high hand. Some of its trolley operations had been questionable under the state laws; many of them were questionable under the Federal Anti-Trust law. No consideration of this sort checked its way. But in Massachusetts the situation was somewhat different.

Massachusetts was corporation-ridden, like the other states, but the riding of the corporations had never gone quite so far as to trample with impunity upon explicit laws of the state. One of these laws, enacted in 1874, provided in the plainest terms, that without the consent of the legislature no railroad corporation could directly or indirectly hold any of the stock of any other corporation whatsoever. The New Haven Company was a Massachusetts corporation, but in open defiance of the Massachusetts law it proceeded to acquire and to hold the stocks of the various Massachusetts trolley companies that it was now sweeping into its net.

The philosophic mind will always note with curious interest by what slender threads important events may hang. For some time the New Haven went its way triumphantly walking over the Massachusetts law and piling up Massachusetts trolley upon trolley. It obtained the Worcester & Southbridge Street Railway Company, the Worcester & Blackstone Valley, the Webster & Dudley, and the Berkshire Street Railway. It next started to acquire through the Springfield Railway Companies (which was its holding concern) the extensive trolley system in and about Springfield.

But at this huge gulp the people of the region began to protest. They understood that the proposed absorption was utterly illegal; they demanded that their laws be enforced.

Just at this juncture fell in the incident psychologically required. The Boston & Maine had carefully observed the law that forbids a railway company to hold stock in another corporation; but it was beginning to be pinched severely by trolley competition, the lines acquired by the New Haven and by still others. Therefore, the Boston & Maine, having some respect for the law, went before the legislature and petitioned for the necessary permission to acquire certain competing trolley lines.

With astounding effrontery the New Haven, represented by a powerful lobby, came upon the field to oppose this petition. The substance of its argument, therefore, was that the Boston & Maine should not be allowed to do lawfully the identical thing that the New Haven was doing in violation of the law. Beyond this height of impudence it does not seem humanly possible to soar; but the extraordinary thing is that the New Haven got away with its colossal bluff. It actually succeeded in inducing the legislature to defeat the Boston & Maine's petition. As to just how it wrought an achievement so marvelous, history is silent, but those to whom the American legislature is no mystery will not be seriously troubled by the omission.

The fight endured for two legislative sessions, those of 1905 and 1906. At the end, on June 23, 1906, when the New Haven came victorious from the final encounter, Governor Curtis Guild, Jr., addressed to the legislature a message of congratulation, but took the opportunity to strike a smashing blow at the victor. There was a corporation, the governor warned the legislature, controlled by men not citizens of Massachusetts, that was seizing upon all the transportation facilities of the state and turning them into a monopoly, and he therefore urged upon the legislature, "with all the strength that is in me," he said, the passage of acts that would meet this menacing situation.

He might have been astonished at the result. Immediately there broke out a wide-spread public clamor against the New Haven octopus that he had denounced; the people irresistibly demanded action at once upon the lines of the governor's recommendation.

At first, the New Haven, affording another pleasing illustration of brazen assurance, had the hardihood to assert that although it was chartered by the state of Massachusetts it was not amenable to Massachusetts law because it had also a charter from the state of Connecticut. Finding that this position did not add to its popularity and might have serious results, it quickly shifted its ground. It now, through its officers, expressed astonishment at the state of public feeling, announced its entire willingness to have its rights adjusted, protested against any legislative action, and proposed instead that the attorney-general of Massachusetts bring a suit in the courts by which the rights of the company might be definitely ascertained.

Mr. Charles S. Mellen, president of the New Haven, went farther. He appeared before the railroad committee of the legislature and solemnly promised that if the legislature would adjourn without taking any hostile action, his railroad would at once cease from all efforts to control competing lines, either directly or indirectly. He made this pledge through a written statement, which his counsel handed to the chairman of the committee, the Hon. Joseph Walker, afterward speaker of the House of Representatives, and which Mr. Walker read aloud to the committee. The legislature was convinced of Mr. Mellen's good faith and adjourned without acting upon Governor Guild's suggestion.

Under the terms of this treaty, the attorney-general of Massachusetts began a suit to test the law of 1874 that the

New Haven had violated by acquiring the stocks of other corporations. Having perfect confidence in their courts and much faith in Mr. Mellen, the people were satisfied and the agitation ceased.

The legislators had hardly reached their homes when the news came that the New Haven had bought the Milford, Attleboro & Woonsocket, the Hartford & Worcester, the Uxbridge & Blackstone, and the Worcester & Holden, four Massachusetts trolley lines, whose purchase was absolutely illegal if the law of 1874 was valid. How these purchases could be squared with Mr. Mellen's promises has never been explained.

But something still more formidable impended.

In the last days of the legislative session of 1907 the astounding news began to be circulated that the New Haven had secured control of the Boston & Maine by quiet purchases of stock from small holders. This acquisition violated the law of Massachusetts and the law of the United States no less. The legislature now took the unusual step of passing a law to forbid the violation of law. It passed an act forbidding the New Haven to purchase any more stock of the Boston & Maine, or to exercise any control over that railroad until May 1, 1908.

On June 23, 1908, the supreme court of Massachusetts decided the attorney-general's action to test the validity of the law of 1874 and the New Haven's trolley road purchases. The decision upheld the law without qualification, found against the New Haven on every point, and ordered the railroad to divest itself of the vast system of trolleys it had acquired.

Mr. Mellen obeyed the order of the court in this manner:

There was registered a concern called The New England Investment and Securities Company. This concern is what is known in Massachusetts as a "voluntary association"; that is, it has the right to issue and sell stock, but its form of charter does not compel it to make any reports to the state corporation department. The voting power of the New England Investment and Securities Company is vested in one thousand shares of common stock, seven hundred and fifty of which shares are distributed among gentlemen that are directors in or are closely allied with New Haven interests.

This New England Securities Company took over vast systems of trolleys that the supreme court had decided the New Haven could not own.

Next, Mr. Charles F. Choate, Jr., of counsel for the New Haven, offered before the legislature another written statement in which the railroad company virtually acknowledged that its purchase of Boston & Maine stock had been in violation of the law, but excusably so because it had been done on the advice of eminent counsel.

The next thing men knew, the New Haven had quietly taken all its Boston & Maine shares outside of the state and nominally "sold" them. The trolley decision was dangerous; this reckless court might next order the New Haven to divest itself of these Boston & Maine shares. They were worth $16,000,000, and, according to the railroad company, they had been "purchased" by Mr. John L. Billard, a coal dealer in Connecticut. Mr. Billard is said to be worth less than a million dollars.

This took them out of the jurisdiction of the Massachusetts courts.

The next move was to introduce in the Massachusetts legislature a bill that would sanction the holding of the Boston & Maine stock by the New Haven Company—that is to say, to legalize the merger.

As soon as this adroit scheme became generally known, the statehouse was turned into a battlefield, where for weeks the people fought the octopus and its able agents. Not in a generation has the commonwealth been so stirred. The labor unions, the merchants, the manufacturers, the boards of trade and chambers of commerce were fighting the merger; the lobbyists, the politicians and the trimmers fought for it. The labor organizations alone sent 500 delegates to appear against the bill before the railroad committee of the legislature. In favor of it was one organization. This was called the "Business Men's Merger League." It consisted of forty members and was organized by Allen Buttrick, then a legislative agent for the New Haven, since created by Governor Draper a judge in Boston.

The fight was carried on with savage energy. One of its results was the development of a man that for a time gave promise of being an efficient leader on the side of the people and against the monopoly. Norman H. White was a member of the House of Representatives from Brookline. In Boston he was interested in a publishing house and also a large book bindery. Hardly another business man in Boston had less personal concern in the merger, for his was a business not particularly affected by freight rates. Mr. White perceived that very great public interests were at stake, and without regard to his personal advantages he threw himself into the struggle and became its temporary champion.

In the legislature he fought every inch of the ground; outside he devoted his time to informing the public of the situation and arraying it against the proposed deal. His activities before the public supplemented and supported the work of Louis D. Brandeis, who had given his services as an attorney against the merger and whose dissection of the actual financial condition of the New York, New Haven & Hartford became a monumental work in railroad analysis.

Mr. White did these things at his own risk in more ways than one. Like every man engaged in large business enterprises, he was and is a borrower at banks. Soon after he began his fight on the New Haven, he found that for no apparent reason his credit was discontinued.

I wish that in some way I could emphasize this fact, because it shows what this Power really is—how tremendous, how many-sided, and how long-armed. It was through similar influence that Francis J. Heney was defeated in San Francisco, and many business men in this country it has by the same means whipped into silence or support, for through these means it exercises across the continent an influence upon our affairs prodigious and unparalleled.

The effort to silence White was a failure. He and his associates went up and down the state preaching against the merger, pointing out the evils it would inflict, but laying most stress upon the fact that the action of the railroad was grossly illegal and immoral.

Meantime, in the state senate the New Haven had won. The bill went to the House. There Mr. White and his associates, among them Robert M. Washburn of Worcester, chairman of the powerful railroad committee, and Charles Brown of Medford, attacked it incessantly with amendment after amendment, until they amended from it every feature that could be of the least use to the New Haven. Therefore, the New Haven was more than willing to have the measure die—for that session.

Meantime, also, the United States Government had been induced to take a hand in the fight. Louis D. Brandeis went to Washington with his analysis of the New York, New Haven & Hartford. Federal District-Attorney Asa P. French, at Boston, had been studying the story of New Haven's acquisition of the competing trolley lines also and was convinced that the Federal law had been violated.

In May, 1908, supported by Attorney-General Bonaparte, French began a suit on these grounds against the New Haven, the Consolidated Railroad Company, and the Providence Securities Company.

This suit was hailed by the people of Massachusetts with infinite satisfaction. It promised to put out of business a monopoly that had seized or was threatening to seize the commercial traffic of all New England, and at the same time to relieve the state from the task of enforcing its decrees upon a Power apparently too great for any one state to control. Only the United States Government could deal adequately with such an institution, and now the Government had taken it in hand.

A feeling of relief cheered all the anti-merger fighters, and at the next state election, that of 1908, the merger was not a prominent issue. There was also a general impression that a kind of truce had been tacitly proclaimed until the Government's suit should be decided. If there be anything most of us love better than a truce it is an excuse for the notion that the Federal Government will take care of our troubles. That lets us out so we can return to our balance sheets and automobiles.

On January 1, 1909, Eben S. Draper, the Business Governor of Massachusetts, was inaugurated. Mr. Draper was the candidate of the safe and sane element. Before making his campaign for governor he resigned from the directorate of the Shawmut National Bank—popularly known as the Morgan bank of New England. On the board of the Shawmut Mr. Draper was associated with Vice-President Byrnes and Charles F. Choate, Jr., of the New Haven. He had been elected when the merger issue had ceased to disturb men's minds and when what we most thought about was the Grand Old Party and the balance sheets.

Early in April, without the least warning, Governor Draper sent to the legislature a special message on the railroad situation. It was somewhat vague, but in a general way it suggested that matters were in an unsatisfactory shape and the legislature should do something to settle them.

Soon after, there appeared in the legislature a bill to create the Boston Railroad Holding Company, under which innocent name was disguised an arrangement to authorize the New Haven to hold the Boston & Maine stock.

It is asserted that several drafts were made of this bill and submitted to Mr. Mellen, the one finally appearing before the legislature being the only one which he was willing, in the language of a high state official, "to stand for."

When the real purpose of the Boston Railroad Holding Company became apparent, the old fight began again.

This time there were new tactics. In the previous campaign the New Haven had appealed to the public; now it confined its attention to the legislature, to members of which it was most considerate and courteous. Mr. Mellen entertained as his guests the members of the railroad committees. They went out to Council Grove Farm, Mr. Mellen's country place in the Berkshires, and had a very pleasant time. They inspected the farm and particularly Mr. Mellen's prize poultry yard. Some of the fowls therein contained were of very rare breeds, and the legislators were much impressed by the fact that these fowls were worth $500 each. President Allen T. Treadway, of the Massachusetts senate, a personal friend of Mr. Mellen, and Representative R. de Peyster Tytus, of the lower House, were also present and much enjoyed the occasion.

All the geusts went for an automobile ride over the proposed route of a trolley extension that Mr. Mellen had planned for his lines, and saw just what Mr. Mellen desired to do. On their return they visited the Red Lion Inn, of which Senator Treadway is the proprietor. And who should meet them there but Mr. Mellen himself and his secretary, Mr. Fabian! Yes, it was a delightful circumstance, as all can see; in fact, quite a coincidence. Mr. Mellen is such a nice gentleman. Mr. Fabian is a nice gentleman, too. So it was altogether a nice occasion, and all present enjoyed it to the utmost.

Previous to that day there had been dissension in the committee over Mr. Mellen's little Holding Company bill, but after that day there wasn't so much. A few days later the bill was reported favorably and slated for passage.

There were still rude, rough men that fought against it. The chairman of the railroad committee, Mr. Washburn, opposed his colleagues unswervingly. Mr. White went at it again as fiercely as ever. He had won his way back to the House in spite of the utmost efforts of the New Haven, which had gone into his district to beat him; he was a member of the Committee on Ways and Means; he was of much influence and reputed courage. It was in these words that he summed up the bill and its true meaning:

"It means complete monopoly of transportation on land and sea, uncontrolled and uncontrollable; a monopoly of all the commerce of New England under a single management. Such a monopoly and management exceeds the limits of greatest efficiency and economy. It involves an increase in power in the hands of a few men over all lines of business. Such a monopoly of transportation and business is dangerous to the political and financial independence of the people of Massachusetts and all New England."

But the lobby worked on, unperturbed by these certain truths. It was directed with great skill. From time to time it adroitly spread the impression that the national party management and certain great Republicans at Washington desired to have the bill passed. Then the feeling grew up that it was a party measure; that the faith of the party was pledged to it; that the men back of it were all fine men, sturdy supporters of "our party" and contributors to the campaign fund by which it had been enabled to defeat the wicked Democrats.

What basis the reports of Washington influence may have had I cannot assume to say, but there is no doubt that with a certain order of mind they were very effective. However, they must have been supplemented by others, for this line of talk does not go far with gentlemen of ripe experience. Some of the other arguments are said to have been quite weighty, so weighty, in fact, that they were brought up Beacon Hill in a suitcase.

While the fight went on, many observers were surprised to note that Governor Draper was much in favor of the bill. At times the governor's room at the statehouse was used as President Mellen's headquarters, and through Governor Draper Mr. Mellen informed the legislators that unless the pending bill were passed the Boston & Maine stock then in the hands of Mr. Billard, the coal dealer in Connecticut, would remain out of the state. But if the bill were passed, said Mr. Mellen, he would bring the stock back into the state. Were this stock brought back into Massachusetts, the state courts would have jurisdiction over it.

In either event Mr. Mellen had the situation cinched except for the hope of the Federal suit, so what was the use? As to the Federal suit, on May 19th, before the railroad committee, Mr. Harold J. Coolidge, a relative of one of the New Haven directors, was good enough to say he had "certain information from Washington that the suit would not be pressed." At the time nobody believed him. What on earth could keep the Government of the United States from pressing a suit like that?

The lobby won, Mr. White and his forces were defeated, and the bill passed on June 18, 1909. Governor Draper signed it, and soon after, we may suppose, Mr. Billard, the coal dealer in Connecticut, was relieved of the responsibility of caring for $16,000,000 worth of stock on less than a million of total wealth.

The Boston Railroad Holding Company, created by this act, had a capital stock of $100,000. This concern can issue any amount of stock, subject to the approval of the Railroad Commission. Its incorporators were Walter C. Baylies, Robert M. Burnett, Frederick C. Dumaine, and some others. One of these gentlemen, I note with pleasure, is a director in the Fore River Shipbuilding Company, whose ownership and whose contracts with the United States Government will some day, I hope, be investigated. Another was formerly a legislative agent for the gas interests. Another is a director in the Shawmut National Bank, which is one of the many financial institutions controlled by the New Haven—and is known as the Morgan bank of New England.

All the voting stock in the Boston Railroad Holding Company is held by the New Haven. Blest be the tie that binds. The Holding Company is authorized to hold Boston & Maine stock for the New Haven. Incidentally, it can hold the blanket while an able construction company milks the Boston & Maine for the New Haven, if that be thought desirable. Such things have been known, little children.

The people of Massachusetts still pinned their faith to the Federal government's suit as their hope of rescue from the danger of the merger. They believed that the anti-trust laws of the nation fully covered the case and would be rigidly enforced.

They were not long of that opinion. It was on April 20, 1909, that Governor Draper sent his special message to the legislature, paving the way to the Holding Company bill. Two days later, in Washington, a conference was held at the Department of Justice between Attorney-General Wickersham and Mr. E. D. Robbins, of counsel for the New Haven. It was admitted that what they were talking about was the merger suit. Mr. Wickersham said that Mr. Robbins wanted to have it tried quickly or dismissed.

Please note.

Governor Draper signed the merger bill on June 18th.

On June 25th came the amazing news from Washington

that the Government had dismissed its suit against the New Haven.

When asked for an explanation of this remarkable conclusion of the case, Attorney-General Wickersham said to the press:

"In view of the fact that the suit of the United States now pending against the New Haven and the Boston & Main Railroad companies for a violation of the anti-trust act rests almost entirely upon a claim that these companies had already consolidated by means of stock ownership, and since the community most directly affected is the state of Massachusetts, whose laws now expressly authorize such consolidation, the Attorney-General has determined to dismiss the Government's action."

This in spite of the statement in the Government's petition that the merger affected "the whole of the New England states" and commerce "between these states and the rest of the United States"; in spite of the fact that this statement is most obviously true; in spite of the fact that one state cannot nullify the law of the nation.

As to the trolley roads, the Attorney-General said that so much of the case as was founded upon their acquisition had been disposed of by the decision of the Massachusetts supreme court declaring such acquisition to be unlawful. Since which time, said Mr. Wickersham, the New Haven Company had been parting with its trolley properties.

Yes? And to whom had it parted with them?

To the New England Investment and Securities Company, an institution it had formed for that express purpose, and in which it holds the controlling interest. It has merely passed them from one hand to the other.

This is the way the case stands now, except that the legislature has appointed a committee consisting of the state bank commissioner, the tax commissioner, and the railroad commission to examine the physical property and assets of the New Haven. This committee was appointed after the attorney-general of the state had informed the legislature that the Massachusetts charter of the New Haven was forfeited because the road had issued some forty million dollars of stock and bonds contrary to law. The committee has the authority of the legislature to validate these stocks and bonds if it finds that the assets of the company warrant it. You may be sure that the stocks and bonds will be validated.

Meanwhile the merger is complete; the New Haven has in its grasp the commerce of New England, a vast empire of rich traffic; and Mr. Mellen is president of the Boston & Maine as well as of the New Haven.

Monopoly has won the day.

The total capitalization of the New Haven has been increased from $85,446,600 to $356,737,975.

What does all this mean for the public?

Passenger rates have already been increased five per cent, and Mr. Mellen is arguing in favor of an increase of freight rates.

Then, who pays the bill?

Also, who are the real rulers of America?

For by what power do you suppose the United States Government was compelled to become the assistant of the New York, New Haven & Hartford in these transactions?

To those that have interest in these speculations I recommend a perusal of the following list of the New Haven's directors:

William Rockefeller.
J. Pierpont Morgan.
George MacCulloch Miller.
Lewis Cass Ledyard.
Charles M. Pratt.
George F. Baker.
Nathaniel Thayer.

Frederick F. Brewster.
I. DeVer Warner.
Edwin Milner.
William Skinner.
D. Newton Barney.
Robert W. Taft.
Thomas DeWitt Cuyler.

Amory A. Lawrence.
Alexander Cochrane.
Charles F. Brooker.
George J. Brush.
Charles S. Mellen.
James S. Hemingway.
A. Heaton Robertson.

James S. Elton.
James McCrea.
Henry K. McHarg.
John L. Billard.
Augustus S. May.
Arthur E. Clark.

Before Mr. Wickersham was Attorney-General he was a member of the law firm of Strong & Cadwalader, of which Mr. Henry W. Taft, the President's brother, is also a member.

We are not yet at the end of this story.

In October, 1910, Mr. Draper, the New Haven's great and good friend, was a candidate for re-election, having been renominated by the Republican state convention.

Before the Democratic state convention met the one opinion among all judicious observers was that the Republicans had not a ghost of a show, and the Democrats, if they were harmonious, were certain to win at the polls.

The Democratic convention met, and instead of being harmonious, some malign influence plainly at work caused it to be deadlocked over the nomination for governor.

Two factions appeared with irreconcilable aims. One wished to nominate Congressman Eugene N. Foss, an anti-corporation Democrat; the other wished to nominate Mr. Charles S. Hamlin, who was Assistant Secretary of the Treasury in Mr. Cleveland's second administration. Mr. Cleveland's administration, it will be remembered, was extremely kind to Mr. Morgan, particularly in the matter of certain bond deals.

These two factions split the party wide asunder, and their dissension promised to ruin utterly the Democratic chance of success.

Many persons wondered greatly at the strength of Mr. Hamlin's support. Mr. Hamlin has never been a popular favorite nor regarded as good material for a candidate.

Yet the faction that supported him was utterly resolved to have Hamlin or nobody.

In the course of this bitter row, Mr. George Fred Williams, who was leading the fight for Foss, suddenly turned up the fact that Mr. Hamlin was, and for thirteen years had been, in receipt of an annual retainer of $10,000 from the Boston & Maine, which is controlled by the New Haven.

It also appeared from an examination of Mr. Hamlin's tax returns that this annual retainer of $10,000 constituted four-fifths of his professional income.

As Mr. Hamlin was not of the railroad's acknowledged counsel, and his employment by the railroad had never been known, the discovery caused some speculation.

This was clarified by the further revelation that the president of the Boston & Maine had explained to his directors the nature of Mr. Hamlin's employment. The services were "of a light and inconsequential" nature, but as Mr. Hamlin was of much influence in the Democratic party, said the president, the retainer was well justified.

Who rules America and whose is the long arm that reaches out from New York and upsets a Democratic convention? Who forces the employment of men whose influence in a political party makes them valuable to certain projects of finance?

If you are unprepared to guess on this subject, let me beg your attention to this comment by former Governor Curtis Guild, Jr., in his newspaper, the *Boston Commercial Bulletin*, of February 19, 1910:

"Both of these men [meaning President Mellen and Vice-President Byrnes of the New Haven] and others of their kind are but hired megaphones, through which a beefy, red-faced, thick-necked financial bully, drunk with wealth and power, bawls his orders to stock markets, directors, courts, governments, and nations.

"We have been listening to Mr. Morgan."

Now go back for only a moment.

Each successive step in these developments has been marked by the issue of new capitalization of the New Haven. This capitalization is stocks and bonds. On these stocks and bonds interest and dividends must be paid.

To this total extent:

	1903	1909
Capital Stock	$70,897,300	$121,878,100
Funded Debt (Bonds)	14,549,300	234,859,875
Total Capitalization	$85,446,600	$356,737,975
Increase		271,291,375

In the same time the annual net earnings by which this capitalization must be supported have increased $7,051,576.98.

The total capitalization has increased 317 per cent, the gross earnings have increased 15 per cent, and the net earnings 58 per cent.

The disproportion between the increase of gross earnings and the increase of the net earnings indicates a decrease of operating expenses and of maintenance charges.

In other words, the increased interest charges have been dug out of the traveling and shipping public and out of the property itself.

What has become of the $271,291,375 of increased capitalization?

Part of it has gone for extensions, purchased properties, and track elevations. What has been done with the rest?

You can obtain a basis for a guess by returning to the stories of the Vanderbilts, Mr. Hill and the Southern Pacific. Also contemplating the fact that in these six years the fixed charges increased $12,130,711, while the net earnings increased only $7,051,576.

In 1903 the net income from operation exceeded the fixed charges for interest, rentals, and taxes by about $3,500,000. In 1909 the fixed charges for interest, rentals, and taxes exceeded the net income from operation by about $1,500,000.

In other words, the dividends must have been paid in part from some other source than operating profits.

What other source?

Such is the railroad business as at present conducted in America by high financiers.

But do not attack it, for by so doing you impair the stability of our securities abroad, and judging from the protest of the financiers, that must be a terrible thing indeed.

Do not attack it. Quietly go down into your pockets and dig up the increased passenger rates, increased prices for commutation tickets, increased freight rates, increased cost of living.

Because that is your duty as patient, obedient, well-trained American citizens.

But some time, looking over a story like this, you might care to ask of yourselves two little questions:

Who are the real rulers of America?

How long can we continue this process of piling up capitalization and increasing the cost of living?